San Francisco Giants 40 Years

San Francisco GIANTS
40 Years

By Glenn Dickey
Foreword by Chris Berman

Woodford Press
San Francisco

Acknowledgements

For this book, I was able to rely on my own observations, because I have seen the Giants in every season since they've been in San Francisco. Nonetheless, as much as possible, I tried to tell this history through the eyes of those who made it, and I am indebted to those who told me their stories. The interviews were a special pleasure because they allowed me to relive many enjoyable moments from the past.

In alphabetical order, these are the men I interviewed:

Larry Baer, Dusty Baker, Vida Blue, Barry Bonds, Bob Brenly, Corey Busch, Orlando Cepeda, George Christopher, Will Clark, Roger Craig, Alvin Dark, Charlie Fox, Herman Franks, Pat Gallagher, Hank Greenwald, Tom Haller, Frank Jordan, Mike Krukow, Duane Kuiper, Bill Laskey, Bob Lurie, Peter Magowan, Willie Mays, Willie McCovey, Mike McCormick, Stu Miller, Joe Morgan, Gaylord Perry, Bill Rigney, Frank Robinson, Al Rosen, Hank Sauer, Jack Schwarz, Lon Simmons, Chris Speier, Leigh Steinberg and Matt Williams.

Bob Rose and his public relations staff with the Giants helped trace many former players and managers for me, so I could conduct these interviews. Pat Gallagher arranged the interviews with Willie Mays and Willie McCovey, which were very productive sessions and particularly enjoyable because both men were great heroes to me in my early career as a sportswriter.

Thanks also to Nancy Donati and Missy Mikulecky, of the Giants Publications Department, for their efforts in providing archival photographs for this project.

Finally, a special word of thanks to my father, who first taught me the joys of baseball, and my mother, who had to endure so many dinner table conversations about the sport.

Dedication
To my wife, Nancy, and son, Kevin Scott, who have made my life complete.

Editorial Director: Pat Gallagher
Edited by C. David Burgin, Laurence J. Hyman and Tony Khing
Design by Laurence J. Hyman and Jim Santore
Photography research by Dennis Desprois and Dick Dobbins
Distribution by David Lilienstein and Paul Durham
Cover assemblage by Ray Ward Studios
Editorial assistance by Debbie Fong

ISBN: 0-942627-50-5
First Printing: December, 1997
Printed and bound in the United States of America

Woodford Press is the book division of Woodford Publishing, Inc.
660 Market Street, Suite 206, San Francisco, CA 94104

Contents

Willie Mays crosses home plate after a home run in 1970. Bobby Bonds (left) and Ken Henderson (right) offer congratulations.

Preface

Home runs splashing into the bay. Views of the Bay Bridge, of the San Francisco skyline, of boats anchored in the marina. A park with all the modern facilities and amenities and yet with the look of beloved old parks like Wrigley Field in Chicago and Fenway Park in Boston.

That's what Giants fans can expect when the first game is played in Pacific Bell Park in China Basin in the year 2000.

When the new ownership group bought the Giants before the 1993 season, it was only on the condition that a new ball park be built for the team. "We knew the old strategies for getting a park hadn't worked," said Giants President and Managing General Partner Peter Magowan. "We told the other National League owners that we'd come up with a different strategy, but we didn't know at that point what it would be."

The Giants' fan base had long been a regional one, with fewer than 20 percent of those at the games actually living in San Francisco, so Magowan's first thought was to put together a regional sports authority which would tax everybody in the area a small amount.

"We thought that made sense, but when we tried to set it up, it just looked like a mess," said Magowan. "We saw we'd run into the argument from, say, people in San Jose asking why they should pay for a stadium in San Francisco. We quickly came to the conclusion that it wouldn't work."

The Giants did extensive polling with focus groups, and the message was clear: There was great interest in a new park, but only if public financing wasn't involved. Even though there was, by that time, information about how new parks in Denver, Baltimore and Cleveland were creating jobs and revitalizing downtown areas, that didn't change the minds of the San Franciscans interviewed.

So, the next step was to look into private financing, using the model of arenas built around the country.

"It's definitely easier for an arena because it has more uses—basketball, hockey, concerts, ice shows," said Magowan, "but we began to see how it could be done with baseball.

"We're in an unique situation in San Francisco because of the beauty of the site and the number of high-class organizations. We had the opportunity to hit the corporate market in a way people in Cincinnati or Minneapolis could not.

"The idea of Charter Seats came up. Our program is different than the Personal Seat Licenses that have been sold by other teams. We're not selling all the seats, only about a third of them. People know the money is going into building the stadium and not into an owner's pocket, and that they'll own the seats forever."

Late in 1995, the Giants came forth with a proposal to build a privately-financed stadium, the first in baseball since Dodger Stadium had opened in 1962. Because zoning had to be changed to eliminate the 40-foot height limit in the area, the proposal was put on the ballot in March, 1996. It passed by a two-thirds majority.

There were still many skeptics who believed that, though the proposal had been passed, the Giants wouldn't be able to pay for the park. But eight days after the election, the Giants and Pacific Bell announced that the telecommunications company would be paying $50 million for naming rights for the stadium, which put the Giants well on the way to the $262 million they needed.

The new park will be a beauty, with a brick facade in the front that is very reminiscent of old parks. A statue of Willie Mays—the greatest player in Giants history—will be in a plaza in front of the park, and there will be retail shops and entertainment in the concourse area, so fans may spend several hours at the park before or after the ball games and even visit on non-game days. There will be a portwalk with openings so that passersby can see into the games, like in the days of the "knothole" gang.

The park is a throwback to earlier days in its playing dimensions, too. Earlier baseball parks were built in the middle of cities, and they were shaped to fit into the property. "Fenway Park has its 'Green Monster' in left field because it comes up against Lansdowne Street," said Magowan.

PACIFIC BELL PARK
HOME OF THE SAN FRANCISCO GIANTS
APRIL 2000

"The old Polo Grounds was only 258 down the left field line and 279 down the right field line but it was 485 feet to center."

In recent years, baseball has dictated minimum distances of 330 feet down the lines. Because the China Basin site was so small, that was impossible; the right field line will be only 308 feet.

The baseball people didn't like that. Magowan told them, "You come out here and explain to the public that you're going to turn down our new park because it doesn't meet your specifications." The Giants got their approval.

"I think it makes for a much better stadium," said Magowan. "We want high walls and low walls and a lot of angles where the ball can ricochet. When the ball is hit off the right field fence, you're not going to know whether it will be handled by the right fielder or the second baseman or first baseman. I think this is a big part of baseball's character because it used to be that every park was different. With the new circular parks built in the sixties, you don't know where you are.

"We'll have a streetcar line stopping in front of the park, ferries in the bay bringing in people. It will be unique. We'll have left a magical facility, long after we're out of baseball. It will be a nice legacy, I think."

There's one other significant advantage to the park: It brings a sense of permanency to the franchise.

"For more than a decade, there's been uncertainty about whether the Giants would get a new park or not, whether they'd be here or moved," said club Executive Vice President and Chief Operating Officer Larry Baer. "Now, that's all settled. The Giants will be in their new park and they're staying. With the economics of the new park, we'll be able to sign up players for the long term, as they did in Cleveland when they knew they were getting a new park."

So, as we enjoy looking back at the glory days of the past, we can also look forward with confidence to a bright future for the Giants as they head into their next 40 years.

— *Glenn Dickey*

Foreword

The Smile. The Stretch. The Kick. The Bull. Every one of them is an everlasting symbol of the San Francisco Giants, and every one of them has a special place in our hearts.

Every one of them also has a special spot in my den at home.

One of the no-no's you learn early on about being a TV, radio or newspaper reporter is that you do not ask for autographs while on the job, or even off it. For that

Left to right: The Bull (Orlando Cepeda), The Stretch (Willie McCovey), The Kick (Juan Marichal) and The Smile (Willie Mays).

reason, I have very few signed balls. But in my Connecticut home, 3,000 miles from the Bay Area, on one shelf sits the essence of the San Francisco Giants—signed baseballs by Willie Mays, Willie McCovey, Juan Marichal and Orlando Cepeda. The Smile. The Stretch. The Kick. The Bull.

There is nothing deeper in sports than the love for one's childhood baseball team. In fact, I am convinced there are only three things in our society you cannot change—date of birth, social security number and your childhood baseball team.

In 1962, that landmark year in San Francisco Giants history, I was all of seven years old. I grew up an hour out of New York. But I had no recollection of the New York Giants, nor was my father a Giants fan. In fact, that year he had taken me to my first games at Yankee Stadium. You would think at that age, at least for awhile, I'd cling to the Yankees. But one of my first baseball recollections is watching on TV as Chuck Hiller hit a grand slam for San Francisco in Game 4 of the World Series against the Yankees in New York, and me cheering wildly. I was hooked forever.

I already knew about Mays, McCovey, Marichal and Cepeda. I quickly learned about the Alous and Jose Pagan and Tom Haller and Jim Davenport. Gaylord Perry and Jim Ray Hart would soon follow.

The first time I saw the Giants in person was in 1963 against the Mets. Fittingly, it was in the Giants' original home, the Polo Grounds, which would be torn down the following year. Dad took us there for my eighth birthday party, and the Giants clobbered the Mets, 17-4, and hit six home runs, two by Cepeda. I will have to canvass my parents' attic, but I'm sure the game program still is up there.

One thing I learned at an early age is that being a Giants fan builds character. They were always good, but seemingly never quite good enough. Every year from 1965 through 1969 they finished second, sometimes being alive until the last day of the season. In 1966, for example, I listened in vain to the radio as the Dodgers beat the Phillies to edge the Giants by one-and-a-half games.

If that didn't teach patience, then try to get scores from the West Coast while growing up in Connecticut! There was no cable TV or even all-news radio. You'd get Tuesday night's box score in Thursday morning's paper.

Through it all, though, being a Giants fan bred class. Plus, you had to root for arguably the best player of his or any other generation, Willie Mays. And you learned to love a city a continent away, knowing that it was likely the most enchanting city anywhere.

It all merged for me in 1971, when my all-time favorite Giants team won the NL West Pennant. That summer I was 16. As part of a cross country trip, I got to see "The City" for the first time. And that meant my first chance to see the Giants play at Candlestick. I went. They won.

The beauty of 1971 was that it was the Old Guard's last hurrah. Mays and McCovey hitting 3-4 in the lineup, with Marichal and Perry pitching 1-2 in the rotation. Add to it a potential superstar in right field, Bobby Bonds, a lovable double play combo in Tito Fuentes and rookie Chris Speier, an underrated catcher in Dick Dietz, and a savior in the bullpen named Jerry Johnson—all carefully handled by Charlie Fox. And it was a team for the ages in San Francisco—*all* ages.

Down the stretch it was Marichal who stood out. There was the September beanball war against the Dodgers' Bill Singer. There was Marichal's being summoned to nail down the pennant on the last day of the season in San Diego, a game that unfortunately made him available for only one game of the National League Championship Series. That was Game 3 in Pittsburgh, which the Giants lost, 2-1. Back then I was backup goalie on my high school soccer team, and I still can recall listening through an earplug to the game on my transistor radio that was tucked into my sweatpants so the coach couldn't see it.

Who knows what would have happened if the Giants had won that game, or if Marichal could have pitched the first game of the Series, followed by Perry, then returned for Game 4? All we know is that the Pirates won three games to one, then went on to win a stirring World Series.

We also know that by May of the next season, Mays and Perry would be gone. And by the end of 1973, McCovey and Marichal would be gone as well. I vividly recall returning to my college dorm room at Brown University one day before the 1975 season to find out that Bonds had been traded to the Yankees. I was so upset that I hurled every trash can I could find down the hall. It was as if the cost of joy for 1971 had been prohibitive.

So prohibitive that the Giants were one Candlestick gust from moving to Toronto in 1976, until Bob Lurie saved the day. Naturally, Lurie was no different from any other Giants fan. His financial bravery went unrewarded for a decade except for 1978 and 1982. In 1978, McCovey was back in Giants orange and black. Vida Blue was pitching along with one of our personal favorites, John "The Count" Montefusco. And 1982, of course, was the famous "If we can't win the pennant, neither can you" final-day home run by Joe Morgan to knock the Dodgers from the postseason the day after they had eliminated the Giants.

The three outstanding teams in the most recent decade all possessed the same flair—and fatal flaw—that both romanced and tantalized San Francisco Giants fans since 1958. Roger Craig and his "Humm Babies" brought a renewed spirit and energy in 1987 and 1989. The Thrill, Robby, the Hac Man, Candy and Chili took a 3-2 lead over St. Louis in the NLCS, only to see Dave Dravecky lose a heartbreaking 1-0 Game 6 and Jose Oquendo hit a grand slam in Game 7 to propel the Cardinals to the World Series.

Then, in 1989, the year of MVP Kevin Mitchell, there was that rousing homestand in Games 3, 4 and 5, all wins over the Cubs to wrap up the NLCS, 4-1, featuring memorable at-bats by Matt Williams and Will Clark.

Die-hard Giants fan and ESPN announcer Chris Berman.

Finally, the Giants would be on center stage, except for two small problems. One, they were the second best baseball team in the Bay Area. Two, there was the 7.1 earthquake just minutes before the start of the first World Series game to be held at Candlestick in 27 years. After a 10-day delay before Game 3 could be played, the Oakland A's completed their sweep.

Which leads us to the most rewarding season in the 40 years the Giants have been in San Francisco. At the end of 1992, they were gone to St. Petersburg. I flew out to sit in the stands on the final home Wednesday and Thursday because my ESPN football duties would preclude me from seeing the bitter end on the weekend. I bargained with Giants Vice President of Stadium Operations and Security Jorge Costa for a piece of Candlestick turf to be sent to me after the season, turf that still grows in my backyard five years later. It was an awful experience.

Again, there was an 11th-hour savior. This time Peter Magowan and friends stopped the exodus. The reward would be, unlike for Lurie, immediate. The year 1993 saw the best record in San Francisco history, with a new MVP, Barry Bonds, bringing back memories of his dad, Bobby. There were more similarities to 1971, with this, in retrospect, essentially being the last hurrah for Clark, Williams and Robby Thompson.

Royce Clayton was the young shortstop instead of Chris Speier. Instead of Marichal and Perry, it was John Burkett and Billy Swift, and pray for a snowdrift. And instead of the steady hand of Charlie Fox, there was the steady hand of Dusty Baker managing in the dugout.

One of the most rousing games, and a personal broadcasting career highlight, occurred on September 1 in Atlanta. That's when John Patterson's pinch hit home run in the ninth brought down the hard-charging Braves. When "Hero" hit it out, I almost jumped through the ceiling with my headset on. I guess my national TV neutrality took an inning off.

When the dust settled on the season, the Giants had amassed 103 wins! Unfortunately, the Atlanta Braves had 104. More heartbreak, or as Yogi might say, "*Deja vu* all over again."

Forty years of Giants baseball in San Francisco. Okay, so there hasn't yet been a World Series victory. But being a Giants fan is about the paradox of sipping the finest wines, only to find out that we can consume just one glass and never the whole bottle. But connoisseurs will tell you that's the way to drink it anyway.

Here's a toast to baseball's most exhilarating team! It's hardly a coincidence that my only son, Doug, was born on May 6, Willie Mays' birthday. I'm convinced there is a Higher Force at work.

That's why, 3,000 miles away from The 'Stick, I have baseballs signed by the Say Hey Kid, Willie Mac, The Dominican Dandy and Orlando.

The Smile. The Stretch. The Kick. The Bull.

— *Chris Berman*

clockwise, from top:
Giants minor league executives Carl Hubbell (a Hall-of-Fame pitcher for the
New York Giants) and Jack Schwarz; "the Dominican Dandy," Juan Marichal;
the first San Francisco Giants manager, Bill Rigney; "Say Hey," Willie Mays; the
first Alou brother to play for the Giants, Felipe; "Stretch," Willie McCovey;
Rigney and his 1959 coaching staff: Wes Westrum, Bill Posedel, Salty Parker

I

KEEPING THE FAITH

• THE HORACE STONEHAM ERA •
1958 - 1975

O ctober 3, 1962. It would become the most important date in the playing history of the San Francisco Giants, although it did not seem that way as the late afternoon sun began its descent at Dodger Stadium in Los Angeles. The Giants had teased their fans for five seasons, promising a pennant but always falling short. This time would be the worst, because the promise had endured for nearly 165 games. After a season-long emotional and physical roller coaster, the Giants had caught the Dodgers at the wire and thrashed them in the opening playoff game, but had blown a 5-0 lead to lose the second playoff game, and had fallen behind in the third game. Once again, collapse seemed inevitable. Only three outs stood between them and their most painful defeat yet as they trailed the Dodgers, 4-2, going into the top of the ninth.

In his private box, General Manager Chub Feeney was certain the Giants were going to lose. When his good friend and former Giants Manager Bill Rigney said he was leaving to go back to San Francisco, Chub was sure Rigney was just bailing out. In fact, though, Rigney had a feeling that the Giants would pull it out. Call it omniscience or just blind faith, but Rigney remembered 1951, when he'd been on the Giants team which had won a playoff against the Dodgers on Bobby Thomson's ninth inning home run, perhaps the most dramatic in baseball history. "Keep the faith," he told Feeney. "I'll meet you in San Francisco for a victory drink."

In the dugout, Willie Mays was the only one still playing who had been on that 1951 team, though Manager Alvin Dark and Coaches Whitey Lockman and Wes Westrum had also been players on that team. Mays didn't remind his teammates of that magical year because he knew they wouldn't remember it. "You can't go back 11 years in a few minutes," he would say years later. He knew, though, that the Giants had beaten the Dodgers more often than they'd lost since the clubs had moved west, so as he walked up and down in the dugout, he reminded the Giants players of that more recent history, telling them they'd beaten the Dodgers before and they could beat them again. Anything can happen, he told them, and he was right. The finish wouldn't be so dramatic as in 1951, but it would be just as devastating to the Dodgers.

Both teams were emotionally spent, because it had been a harrowing season, with the Giants and Dodgers tossing the lead back and forth for six months, and an especially tense finish.

Going into the final eight days, the Dodgers had owned a four-game lead. The pennant race seemed over.

Not quite. The Giants won on that next-to-last Sunday, and the Dodgers lost, to close the gap to three games. The Dodgers kept losing—five of their last seven—and the Giants won six of their last seven. By the final Sunday, the Dodgers led by a single game.

Giants Manager Alvin Dark kept telling his players not to lose hope, although he had abandoned it himself. "We couldn't control it because we weren't playing the Dodgers," he said. "Even if we'd won every game that last week, if the Dodgers just won three out of seven, they'd win. I couldn't let my feelings known to the players because I wanted them to keep playing hard. Meanwhile, I was watching the scoreboard even while I was managing. I'm sure the players were too."

One of Dark's star players was not. Perhaps because he was locked in the worst slump of his life, Orlando Cepeda was unaware of the drama.

"I went out to dinner with my wife, Annie, that last Saturday night," remembered Cepeda many years later, "and people came up to me, very excited, and said, 'You're just a game out. You could still win.' I was really surprised. I hadn't been keeping up with the Dodgers scores, and I had no idea we were that close."

Yet, everyone else seemed to be, and on that last day of the season, those who were not at the ballpark were listening elsewhere on ubiquitous transistor radios. *San Francisco Chronicle* columnist Herb Caen reported that the intermission at the Curran Theatre, which was showing "Oliver!," was delayed for 25 minutes so theatre-goers could listen to the end of the Giants game at Candlestick. At the Patio Bar in San Carlos, a sign was posted, "Drinks served between innings only! Order ahead." The big Roos/Atkins store at Powell and Post sold only five suits while the Giants game was on, all to out-of-towners.

The Giants did their part, beating Houston, 2-1, on a Mays homer in the eighth inning. At Kezar Stadium, the 49ers and Minnesota Vikings were playing football, but many of those in attendance were also listening on their transistors. As the Vikings came out of a huddle, a roar went up from the stands; the puzzled Vikes had no idea it was because Mays had just hit his home run. There was still an inning to play, but when Stu Miller struck out pinch-hitter Billy Goodman for the final out, he was mobbed by his teammates and the 41,327 fans in the stands at Candlestick rose to their feet to cheer their heroes. At Grace Cathedral, after hearing the end of the game on the radio, verger Charles Agnews rushed to the carillon and banged out Handel's "Hallelujah."

The Dodgers-St. Louis game in Los Angeles was still scoreless when the Giants game ended. Giants announcer Russ Hodges rushed to the clubhouse where Dark and his players were huddled around a radio carrying the Dodgers-Cardinals broadcast, and he relayed information to his radio audience.

Hardly anybody had left Candlestick, because it was Fan Appreciation Day, and gifts, including automobiles, were to be given away after the game.

It was common for those going to games at that time also to listen to Hodges and Lon Simmons (who was broadcasting the 49ers game at Kezar that day) on their transistors, so they heard Hodges' account. For those who didn't, public address announcer Jeff Carter was also relaying reports from the Dodgers game, in between making gift announcements.

Then, Vin Scully announced that Cardinals catcher Gene Oliver had hit a home run in the top of the eighth. When Hodges and Carter relayed that information, a huge roar went up at Candlestick, a lesser one at Kezar, this time unnerving the 49ers players who were coming out of their huddle.

It was by no means over. The Cardinals still had to get the Dodgers out for two more innings. But they did, and the Giants and Dodgers would be starting a playoff for the pennant the next day, the first game in San Francisco, the second and third, if needed, in Los Angeles.

This had happened before, in 1951, when the Giants were still in New York and the Dodgers in Brooklyn, and there would be more similarities to come.

In 1951, the Giants had won the first game, and in 1961, the Giants won the first game again, 8-0, behind Billy Pierce, who had been undefeated in 12 regular season decisions at Candlestick that year. The Dodgers started Sandy Koufax, who had been sidelined with a finger injury in midseason, but Koufax was out of there early, as Mays hit the first of two homers he had in the game; Cepeda and Jimmy Davenport also homered.

Orlando Cepeda (left) and Juan Marichal give each other "five" upon hearing that the Dodgers lost to St. Louis to force a best-of-three game playoff for the 1962 National League pennant. Earlier that day, the Giants defeated the Houston Colt 45s. Had the Dodgers won, the Giants would have ended the season in second place.

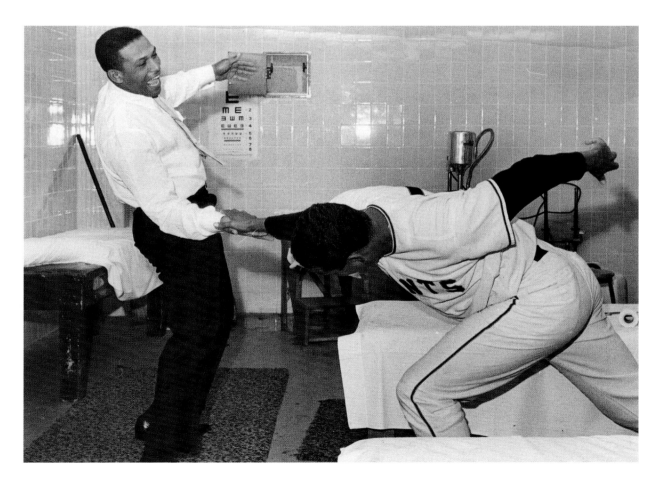

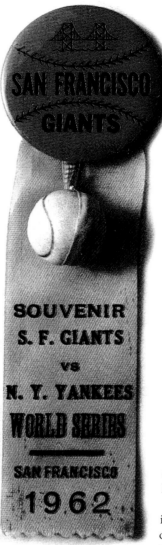

SOUVENIR
S. F. GIANTS
vs
N. Y. YANKEES
WORLD SERIES
————
SAN FRANCISCO
1962

The Dodgers seemed in disarray. New York columnist Dick Young, still smarting because the team he loved had moved from Brooklyn in 1958, labeled the Dodgers last week collapse the worst choke job in baseball history. Koufax had been battered in the first game.

Manager Walter Alston said he would go with Stan Williams in the second game instead of Don Drysdale, who had won 25 games that season, because Drysdale would be pitching with just two days rest. Drysdale was furious. "Are they saving me for the first intra-squad game in the spring?"

Alston changed his mind and started Drysdale, but the manager's first thought was the correct one: The tired Drysdale was rocked for five runs, four of them in the sixth inning, and left with the Giants ahead by 5-0.

At that point, the Dodgers had been held scoreless for 35 straight innings, including Pierce's win and two shutouts at the end of the season, but that streak would end dramatically in the bottom of the sixth.

Giants starter Jack Sanford had scored a run in the top of the inning, coming home from second on a single. Never an example of a well-conditioned athlete, Sanford was tired. When he walked Jim Gilliam to lead off the inning, Dark took him out, though Sanford had a two-hitter at the time, and brought in Miller.

Yet, Miller had nothing that day, and he gave up a double to Duke Snider, a sacrifice fly to Tommy Davis, a walk to Wally Moon and even a single to Frank Howard, who was always his patsy. "That's the game I've always thought got me traded to Baltimore (after the season)," said Miller. "The year before, Alvin had called me the best relief pitcher in baseball, but I don't think he could ever get this game out of his mind, so I was gone. That's baseball."

Dark brought in Billy O'Dell to replace Miller, but he was no more effective. Before Don Larsen finally came in to get the Dodgers out, the home team had scored seven runs to take a 7-5 lead.

The Dodgers eventually won the game, 8-7, when Maury Wills scored in the bottom of the ninth on Ron Fairly's sacrifice fly, but the key play had come an inning earlier. Davenport and Mays singled. When pinch-hitter Ed Bailey also singled to right, Davenport scored and Mays tried for third base, where he was ruled out by umpire Jocko Conlan after Tommy Davis' throw.

"The newspaper pictures the next day showed an angry Mays," remembered Simmons, "but what it didn't show was that Mays was angry at himself because he had broken his own rule: Never to try for an extra base when Jocko Conlan was the umpire."

"It seemed that he called me out all the time, going to second, going to third," said Mays. "When I tried to steal and I looked up and saw Jocko, I thought, 'Uh, oh, I'm out.' But you don't look for that in the playoffs."

The pictures the next day seemed to show Conlan first making a safe signal and then changing it to out, but the feisty little (5-foot-4) umpire insisted he was just starting to bring his hand up for the out sign.

It didn't matter, of course, because the decision had been made and the playoff was tied. A third game would be played, and the Dodgers seemed in command with their 4-2 lead after eight innings.

Pinch-hitter Matty Alou led off the ninth with a single for the Giants, but Harvey Kuenn forced him at second. The Dodgers needed only two more outs. Pitching too carefully to Willie McCovey, who had hit 20 home runs in just 229 at-bats that year, Ed Roebuck walked him on four pitches. Now, the Giants had the tying runs on base, and Roebuck was clearly feeling the pressure. If he couldn't get a double play, he would have to face Willie Mays. It got worse. Roebuck also walked Felipe Alou, and the bases were loaded for Mays. Disaster loomed. On the Dodgers' side of the field, you could hear hearts murmur.

Mays lashed a liner back through the mound. Roebuck deflected it, which kept the ball from going through to center field to score the tying runs, but he could not make a play. One run scored. Stan Williams replaced Roebuck and the slump-ridden Cepeda tied the game with a sacrifice fly to right.

Williams had won the second game in relief, but Alston always had to hold his

Ernie Bowman (right) and Gaylord Perry give each other a champagne shower after the Giants rallied with four runs in the top of the ninth to beat the Dodgers in Los Angeles for the 1962 National League pennant.

breath when he used him because the towering righthander was unpredictable. He could be overpowering, but there were other times when his adrenalin was pumping so hard that he overthrew, and his pitches would sometimes come closer to the on-deck circle than the plate. This was one of those bad days, as became quickly evident when he threw a wild pitch with Bailey at bat, giving Kuenn and Mays a chance to advance a base. Dodgers Manager Walt Alston then ordered Bailey walked intentionally to load the bases and gave the Dodgers a play at any base. But Williams' always fragile control had totally deserted him, and he walked Davenport, which forced in the winning run. A funereal pall settled over Dodger Stadium, or at least over those who had not left to beat the traffic before the start of the inning.

The Giants got an insurance run when Dodgers second baseman Larry Burright booted a ground ball, but they didn't need it. Dark brought in his Candlestick ace, Pierce, who went 1-2-3 against the stunned Dodgers in the bottom of the inning. The Dodgers went into their clubhouse and didn't open their doors to the press for half an hour.

In San Francisco, it was pandemonium as hundreds of thousands of fans gathered around their radios and erupted in cheers and celebration, and poured onto downtown streets, swarming in front of landmarks like the Samuels clock on Market Street, past the fish tank at Bernstein's Grotto and the famous restaurant Omar Khayam's on Powell Street. Even the side streets were jammed; on Ellis Street, Sam's Grill, site of many scenes from the Dashiell Hammett novels, had virtually disappeared from sight. The crowds blocked traffic on Market Street and other main thoroughfares. The fabled cable cars weren't climbing halfway to the stars; they were not, in fact, going anywhere. Confetti streamed from windows and fans wreathed the cable cars in serpentine-like fashion.

Market Street buzzes with excitement following the Giants' 6-4 win pennant-clinching win over the Los Angeles Dodgers on Oct. 3, 1962.

Jubilant San Franciscans on Montgomery Street celebrate after the Giants beat the Dodgers in a three-game playoff to win the 1962 National League pennant.

It was joy mixed with hysteria, tears mingled with laughter, as people tried to grasp the intensity of what had happened. Strangers hugged strangers. Everyone seemed to be screaming. It was compared to V-J Day in 1945 by those who had been around for the earlier celebration.

There was a romance going then with San Franciscans and their Giants. "Women would go into supermarkets and ask the score," remembered Lon Simmons, who started his Major League broadcasting career with the Giants in 1958. "People would go to the opera with transistor radio plugs in their ears, so they could listen to the games."

But that was mundane compared to this celebration. At the airport, some 25,000 fans had poured onto the runways, blocking off two of them, hoping to get a glimpse of their heroes when they landed. The Giants' plane actually had to circle a few times before the controller could be certain there would be an open area for it to land.

When the players boarded a bus to take them into the city, fans rushed over to the bus, pounding on the sides, even breaking a couple of windows in their enthusiasm. The players were astounded, and more than a little frightened, by the ardor of their fans. The Giants had a reserve outfielder, Carl Boles, who bore an amazing physical resemblance to Mays, and some players suggested that Boles leave the bus and do a Mays impersonation to distract the fans, a suggestion Boles wisely resisted. Willie himself had somehow managed to slip away to catch a cab to his penthouse apartment in the city. A frightened Cepeda saw the mob and fled. "I walked out to the freeway to catch a ride home," said Cepeda.

It was the climactic point in the history of the San Francisco Giants. The Giants had benefited from the novelty of Major League Baseball on the West Coast, and the first two years had been very exciting, even more so the second, when they were in the race until the final week. The opening of Candlestick had created more excitement,

The Giants raise their 1962 National League Champions banner in downtown San Francisco prior to the World Series.

and an attendance record was set in the first year that lasted for 27 years. By 1962, though, the novelty was starting to wear off. The shortcomings of Candlestick were becoming obvious, and the frustrations of the near misses were telling on fans, who were beginning to wonder if the Giants would ever win.

But when they won the pennant in the most exciting way possible, the riotous excitement erased any doubt that the Giants move from New York was a success. Nobody could have been more satisfied than George Christopher, who had engineered the move in 1957.

In the mid 1950s, Christopher had begun thinking of getting a Major League Baseball team to move to San Francisco. He loved baseball, having played it as a youngster, but his motive was practical, not emotional. "I knew that if we had a big league team here, after every home game there would be San Francisco datelines in newspapers around the country and even in foreign countries," he said.

Both San Francisco and Los Angeles had major league football teams, the 49ers and Rams, but baseball was unquestionably the country's most popular sport at that time. Christopher knew that he needed a Major League Baseball franchise to make San Francisco a major league sports city.

He thought first of the Boston Red Sox. "Joe Cronin, a native San Franciscan, was the Red Sox general manager, so that would have been a natural tie," he said. But Cronin told Christopher that the Red Sox's roots in New England were too strong for them to move.

Soon, though, Christopher began seeing stories that New York Giants Owner Horace Stoneham was unhappy and that Brooklyn Dodgers Owner Walter O'Malley was threatening to move if he didn't get a new stadium.

Through conversations with O'Malley and Los Angeles Mayor Norris Poulson, Christopher learned that O'Malley had his eye on Los Angeles. In fact, in 1956, O'Malley had bought the Los Angeles franchise in the Pacific Coast League from the Chicago Cubs. Though he continued to say publicly that he wanted to stay in Brooklyn, O'Malley was already talking in specific terms with Poulson about what it would take to get the Dodgers to move to Los Angeles.

Yet Stoneham was talking about moving the Giants to Minneapolis, where the Giants had their Triple-A farm club.

"That didn't make sense to me," said Christopher, "because there would be no Dodgers-Giants rivalry if the Giants were in Minneapolis." Jack Schwarz, then the farm secretary for the Giants, concurred. "The Dodgers were our meal ticket," he remembered. "We'd always get a very good crowd for the 11 games they played in the Polo Grounds."

Christopher proposed to Stoneham that the Giants move to San Francisco and the Dodgers to Los Angeles. (He dismisses the oft-told story that O'Malley gave Stoneham a choice of cities: "No way. O'Malley always had his eye on the bigger market").

It was an audacious thought. At the time, Major League Baseball was confined to the eastern half of the country; St. Louis, perched on the western bank of the Mississippi, was the furthest west of any franchise.

There had been only two franchise moves in the century, the Boston Braves to Milwaukee and the St. Louis Browns to Baltimore, where they became the Orioles. In both cases, the teams had been largely unsuccessful, both on the field and at the gate.

In contrast, the Giants had been a bulwark of the National League, having won 14 pennants, more than any other team, the last one as recently as 1954. The Dodgers were tied with the Cardinals for second, with nine pennants, six of them coming in the 1947-56 period. It was unthinkable that these teams would move.

The negotiations were kept as secret as possible. "When I'd fly back to New York,

A commemorative record album, complete with play-by-play highlights, came out after the 1962 season.

The first San Francisco World Series press pin.

In August 1957, Horace Stoneham, with team Secretary Edward T. Brannick on his right, told the New York press that the Giants were moving to San Francisco.

they had me stay at third-rate hotels, so nobody would know I was there," said Christopher. "I'd have been very embarrassed if anybody who knew me had seen me at those hotels." O'Malley had already made his decision to move; now, he worked with Christopher to get Stoneham to move to San Francisco, to keep the Giants-Dodgers rivalry alive.

Although O'Malley made his decision earlier, it was Stoneham who made the first announcement: On Aug. 19, 1957, the Giants board of directors voted, 8-1, to move to San Francisco for the 1958 season. The lone dissenter was M. Donald Grant, who would later serve as the chairman of the board for the New York Mets.

A reporter asked Stoneham how he felt about taking the Giants away from the kids of New York. "I feel bad about the kids," said Stoneham, "but I haven't seen many of their fathers lately."

On Oct. 8, the Dodgers also made it official: They were moving to Los Angeles. Major League Baseball would never be the same again.

But first the Giants needed a place to play. Stoneham was willing to play the first two years in Seals Stadium, a cozy little minor league park that seated only about 22,000, but he insisted that San Francisco build him a new stadium. Convinced that the lack of parking at the Polo Grounds in New York had doomed his franchise, he insisted that there be 10,000 parking places for the new stadium.

"There was no parking at Seals Stadium," said Christopher, "and to provide the 75 acres we needed for that parking, we would have had to take over property on Potrero Hill through eminent domain, which would have closed a lot of businesses and put people out of work. I didn't want that."

"I took Horace around and showed him the possibilities. He didn't want a downtown stadium because there was no parking. He didn't want Seals Stadium because there was no parking."

So Christopher took Stoneham out to Candlestick Point, where contractor Charles Harney owned land. "He saw that and said, 'This is what I want.' He saw there was enough room for parking and he thought it would be a good spot because it was accessible to people on the peninsula."

Candlestick Park was opened in 1960, and has been the butt of jokes since, although then Vice President Richard Nixon proclaimed it, "The most beautiful park in America," due to its location on San Francisco Bay.

There since have been unfounded reports that Harney made a killing on the deal, though the total cost of stadium and land was only $11 million, a bargain even adjusted for inflation, and that shortcuts were taken on construction. In fact, Candlestick came through the 1989 Loma Prieta earthquake with only minor damage, while a part of the Bay Bridge went down. The design was faulty but the construction was not.

In the end, said Christopher, the decision to build at Candlestick Point was a no-brainer. "I had the choice of building the park there or not building it and losing the Giants."

"It was a perfect time for the team to come out," said Bill Rigney, who had been the team's manager the last two years in New York and would continue in that role in San Francisco until he was fired before the mid-point of the 1960 season. "The Giants had won in '51 and '54, but the team was growing old and going downhill. But it still had Willie Mays and the farm system was really beginning to put out good players."

Had the Giants stayed in New York, it might have been difficult to sell fans on an almost total overhaul of the team, as happened when the club moved to San Francisco. Conversely, that scenario worked perfectly in San Francisco, where fans wanted to see players they could call their own, and not transplanted New Yorkers.

For the most conspicuous transplanted New Yorker, Willie Mays, the move was not good news. "It bothered me," Mays said frankly when he was interviewed for this book. "I had only played in New York at that time. I was just getting adjusted to New York. At that time, in the '50s, New York was very, very good. You could walk the streets then. I really liked New York, and now I had to adjust to a new city."

And, the fans had to adjust to Mays. On both sides, there was a lot of early friction. "Naturally, when we came out here," said Rigney, "we told everybody what a great player Mays was, because he was the one proven guy we could brag about. Well, the attitude, from both writers and the fans, was, 'Show us.'"

"I thought, 'Hey, wait a minute. I've been in the league for five years. Why do I have to prove myself?'" said Mays. "When I came out from New York, I already had close to 200 home runs (187). And I have to prove myself?"

San Franciscans welcome their new Major League Baseball team during a parade in downtown San Francisco.

Bay Area native Bill Rigney returns home as manager of the San Francisco Giants.

The "George" who brought the Giants to San Francisco was Mayor George Chirstopher.

Manager Bill Rigney and Giants Owner Horace Stoneham.

Mike McCormick, who had been with the Giants in New York, saw the situation clearly. "Most of us were very happy to come to San Francisco," he said, "because the last year in New York was pretty dreary. Except for the games with the Dodgers, nobody came out. We used to sit out in the bullpen and see if we could count the fans in the stands.

"So it was pretty exciting to come out here and see all this enthusiasm, but I don't know how astute the fans were. There had been a lot of Major League players who came out of San Francisco, but they hadn't been watching Major League Baseball. I think they were expecting perfection. They seemed to think Mays should never do anything wrong and hit maybe .800."

To try to please the fans, Mays concentrated on hitting for average, and his .347 average was the highest of his career, but he felt his overall game suffered. "I had always been the type of player who did everything well," he said, "but I felt that year that people expected me to do something different, so I went after the batting championship (he finished three points behind Richie Ashburn's league-leading .350). After

Giants skipper Bill Rigney directs his players onto the field for the San Francisco Giants' initial Spring Training session.

Seals Stadium, named after San Francisco's entry in the Pacific Coast League, was the Giants' home in 1958 and 1959.

Let me in! Fans rush into Seals Stadium to get their first look at the San Francisco Giants.

OFFICIAL BATTING ORDER
CLUB SAN FRANCISCO DATE 1958

	ORIGINAL	CHANGE
1	Mays	
2	Davenport	
3	Kirkland	
4	Wagner	
5	Cepeda	
6	Rodgers	
7	Schmidt	
8	O'Connell	
9	Fitzgerald	

Lineup card from the 1958 season filled out by Manager Bill Rigney.

that year, I thought, 'Hey, wait a minute. I should do what I want to do, not what other people want me to do.' So, I went back to playing my regular game."

But it was in the field that Mays was most frustrated. In the Polo Grounds in New York, which had an enormous center field, he had made many spectacular catches. In Seals Stadium, whose center field fence was only about 400 feet from home plate, he had much less room to make those catches. "He'd come into the dugout after a home run was hit to right center or left center," said Rigney, "and he'd tell me, 'I could have caught that if I'd had room.'"

The fans, who had never seen Mays in New York and didn't understand that, wondered where the spectacular catches were that they'd been told about.

"I couldn't make spectacular catches if I didn't have room," said Mays. "I had to change the way I played center field. At Seals Stadium, I played very, very shallow because I knew I could still get back to the wall. That probably made me a better center fielder. That gave me a little different dimension."

In time, as fans became more knowledgeable about Major League Baseball, they came to appreciate the very special talents of Mays, regarded as the best player of his generation by those who saw him play. That first year, though, they were more

The Giants and the Dodgers participate in the traditional Opening Day ceremonies at Seals Stadium prior to the first regular season Major League Baseball game on the West Coast. The Giants are standing down the first base line.

enthralled by the young players the Giants were bringing to San Francisco, and they had reason, because the Giants had some very good and exciting young players.

"I had seen Orlando Cepeda in Puerto Rico, so I knew how good he was going to be," said Rigney. "Carl Hubbell had told me about Jimmy Davenport, and we had a whole bunch of good outfielders coming along—Willie Kirkland, Leon Wagner, Felipe Alou and his brothers, Jackie Brandt. I didn't even know about Willie McCovey yet, but he came along the next year."

The Giants' farm system director was Hubbell, who had been a Hall of Fame pitcher for the team in New York, but the man who really made it work was Jack Schwarz, who was working under Hubbell.

The Dodgers had gotten a jump on everybody by breaking the color line with Jackie Robinson—and following up with Roy Campanella and Don Newcombe, amongst others—but the Giants weren't far behind.

"We realized there was a huge talent pool that hadn't been tapped," said Schwarz. "We had a tenant at the Polo Grounds, a team in the Negro League that was run by Alex Pompez. So I went to Alex and asked him for help."

Pompez recommended players to the Giants, and Schwarz also asked his opinion whenever one of his scouts made a recommendation on a black player. One time, for instance, Eddie Montague called and told Schwarz that he'd been watching the best player he'd ever seen, who was then playing for the Birmingham Black Barons. Because teams had to pay to get players from the Negro League, it would cost the Giants $10,000.

At Schwarz's request, Pompez went down to Birmingham and reported back that the player was indeed worth $10,000, so the Giants signed him.

The player was Willie Mays. "And what a beauty he was!" said Schwarz. Mays was sent down to Minneapolis for a couple of months, but the Giants brought him up when he was hitting .477 in May, and that was the end of Mays' minor league career.

Pompez also had contacts in Latin America, and he told Schwarz that the Dominican Republic was the best place to scout for players. The Giants did so and came up with Juan Marichal, Felipe, Matty and Jesus Alou, and Jose Pagan. Pompez also tipped the Giants to Cepeda in Puerto Rico.

Schwarz had worked at putting together a group of excellent scouts. One of the best was George Genovese, who operated in Southern California. "There was a period in the early '70s," said Charlie Fox, manager of the team then, "that six players Genovese had signed were on the team."

Schwarz also had a system of "bird dogs" in the United States, many of them former players who liked to watch baseball games. They would call when they'd spotted a player they thought could make it, and Schwarz would then have the player checked out by a full-time scout. The bird dogs got payments which depended on how long a player lasted and how high he got in the system.

Now, scouting is more sophisticated and every team knows the best prospects, but for perhaps the first 20 years the Giants were in San Francisco, the bird dogs spotted players that had been otherwise missed. One Schwarz remembers in particular was Bobby Bonds. Tipped by a bird dog, Schwarz sent Genovese to look at Bonds, and Genovese immediately recommended that Bonds be signed.

As Rigney noted, the farm system was really beginning to pay dividends by 1958. Cepeda was the National League Rookie of the Year, Bob Schmidt was an excellent young catcher, Jimmy Davenport quickly earned a reputation as the best-fielding third baseman in the league.

The Giants had so many good young outfielders, they couldn't work them all into the lineup.

"We probably had too many good outfielders," said Rigney. "We had to platoon them, so maybe they didn't develop as much as they could have. Willie Kirkland, for instance, was an underachiever. I really thought he was going to be an outstanding outfielder, but he never really made it."

The Giants, in fact, traded away their outfield surplus quickly. Kirkland went in a trade for Harvey Kuenn, Brandt went in a trade for Billy O'Dell, Wagner was part of a trade for Don Blasingame.

One of the fans' favorites was Wagner, who went by the nickname "Daddy Wags." Wagner was an excellent hitter but as an outfielder. . . well, let's just say that he was a

Alex Pompez was the scout who recommended that the Giants sign Willie Mays and helped them find players such as the Alou brothers, Orlando Cepeda and Juan Marichal.

Orlando Cepeda crosses the plate after belting his first Major League home run during the Giants' inaugural game in San Francisco.

"Daddy Wags," Leon Wagner, had a reputation as an outstanding hitter.

Don Blasingame was in the Giants' 1960 Opening Day lineup as the second baseman.

Willie McCovey during 1958 Spring Training.

designated hitter who came on the scene too early. His outfielding varied from merely inept to comical.

The other young Giants weren't much more disciplined than Wagner, especially on the bases. Salty Parker, the Giants third base coach, was often booed by fans when a Giants runner was thrown out at third, although it was seldom his fault. The baserunners, especially Cepeda, just kept running even when Parker tried to signal them to stop. "Orlando was trying to be like Mays," said announcer Lon Simmons, "so when he got on base, he'd never stop at third. He wanted to score."

But even when the players made bonehead plays, the fans loved them. "The fans were so enthusiastic in that little park," said Rigney. "They were just thrilled to see Major League Baseball. They'd had the Pacific Coast League, and that was a pretty good league, but people realized the difference as soon as they saw the Giants."

Being the first San Francisco manager of the Giants was a special thrill for Rigney, too, because he had grown up across the bay in Alameda and had played in the PCL himself, with the Oakland Oaks. He knew what to expect. "San Francisco had always been a good baseball town. There were all kinds of players who came out of there in those days (the DiMaggio brothers, Frank Crosetti, Tony Lazzeri, among many others) so the people really knew baseball and they loved it."

And the Giants were playing very exciting baseball—even when they lost. Simmons remembers one game when the Giants trailed the Pirates by 10 runs going into the bottom of the ninth and scored nine runs.

"Bill Mazeroski saved the game with a great diving catch of a pop fly in right field. It was the second out he'd made in the inning. Earlier, with Mays on first, Dick Groat had booted a double play grounder, but Mazeroski stretched out lying on the ground with his foot just touching the bag and grabbed the ball as it bounced away from Groat, so Mays was out. If he hadn't made both of those plays, the Giants would have won the game, and it would have been an incredible comeback. That's the way it was all year. It was just a wild first year."

Buoyed by the enthusiasm of their fans, the Giants finished a surprising third that first year, though a distant 12 games behind the Milwaukee Braves, who won the National League pennant. Cepeda was the National League Rookie of the Year, and the San Francisco fans named him the Most Valuable Giant, though Mays' statistics were better in almost every regard. "I didn't think it would come to the point that, 'We're just going to do it no matter what you do,'" said Mays, still obviously nettled by that vote nearly 40 years later.

Trying to close the gap with Milwaukee, the Giants made two big trades with the St. Louis Cardinals before the 1959 season, trading young first baseman Bill White (who much later became the National League president) for pitcher Sam Jones and Wagner and Spencer for second baseman Blasingame. They also traded catcher Valmy Thomas and pitcher Ruben Gomez, the Opening Day starter in 1958, to Philadelphia for pitcher Jack Sanford.

The first trade was an example of a perfect baseball trade, one which worked out for both teams. Jones pitched only three years for the Giants, but the first two were excellent ones, as he won 21 games in 1959 and another 18 in 1960. White went on to have an excellent career, eight of his 13 years in St. Louis, but he was surplus for the Giants.

White had come up to the Giants in 1956, when they were still in New York, but had then been called into the service. When he got out in 1958, Cepeda was at first base and Willie McCovey was at Triple-A.

"We had no place for him," said Rigney, "and we really needed a pitcher like Sam Jones. We played White a little in the outfield, to show his versatility, and we gave the Cardinals their choice: White or Kirkland. They made the right one. White went on to have the kind of career we always knew he would have, but we just didn't have room for him."

The Sanford trade also worked out well, with Sanford winning 15 games before suffering a hand injury that ended his season a month early.

The second trade with St. Louis, though, was a huge disappointment. "I saw (Cardinal Manager) Fred Hutchinson in the off-season," said Rigney, "and he told me, 'You got my best player.' But Blas never really got untracked with us. I remember a game in Spring Training when he made an error which cost us the game, and that seemed to prey on him. He never was the player for us that he had been in St. Louis."

Blasingame had been a steady fielder and an improving hitter for St. Louis, batting

.289 in his final season with the Cardinals. With the Giants, he was erratic in the field and hit just .235. He was traded away in 1960.

Weak infield defense would plague the Giants throughout the 1959 season, but with Jones bolstering their pitching and a strong hitting attack, they were in the race with the Los Angeles Dodgers and Milwaukee Braves all season. And in mid-season, their already potent attack got even stronger when they brought McCovey up from Phoenix.

McCovey had been devastating the Pacific Coast League, hitting .372 and leading the league in RBI. (In fact, he wound up leading the league with 29 home runs, though he missed more than a third of the PCL season).

"I really should have been brought up at the start of the year," said McCovey, "because I had already proved myself the year before at Phoenix. I was too good for Triple-A. But Cepeda was at first base and they still had Bill White (before the trade was made in Spring Training), so they sent me back to Phoenix."

The day McCovey came up, he was hustled off the plane and out to Seals Stadium, too late even to take batting practice. It didn't matter. He went four-for-four in the game off Robin Roberts, a pitcher on his way to the Hall of Fame. "I was in the middle of a hot streak that started in Phoenix, and I continued that way the rest of the season," said McCovey, who hit .354 with 13 homers and 38 RBIs and was named NL Rookie of the Year, though he played in only 52 games. "It didn't matter who was pitching that year. I hit them all."

Very quickly, too, Willie became a fan favorite, with fan clubs springing up all over Northern California. "I had a big one down by Monterey," he remembered. "They used to come up in droves. There were some ladies who used to sit behind home plate and one of them, I think her name was Beulah Trent, got wind of the fact that I liked macadamia nuts, so every home run I hit, she'd give me a can of macadamia nuts.

Salty Parker was one of Manager Bill Rigney's coaches on the 1958 Giants.

An ecstatic Orlando Cepeda receives the 1958 National League Rookie of the Year Award from *San Francisco Chronicle* baseball writer Bob Stevens.

Al Worthington won 11 games in 54 appearances (12 starts) for the 1958 Giants.

Lonas Edgar Bailey, as announcer Russ Hodges would occasionally refer to him, was acquired from Cincinnati during the 1961 season. He played in two All-Star Games as a member of the San Francisco Giants, one as a starter.

Jackie Brandt was the Giants' starting left fielder in 1959.

Two major participants in the Giants-Dodgers battles of the 1960s, Willie Mays (right) and Los Angeles shortstop Maury Wills.

When we'd go on a long road trip, sometimes I'd hit a lot of home runs, so when we came back, the cans would be there in the clubhouse, and they'd all be numbered, so I could tell which can was for which home run. That's the way the fans were in those days."

McCovey's presence forced Cepeda to move, first to third base and then to the outfield. Cepeda had started his career in the minors at third base, but he was a disaster in the four games he played there in 1959. "I wasn't prepared emotionally," he admitted. "I couldn't handle that." He played reasonably well in the outfield, and keeping both his bat and McCovey's in the lineup more than balanced-out what they lost with Cepeda's defense in left field.

What really hurt the Giants, though, was the erratic play of shortstop Andre Rodgers, who had been a teammate of McCovey's at Phoenix in 1958.

Rodgers was a former cricket player from Nassau who had great athletic ability. He had led the PCL in hitting at .354 in 1958, and he was also an excellent fielder.

"I never saw a guy have a better year than he had at Phoenix," said McCovey. "I thought he was going to be the kind of player Alex Rodriguez is for the Mariners now.

"He was really a great fielder, too. People talk about Shawon Dunston's arm, but he had nothing on Rodgers. He could go get a ball in short left field and he'd throw something that was just skirting the ground when he let it go, but by the time it got to me, it was waist high.

"But, it never worked out for him up here. He made some errors and people got on him, and he just couldn't handle that."

In fact, Rodgers made 22 errors in just 71 games and had a shockingly low fielding percentage of .933 that year. He was a factor in several early Giants losses, and he became a point of debate between Manager Bill Rigney and Owner Horace Stoneham, who loved Rodgers' potential and thought Rigney should continue to play him. Rigney, though, decided to bench Rodgers and play Eddie Bressoud, a proven shortstop.

"Horace always had players he liked and players he didn't," said Rigney, "and Bressoud was definitely one he didn't like."

Herman Franks, then a coach for the Giants and later their manager, told Rigney, "Play Rodgers. The owner likes him." But, Rigney countered, "What do I tell the other 24 players?"

Rigney got his way but his show of independence was probably a big factor in Stoneham's decision to fire Rigney in mid-season in 1960.

With Bressoud at shortstop, the Giants went into the final 10 games of the season with a two-game lead. The first five of those games were at home, but the homestand ended disastrously when the Dodgers swept a three-game series. That dropped the Giants to third place, and that's where they ended as the Dodgers won the pennant.

Willie McCovey receives the 1959 National League Rookie of the Year Award from long-time *San Francisco Examiner* baseball writer Bucky Walter in an on-the-field ceremony prior to a 1960 game at Candlestick Park.

Disappointing as that finish was, there was still next year, and Rigney thought it would be a good one. "I always thought the '60 club was the best I had," he said. "We had a good balance. The younger players had enough experience by then, going through a pennant race, and we still had good veteran pitching, with Sam Jones and Johnny Antonelli. And, of course, we still had Willie Mays."

They also had a new stadium, Candlestick Park, named after the point of land on which it was built, though some thought it should be named after Lefty O'Doul, the former player and Seals manager who represented baseball to many San Franciscans. Builder Charles Harney thought it should be named after him. Years later, some thought that would have been a good idea, as a means to fix the blame.

Many years later, after all the verbal and written abuse Candlestick has taken, it's hard to remember the excitement at its opening. Then Vice President Richard M. Nixon came out for Opening Day and proclaimed it the most beautiful park in the country. In truth, it was a beautiful sight that day, with the San Francisco Bay just beyond it.

The park's shortcomings, though, became painfully obvious when the novelty wore off. Some of them had to do with the players. The Giants dugout along the first base line had a tunnel to the dressing room, but the visitors had to walk all the way in from behind the bullpen, along the right field line to their dugout on the third base line. That was a considerable home field advantage for the Giants because they could duck into their dressing room momentarily, to get warm on the cold nights, while the visiting team had to stay in its dugout. McCovey used to put balm on his always aching knees; in his short time with the Giants later, Bobby Murcer would put his bats in the sauna.

There was another design flaw: There was no door on the toilet in the Giants dugout. "Where is your wife sitting?" Rigney asked architect John Bolles. "In a first base box," said Bolles. "Can she see into the dugout?" asked Rigney. Bolles nodded yes, and then realized what Rigney was saying. A door was quickly put on the toilet.

San Francisco Supervisor Clarissa McMahon had insisted that radiant heat be installed

Candlestick Park Dedication Dinner

MONDAY EVENING, APRIL 11, 1960 AT 7

GARDEN COURT, SHERATON-PALACE HOTEL • SAN FRANCISCO

The commemorative program from the Candlestick Park dedication dinner.

beneath the seats at Candlestick, to ward off the cold, but the heating system didn't work because the pipes were installed an inch from the concrete, instead of being imbedded in it. Flamboyant attorney Melvin Belli later sued because he claimed the Giants had not lived up to their promise to provide heat for the six-seat box he had purchased. Belli won his suit and donated the money to the city to buy trees, with the provision that they not be planted at Candlestick "because they would freeze out there."

And, of course, there was the wind which swept down the hill, freezing spectators, blowing balls off course and causing pain to players. "It blows peanut shells into my eyes," said McCovey.

The fact that the wind blows in San Francisco should not have come as a surprise to anybody who knew San Francisco. There are very few spots in the city where the wind doesn't blow, and certainly Seals Stadium was neither warm nor calm.

But some areas are worse than others, and the Candlestick/Cow Palace area is probably the worst in the city. The wind comes through the gulch from the ocean and gathers force as it travels to hit Candlestick.

The construction planners had thought that the hill in front of Candlestick would block the wind. Wind studies since then have shown that just the opposite is true: When wind hits a barrier, it gathers strength as it finds its way up and around the barrier.

Early visits by Giants executives didn't even hint at this problem because they came in mid-morning, before the wind comes up. When General Manager Chub Feeney came out one afternoon, he was hit by a wintry blast. "Does it always blow like this?" he asked a construction worker. "Only in the afternoon," was the reply. Actually, in the evening, too, as players and fans soon learned.

HORACE STONEHAM

Horace Stoneham, the Giants owner when the club moved to San Francisco, was one of the last of the breed: an owner who had no other business than baseball. Stoneham's father, Charles, had bought the club in 1919 and Horace had inherited it in 1936 when his father died.

Stoneham was a legendary drinker; it was always the first thing anybody mentioned when asked about him. He liked his managers to drink with him, too, though he made an exception for Alvin Dark, whose fundamentalist Christian beliefs precluded alcohol.

His managers, though, usually found excuses not to start drinking with Stoneham because, once you started, it was almost impossible to leave. "I tried it once," said Bill Rigney. "I was sitting there at 3 in the morning and thinking in 5-6 hours I'd have to be getting ready to go out to the ballpark, but Horace could sleep for a couple of days if he wanted. That was the last time I did that."

Horace was known as a "players' owner" because he was generous to his players and treated them well, but he definitely had favorites and players he didn't like. He didn't like Stu Miller, though Miller was a very effective pitcher, and he didn't like shortstop Eddie Bressoud, preferring Andre Rodgers, a former cricket player who was a bust at baseball.

Stoneham also had a strange relationship with club General Manager Chub Feeney. Though Feeney was Stoneham's nephew, those who were around the two in those days said that Stoneham often directed sarcastic comments toward Feeney.

Even before the club moved to San Francisco, Feeney had become the man who generally made the trades, but he tried to ease the strain between him and his uncle by implying that Stoneham was making the decisions. "Before I knew that, I had Chub on the air one day and complimented him on a trade," said announcer Lon Simmons. "He was shaking his head on the other side of the table to try to say he didn't do it."

Rigney, perhaps because he had often played Bressoud instead of Rodgers, or perhaps because he was close to Feeney, was not one of Stoneham's favorites, either. When Rigney was fired, Feeney wanted to put Herman Franks in his place, but he knew better than to propose the idea himself. So he went to Tom "Clancy" Sheehan, a Stoneham confidant, and asked him to propose Franks when Stoneham called a meeting. Sheehan said he would.

When the meeting started, though, Stoneham said, "Tom, we were kind of hoping you would take the job."

Said Sheehan, "I'd be honored."

So Franks had to wait until 1965 to become the Giants manager.

After a few games, Rigney realized that the park was going to favor pitchers, because balls hit to left would die in the wind, not to mention that it's hard for batters to hit when their hands are frozen. "I'll have to manage two ways," he said, "for defense at Candlestick and offense on the road."

Even before that, Mays had made his own evaluations. "That first year, the fence in left field was right up against the stands," he said. "I looked at that and said, 'Nobody's going to hit the ball out of here.'"

Mays immediately changed his batting style for games at Candlestick, adopting an inside-out, golf-type swing to drive the ball away from left field. "I aimed at center field," he said, "because I knew that if I hit it to center field, the wind would blow it to right-center, and I had a chance of getting a home run."

In the field, Mays made another adjustment. "When the ball was hit in the air, I would count 1-2-3," he said, "and then go after it. If you started in the direction the ball was hit, you'd always get fooled, because the wind would take it and blow it in another direction."

Even while adjusting to their new park, the Giants got off to a decent start, generally first or second for the first month. But problems were developing as McCovey, Rookie of the Year the previous season, got off to a very slow start, hitting in the .230 range.

Part of it, McCovey admits, was his own problem. "I wasn't in good shape," he said. "I'd been used to playing ball in the winter, and suddenly, I was not playing. I didn't work as hard to keep in condition as I should have."

But, another part of the problem was that the Giants had decided to change McCovey's hitting style.

"That spring, for some reason, the Giants weren't satisfied with the way I was hitting," said McCovey. "Don't ask me why. I guess they figured here was this big strong lefthanded hitter, so they wanted me to pull the ball. I had always been a hitter who could hit the ball with as much power to left field as I could to right. Even to center. I remember hitting a home run in the L. A. Coliseum to straightaway center field, and not too many hitters could do that.

Scout Buddy Kerr (left) was the man who signed a young pitcher named Juan Marichal (right).

Orlando Cepeda meets serious baseball fan and Vice President Richard Nixon in 1960. Manager Bill Rigney is to Nixon's right and Coach Bill Posedel is in the background.

Willie McCovey, pictured in a minor league uniform, was one of three future Hall of Famers that came from Mobile, Ala. The other two were Henry Aaron and Billy Williams.

"That spring, they sent me to Arizona ahead of everybody else and sent Lefty O'Doul down there with me. We would go out every day and Lefty would want me to pull everything foul. As much as I liked Lefty and respected him, I think that screwed me up."

The Giants' organization at that time seemed determined that their power hitters should be pull hitters, though fortunately, nobody was dumb enough to mess with Mays. Rosy Ryan, a confidant of Owner Horace Stoneham, was down on Cepeda, too, because Orlando often hit to his opposite field, right and right-center.

There was more justification for making McCovey a pull hitter because of the strong wind to right field, but Mays thought the emphasis on pull hitting might even have hurt McCovey's home run totals. "Willie Mac used to hit these high fly balls," he said. "There were many times when he'd hit a ball like that which would start fair and then the wind would blow it foul."

It's hard to say that the Giants did long term damage to McCovey, who ended his career with 521 home runs and has since been voted into the Hall of Fame. Yet, in his rookie year, he hit for a high average without sacrificing power, and he might have been able to do that throughout his career if the Giants had left him alone. "They (opposing teams) pulled some shifts on me you wouldn't believe," said McCovey. "They had four outfielders at times. Being a pull hitter takes away your chances to get base hits."

For the short term, it was certainly damaging to McCovey, who was hitting in the .230s when he was sent to Tacoma of the Pacific Coast League in May. When he was brought back, he was a part-time player the rest of the year and wound up hitting just .238. With McCovey playing a minor role, the Giants weren't as good as Rigney had anticipated they would be, and he paid the price quickly. Though the

Giants were in second place, just five games back in early July, Stoneham fired his manager.

Why? Stoneham's official announcement said the team wasn't hustling, but there was certainly much more to it than that. Rigney thought Stoneham was disappointed because he expected the Giants to be five games in front by then. The dispute over Andre Rodgers played a part. Simmons thought Rigney's friendship with Feeney might have been a factor. "Horace always seemed to distrust those who were close to Chub," said Simmons, who was also a good friend of Feeney's. "Horace 'fired' me several times, but he always forgot by morning."

"You know what bothered me most about the timing of it," said Rigney, "was that I had been pushing to get Juan Marichal up from the minors all season, and the day I was fired, they brought Juan up!"

Marichal immediately showed why Rigney had been eager to bring him up as he shut out the Philadelphia Phillies in a game Simmons remembered for personal reasons. "It was my birthday," said Lon. "In those days, I did the third, fourth and seventh innings, but Juan had a no-hitter going after seven innings and Russ (Hodges) motioned me to keep going. 'I'm giving you a present,' he said. 'I've done no-hitters but you never have.' As it happened, Clay Dalrymple broke up the no-hitter in the eighth."

Rigney's replacement was Sheehan, a scout and close friend of Stoneham's, and so began the most bizarre managing period in San Francisco Giants history. Sheehan, an amiable man with the ability to tell stories (especially about his one-time roommate, Babe Ruth) was admired by Stoneham, but was totally unsuited to the job.

Simmons remembered one game in which Henry Aaron came up with the potential winning run on second base and first base open. Sheehan went out to the mound to talk to his pitcher. Shortstop Bressoud came to the mound and urged that they pitch to Aaron instead of walking him and facing Eddie Matthews. Aaron quickly singled, and the Braves won the game. In the dressing room after the game, Sheehan told the writers, "My shortstop thought we should pitch to Aaron," without ever suggesting that he might have had a voice in that decision.

Perhaps even more indicative of Sheehan's lack of control was a game in which Sanford was being hammered. Head down, Sheehan started to the mound to take him out but Sanford was so angry with himself that he walked off before Sheehan got there and was in the dugout by the time Sheehan got to the mound. "Sheehan never saw him," said Simmons. "He looked up, and all of a sudden his pitcher was gone. He never knew what happened."

At the start of the season, when Rigney was the manager, Sheehan had said, "It would be hard not to win with these players." At the end of the season, he said, "How could anyone win with these players?" Certainly he couldn't; the Giants faded to a fifth place finish.

In 1962, Jim Davenport became the first Giants' third baseman to win a Gold Glove.

On July 19, 1960, Juan Marichal made his major league debut against Philadelphia. He struck out 12 and gave up just one hit—a seventh-inning single by Clay Dalrymple.

Tom "Clancy" Sheehan replaced Bill Rigney as manager during the 1960 season.

Alvin Dark, a key member of the Giants' 1951 National League Champion and 1954 World Champion squads, was named manager after the 1960 season. General Manager Chub Feeney watches Dark address the media following the announcement.

Fortunately, Stoneham realized his mistake and hired another manager for 1961, Alvin Dark, who had played shortstop on the last two Giants pennant winners, in 1951 and 1954.

"I had always thought I would be a manager when I finished my playing career," said Dark. "I think it's easy for a shortstop, second baseman or catcher to become a manager because you're always right in the middle of what's happening and you get to know pitchers, which is really the secret of being a good manager."

Dark had planned to play another year as a reserve infielder for the Milwaukee Brewers, but when Feeney called and asked if he wanted to manage his former club, it was a no-brainer. Because Dark was still a player, the Giants first had to trade for him, so they gave up Rodgers, which was not much of a loss at that point.

Dark was a very demanding manager. He expected something close to perfection from his players and had a set of minor fines he applied if the players failed. "He used to fine us a dozen golf balls if we missed a sign or didn't get a bunt down, things like that," recalled Gaylord Perry. "Well, when I was a rookie, I was only making $7,000 a year, so that meant something. He'd give the golf balls to other players, and they'd come by my locker and say, 'I sure enjoyed playing with your golf balls.' To this day, I can't get much enjoyment out of golf."

Dark was determined to do things his way, and that sometimes led to conflicts with players. Instead of relying on normal statistics, he had a complex system of pluses and minuses, giving more weight to hits in late innings when the game was on the line, for instance, than to hits in pressure situations. Conversely, a strikeout earned more minuses when it occurred in a pressure situation. When Cepeda was holding out during spring training in 1963, he discussed his system with writers and told them that Cepeda had more minuses than pluses. Dark's relationship with Cepeda was never a good one, and that announcement doomed it forever.

Dark also decided that McCovey could not hit left-handed pitchers and platooned him in 1962. "Alvin and I had a talk about that after my career was over and he admitted he was wrong," said McCovey. "Nobody could hit .372 in the Pacific Coast League, as I did, without hitting all kinds of pitching." At the time, McCovey said nothing to Dark. "You didn't talk back to your manager then," he said. Eventually, his bat made his point, as he became the most feared power hitter in the league, against all pitching.

Yet Dark made a brilliant move with Sanford, who had been basically a .500 pitcher since his first year with the Phillies in 1957, when he won 19 games and led the league in strikeouts. Traded to the Giants in 1959, Sanford had been 15-12 and 12-14. Sanford relied heavily on his fast ball, but Dark thought he would be more effective if he varied his pitches more. He had Pitching Coach Larry Jansen force Sanford to start every hitter off with a breaking pitch, which stopped hitters from just laying back and waiting for

Bob Schmidt had 14 homers in 127 games during his rookie season (1958) with the Giants.

Hobie Landrith came to the Giants in a trade with the St. Louis Cardinals after the 1958 season.

DOWNTOWN PARK

In the mid-1950s, when San Francisco was still a minor league city, real estate developer Ben Swig, whose most notable property was the Fairmont Hotel, proposed building a ballpark downtown, to lure an established Major League team.

"When it was broached publicly," said then-Mayor George Christopher, "the department stores were totally opposed to it because they thought it would create so much traffic that people wouldn't come downtown. The managers of Macy's and the Emporium went to the editors at the *Chronicle* and *Examiner* and said they'd move their flagship stores out of downtown San Francisco."

Christopher had been a copyboy at *The Examiner* in his youth, so he knew first-hand how important the store advertising was, and that the stores' opposition would sink

the proposal. He was also sympathetic to the stores. "There was a crying need then for more parking to sustain our department stores," he said, "which is why I worked to get downtown garages. Fifth and Mission, Sutter-Stockton, Portsmouth Square and St. Mary's garages were all built during my administration."

He also hoped that a convention center would be built downtown. "That would increase the traffic because people would be coming from somewhere else and they would be driving cars."

Since then, the Moscone Center has been built in the approximate area where Swig had contemplated building a ballpark, and when Pacific Bell Park is finished in 2000, San Francisco will have both a convention center and a ballpark downtown.

Jack Sanford came to the Giants from the Philadelphia Phillies in 1959. He was second on the staff with 15 wins that year. Sanford won 24 times in 1962—the only time he won 20 games during his 12 Major League seasons.

Tom Haller spent seven of his 12 Major League seasons with the Giants. "Hatch" earned a reputation as a solid defensive catcher who could hit for power—he belted a career-best 27 homers in 1966. After his career ended, Haller served the Giants in various on- and off-the-field capacities—including a five-year stint as general manager (1981-85).

Juan Marichal's feats on the mound always seemed to be overshadowed in comparison to his 1960s contemporaries like Sandy Koufax and Bob Gibson. All Marichal did was win 20 games six times between 1963-69. He either led or tied for the National League in wins four times. Despite winning 243 games, the "Dominican Dandy" never won the Cy Young Award.

Gaylord Perry won 20 games twice while a member of the Giants.

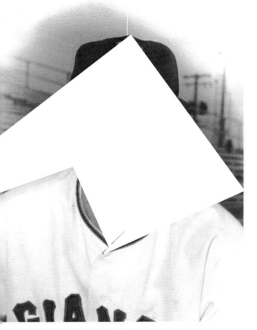

Left-hander Johnny Antonelli was part of the Giants starting rotation from 1958-60.

Sanford's fast ball. Sanford responded in 1962 with the best season of his career, 24-7, as the Giants won the pennant.

As a rookie manager in 1961, Dark did a lot of things right. He realized that the team had become divided into cliques when Sheehan was managing and there was no leadership at the top. Therefore, he met individually with players and as a team, to impress upon them the necessity of being a team.

He also worked with Stoneham and Feeney to make trades to try to balance the Giants, who were loaded with the power hitters Stoneham always liked but had only one good baserunner, Mays. One trade he was especially happy with brought Kuenn for the washed-up Antonelli and Kirkland, who had been a big disappointment. Kuenn could play shortstop, third and left field, which gave Dark some flexibility with his line-ups, and he also had great bat control. "He was really the only player I had who could execute the hit-and-run," said Dark.

There was no doubt that Dark was a brilliant tactician, and his duels with Philadelphia Manager Gene Mauch were legendary. In one game, Mauch warmed up both a left-handed pitcher and a right-hander, trying to make Dark commit to a lineup heavy in hitters who hit from one side. Dark did the same and thought he would one-up Mauch by putting three pitchers in his starting lineup, who he would yank as soon as Mauch committed to his starting pitcher. But Mauch did the same, so their tactics cancelled each other out. During a game, each manager would try to outwit the other, sending up a right-handed pinch-hitter, for instance, and then pulling him to put in a left-hander when the other manager brought in a right-handed pitcher. "You could make changes like that in those days because players didn't complain," said Dark.

Whether it was against the Phillies or any other team in the league, Dark was a total-ly involved manager, and he liked other managers to think that he was calling every pitch, using signs from his position with one foot on the top of the dugout steps.

Not quite, said Tom Haller, who started the season as the Giants catcher, went back to the minors in mid-season but then came up to stay in 1962. "That was before the era when managers called pitches," said Haller. "In those days, you really had to learn your craft. You ran the game. Dark would call pitchouts from time to time (and

A happy bunch of Giants are in General Manager Chub Feeney's office signing their contracts during the early 1960s. Sitting from left to right: Willie McCovey, Willie Mays and Tom Haller. Standing from left to right: Mike McCormick, Feeney and Jim Davenport.

knockdown pitches, a reminder that he had been a player under Leo Durocher) but I called the pitches. It made me feel good because I knew there was a way I could contribute other than just hitting, and it kept me more in the game."

Dark was also a tremendous competitor, with a rage that was hidden just below the surface. After a game in which the Giants lost 1-0 and stranded 12 base runners, Dark exploded in the dressing room, throwing a metal stool against one wall. Part of his little finger got caught in the stool and ripped off, requiring stitches.

Though the Giants' record in Dark's first year, 85-69, was actually their best in their brief San Francisco history to that point, the year was important chiefly for Dark to get to know his team, and vice versa. That was especially true for the pitchers, and Dark had to make a dramatic point in mid-season.

Though relief pitchers were becoming more and more important, and the Giants had one of the best in Stu Miller, starters were still expected to complete games more often than not at that time. In mid-season, though, Miller was becoming seriously overworked because the Giants starters were seldom finishing games. At one point, Miller pitched in seven straight games, a streak which ran through the first game of a doubleheader in Philadelphia. At that point, Dark told Miller to put on his street clothes and join Russ Hodges and Lon Simmons in the announcers' booth, so he wouldn't be tempted to use him again in the second game. "Billy Loes pitched a 1-0 shutout in the second game," remembered Miller, "so Alvin was right, he probably would have used me."

Miller was an unusual reliever because he did not rely on an overpowering fast ball, as most relievers of that day and since have, nor on a trick pitch, like the "forkball" (much like today's split-fingered fastball) that Elroy Face used. He had a sinking fast ball, which hitters could seldom lift out of the park, and a variety of off-speed pitches and a changeup that was probably the best in the majors at the time. "I had a motion which made hitters think the pitch was coming at a faster speed, and I had the control to throw any pitch on any count," said Miller.

By mid-season in 1961, Miller seemed to be a victim of his own success, as starting pitchers were looking for bullpen help more and more. "Dark had told Jack Sanford he wanted six strong innings from him," said Miller, "and I think Jack got to thinking that if he pitched those six innings, that was all that was required.

Dark was very concerned. "I think the starting pitchers were depending on Stu Miller as much as I was," Dark said. "It got to the point where I was afraid he'd get too tired and wouldn't be effective. We were going into Pittsburgh and I told Larry Jansen, our pitching coach, that I was going to leave the starter out there the next three games no matter what, unless there was an injury."

THE WIND

Those who think the wind became a factor at Giants games only when they moved into Candlestick Park never saw a game at Seals Stadium.

Johnny Antonelli lost a mid-July game in 1959 to the Dodgers because Gil Hodges and Charley Neal hit home runs which barely cleared the left field fence, helped greatly in Antonelli's view by the wind.

"A pitcher should be paid double for working here," Antonelli told writers after the game. "It's the worst ballpark in America. Every time you stand up there, you've got to beat the hitter and a 30-mile-an-hour wind."

Newspapers weighed in with editorials blasting Antonelli. *The Chronicle* said Antonelli was notorious for throwing home run pitches, and if he didn't like it here, he should go back to the Polo Grounds. *The Examiner* editorial writer was less pointed, accusing Antonelli only of bad manners in criticizing "our lifegiving summer breeze," but sports editor Curley Grieve called Antonelli a "crybaby."

The Chronicle even sent Jack Fiske, usually the boxing writer, out with a wind meter the next day, to sit in the left field bleach-

ers and record the wind. At times, Fiske reported, the wind gusted up to 32 miles an hour, but at other times, there was no wind at all.

"I never realized how provincial this area was until then," said broadcaster Lon Simmons.

The controversy seemed to have an adverse affect on Antonelli; 14-5 at the time of his outburst, he could only split 10 decisions the rest of the way. In 1960 at Candlestick, he was only 6-7. The Giants traded him, and he retired after the 1961 season, though he was only 31.

Dark picked a good time for his announcement because the next scheduled starter was Marichal, who would go on to complete as many as 30 games in a season and actually finished his career with one more complete game than wins. Well, nobody ever accused Alvin of being dumb. "As it happened, we won three straight," said Dark. "Juan pitched a shutout in the first game and the other two just fell into place."

Given a chance to rest, Miller came back strong and wound up the year with 14 wins and 17 saves, good enough to earn "Fireman of the Year" honors.

It was an exciting season, partly because the Giants had brought in the fences at Candlestick. The power alleys in left- and right-center were reduced from 390 feet to 365 and 375, respectively. Center field was brought in 10 feet to 410 feet, and the distances on the foul lines were reduced from 335 to 330 feet. The results were dramatic: In 1960, only 80 home runs had been hit at Candlestick but there were 174 hit in 1961, 97 of them by the Giants.

Cepeda had a monster year, with 46 homers and 146 RBI, a record for a Giants first baseman. Mays hit 40, and four of them came in an April game in Milwaukee, as the Giants tied a major league team record with eight homers in a 14-4 win.

Yet, overall, the Giants were becoming a frustrating tease for San Francisco fans, good enough to be in contention three of their first four years (even in the off-year, 1960, they had finished above .500, at 79-75) but not good enough to win a pennant.

Meanwhile, the Giants-Dodgers rivalry, although strong as ever, had a different flavor than when both teams were located in the same metropolitan area. No longer were the parks full of fans of the visiting team, but the rivalry between San Francisco and Los Angeles added an extra ingredient to the battle, and Los Angeles sports columnists took particular glee at poking fun at the Giants and their fans.

When the Giants went 10-16 in June in their first season, a writer coined the rhyming term "June Swoon," and that tag hung on for years, flying directly in the face of facts; in the first 10 seasons, the Giants had only three losing records in June. In 1962, *Los Angeles Times* columnist Jim Murray, using his unique technique of humorous exaggeration, noted that you could set your calendar by the Giants. "A business executive standing by his window sees a falling figure shoot past the window. 'Oh, oh,' the man says, glancing at his chronometer. 'It must be June. There go the Giants.'"

Los Angeles Examiner columnist Melvin Durslag wrote of the "gas jobs" the Giants took in losing in 1958 and 1959. "If the Giants are permitted to remain in San Francisco, people there will wind up killing each other."

Against that backdrop, the Giants and Dodgers engaged in one of the most thrilling pennant races in National League history in 1962, a race which ultimately went down to a three-game playoff.

On the Giants side, it was set up by three pitching moves, one that was not made and two that were.

This "special" Croix de Candlestick was handed out at the 1984 All-Star Game to commemorate Stu Miller's "incident" at the 1961 All-Star Game.

Stu Miller

Mention the name Stu Miller to any long-time Giants fan and the response will be, "Oh, yeah, the guy who got blown off the mound in the 1961 All-Star game."

Well, not quite.

"The wind was stronger that day than any time I can remember," said Miller. "I had just come into the game in relief and I was leaning in to get my sign. The wind used to swirl around and come back toward the mound, and this big gust came out and hit me. I kind of leaned a little bit to my left to get away from it. The American League players on the bench started yelling when they saw that, so the plate umpire called a balk. He knew it wasn't intentional on my part, but he had no choice.

"Then, the next day, I saw these big, black headlines: 'Stu Miller blown off the mound.' I asked the writers, 'Did you see me pinned against the center field fence?'"

Miller didn't usually mind the wind. "Actually, it helped me because it gave me such a good break on my pitches," he said. "I remember one time pitching to Yogi Berra (in the 1962 World Series) when I threw a pitch at his waist. Yogi twisted out of the way, and damned if the wind didn't blow it across the plate. Yogi probably still doesn't believe that was a strike because he didn't see the end of the pitch.'"

Miller was an excellent relief pitcher who won 14 games with a league-leading 17 saves in 1961 and had 19 saves when the Giants won the pennant the following year. He had special success against the Dodgers' Frank Howard. Frank had a bad habit of hitting off his front foot, remembered Miller. "He was always lunging at my pitches. I think I struck him out the first nine times I faced him."

But, despite that success, he's still remembered primarily for being "blown off" the mound. "After all this time, that's still the first thing everybody asks about," he said.

Stu Miller had 19 saves when the Giants won the 1962 National League pennant.

Alvin Dark managed the San Francisco Giants to their first National League Championship in 1962.

Eddie Fisher, who made his Major League debut with the Giants in 1959, was part of a six-player trade that brought left hander Billy Pierce from the Chicago White Sox prior to the 1962 season.

The non-move involved pitcher Billy O'Dell, called "Digger" by his teammates after a character on the Fibber McGee and Molly radio show of the 1940s. The left-handed O'Dell was a hot-head who sometimes let his temper get the best of him. Simmons remembered one game when he was constantly arguing calls with the umpire, and then served up a fat one that the batter hit far out of the park. O'Dell yelled at the umpire, "Was that f—ing pitch a strike?" Dark was on his way out to the mound to take O'Dell out, but the umpire tossed him before Alvin got there.

Partly because of his temper and partly because he had won only 15 games in his first two years with the Giants, he had originally been put on the list of players available in the expansion draft to the new Houston Colts 45s and New York Mets. At the last moment, however, the Giants pulled him off and substituted reserve infielder Joey Amalfitano. O'Dell went on to post a 19-14 record, the best of his career, for the 1962 Giants.

The Giants also made a significant trade, sending four little used players—pitchers Don Zanni, Eddie Fisher and Verle Tiefenthaler and outfielder/first baseman Bob Farley—to the Chicago White Sox for Don Larsen and Billy Pierce. Larsen helped with five wins and nine saves, but it was Pierce who was really the key to the trade.

It didn't seem that way in Spring Training, when Pierce was consistently rocked. "Every time he pitched," said Cepeda, "all I could see was No. 44 (McCovey) or No. 24 (Mays) going to the wall as they chased balls."

Yet, that was both Arizona, and the spring, where good pitchers often have poor results. It was much different during the season. "I had been after Chub Feeney to

Veteran Don Larsen provided depth in the Giants bullpen during 1962. He saved 11 games, second on the club to Stu Miller's 19.

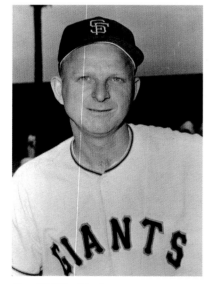

Carroll "Whitey" Lockman was an outfielder for the 1958 San Francisco Giants and served as coach from 1961-64.

Lefty Billy Pierce came from the White Sox prior to the 1962 season. He wound up winning 16 times during that pennant-winning season.

get us a left-handed pitcher," said Dark, "and when we got Billy Pierce, I thought we had a real good chance. We needed a left-hander to pitch in Candlestick, because the wind was so strong out to right field. I would always try to pitch Billy on the first day of a home stand and also the last. I didn't want to use him too much on the road because he'd get tired in the heat in the east and midwest."

Dark's strategy worked perfectly. Pierce was a perfect 12-0 at Candlestick (16-6 overall) and won a playoff game and a World Series game, both at the 'Stick.

"We knew we had a very good team, a team that was capable of winning a lot of games," said Haller. "We had good pitching, we had the big stars, we had Jose Pagan playing well at shortstop. Ed Bailey and I split the catching, and between us we had 35 home runs and 100 RBI. We had Alvin Dark in his second year of managing, and he was a very good baseball man."

To win a pennant, a team usually has to get unexpected help from players below the star level, and they got that from their double play combination of Pagan and second baseman Chuck Hiller.

Pagan played 13 years in the majors, mostly on the strength of his season in 1962, by far the best of his career. He had a great year in the field and made surprising offensive contributions, scoring more runs (73) and knocking in more (57) than in any other season he played.

Hiller was even more of a surprise. He had been up for 70 games the previous year, when the writers had fun with their "Haller-Hiller, Killer-Diller" rhyme, but was regarded as a marginal player, neither a great defensive player nor a strong hitter; he wound up hitting just .243 in an eight-year career. In 1962, though, he worked well with Pagan defensively and was an effective hitter, with a .276 average and 94 runs scored. Three years later, both he and Pagan had deteriorated so much that they were both traded early in the season, but in 1962, they were very important to the team's success.

The Giants also had the best-balanced pitching staff they had in those early years. Pierce and O'Dell provided strong left-handed starting. The relief pitching was solid with Larsen complementing Miller, who had 19 saves, an excellent figure in that era. Sanford had his best year with 24 wins and Marichal won 18, the precursor to a stretch when he won 20 or more games for six of seven seasons.

Haller had caught Marichal in the minors—Marichal had come up just a half season before Haller—so he already knew what others were just learning, that Marichal was not only a great pitcher but an original.

"He had four basic pitches, a fastball, a slider which had a very sharp break, an overhand curve and a changeup," remembered Haller. "A little later, he also added a screwball. He could throw pitches from different angles, which made it seem that he had even more pitches. If he got two strikes on a right-handed hitter, for instance, he'd drop down (pitch sidearm) and that would really mess with the batter. What really made him was his control, because he could put any pitch wherever he wanted. Plus, he had that big windup, which bothered hitters even more.

"Because I had caught Juan in the minors, we knew each other very well. I always talked to pitchers before games to try to find out what they were thinking, because it was better if you were on the same wavelength. Ideally, you always wanted to be calling the pitch the pitcher wanted to throw. He made the ultimate decision, because he could shake off your sign, but you didn't want him doing that a lot because that messed up his psyche. With Juan, there was never any problem because we spent so much time talking about what he could do. I remember suggesting he might try coming in sidearm early in the count against a right-handed hitter to get him looking for it, and then come in overhand and surprise him."

It was a wild season, with the Giants and Dodgers exchanging first place five times. The Dodgers took a big hit in July when Sandy Koufax, who had already won 14 games, was lost for the season with a finger injury, but it didn't stop the Los Angelenos. In early September, the Dodgers had a 5-1/2 game lead as they came to Candlestick for a three-game series that showed Dark at his ingenious best—or worst, as the Dodgers claimed.

The classic high-leg kick of Juan Marichal was just one of the many ways he baffled hitters during the 1960s.

Shortstop Jose Pagan (left) and second baseman Chuck Hiller (right) served as the Giants' double play combo during the memorable 1962 season.

Jose Pagan set a Giants record by playing in 164 games during the 1962 season.

In a nice start to the memorable 1962 season, Willie Mays and Juan Marichal share a happy moment after the Giants' 6-0 win over the Milwaukee Braves. Mays hit a solo homer in his first at-bat, while Marichal pitched a three-hitter and had a two-run single.

Chuck Hiller and Tom Haller

Giants groundskeepers try to fix a muddy situation around first base by adding dirt during a July 6, 1962 contest against the Dodgers at Candlestick Park. The Dodgers claimed the additional dirt, along with the mud, slowed down their runners, especially Maury Wills, who went on to steal 104 bases that season. The Giants won this game, 12-3.

The Dodgers had opened their new park in 1962, and it was clearly a pitcher's park, tailored to the Dodgers team, which had strong pitching and very little hitting. The big-inning concept by which championship teams had lived since the days of Babe Ruth was foreign to the Dodgers. They scratched out one run at a time, and the key man in their offense was Maury Wills, who set a season stolen base record with 104 that year.

To give Wills even more of a chance to steal, the Dodgers used a steamroller over their infield to harden it to nearly the consistency of an airport landing strip. Even the artificial turf surfaces that came later didn't give a baserunner better traction than that infield.

Dark had tried various strategies to counter Wills, once even telling first baseman Cepeda to take a fielding position in the basepath, rather than holding Wills on, to force him to take a wider path to second. But, since Wills could take a longer lead with Cepeda off the base, he was still able to steal second.

For this series, Dark tried another tactic, telling groundskeeper Matty Schwab to water the area around first base extensively. When asked about it, Dark said innocently, "I guess a pipe broke." The Dodgers complained to the umpires, who told the Giants to bring out sand to soak up the water. That was fine with Dark, because adding sand to the mix just made the footing even more treacherous.

Writers nicknamed Dark the "Swamp Fox." In his column, Melvin Durslag of the *Los Angeles Herald Examiner* claimed, "There was enough water there to run a hydroelectric plant." Jim Murray of the *Los Angeles Times* commented that, "An aircraft carrier wouldn't have run aground. . .instead of coaches, lifeguards should be stationed on the bases."

Helped by this tactic, the Giants swept the series to climb within 2-1/2 games of the Dodgers.

And, after the season, the Giants players voted a full World Series share of $7,290 to Schwab.

Despite losing that series, the Dodgers maintained their lead until falling into a tie

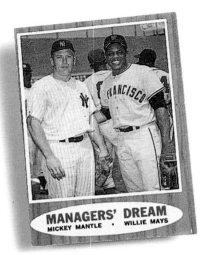

A 1962 Topps Baseball Card depicting the two key players of that year's World Series.

on the last day of the season, and then losing in the playoff—on their own, dry field.

After winning the playoff, the Giants were happy and relieved—and tired. "We got back late from L.A.," remembered Cepeda, "and we had to be at the park at 10 the next morning because it was a noon game. We were all so tired. The first game was a letdown."

Or, as Mays put it when he was asked if he'd be tense for the Series, "Man, I'm all out of tense."

The Giants also had to face the great money pitcher of the New York Yankees, Whitey Ford, and Ford beat O'Dell, 6-2. It wasn't a typical game for Ford, though, especially by the high standards he had set for himself in the World Series. The Giants stopped Ford's Series record for consecutive scoreless innings at 33-2/3 with a run in the second, and he seemed to be going to a three-ball count most of the game. It was 2-2 after six innings, but Boyer homered in the seventh for the go-ahead run, and the Yankees added two runs in the eighth and another run in the ninth while holding the Giants scoreless.

"The first game of the World Series was like '51 when we won the playoff and had to start the Series the next day," said Dark. "You're just so tired, and the Series seems anti-climactic after what you've been through. But the second day, you start to get caught up in the excitement of the World Series, and I think that's what happened to our players in '62."

The Giants did-in fact, win the second game as Sanford threw a three-hitter to beat Ralph Terry, with McCovey hitting a home run for the second run in a 2-0 game. The hard-throwing Sanford was notorious for running out of gas—he'd completed only a

Three reasons why the Giants won the 1962 National League pennant: Orlando Cepeda, who hit .306 with 35 homers and 114 RBI; Willie Mays and his league-leading 49 home runs; and Harvey Kuenn, with his .306 average.

Jack Sanford's three-hit shutout in Game Two of the 1962 World Series evened the series with the Yankees at one game apiece. Chuck Hiller (26), Giants Manager Alvin Dark (in jacket) and catcher Tom Haller congratulate Sanford.

third of his 39 starts that season—and Dark had told him, "Just throw as hard as you can as long as you can." Dark was assuming that would only be about six innings, and he had his bullpen ready at that point. But Sanford was in control for the whole game.

In the ninth, Sanford had to face the heart of the powerful Yankees batting order with just that two-run margin, but by this time, Dark had so much faith in the powerful right-hander that he didn't have anybody warming up in the bullpen. His confidence seemed justified when Sanford quickly got two outs, on a groundout by Bobby Richardson back to the mound and another groundout by Tom Tresh, this one to Hiller at second base. Then Mickey Mantle powered a Sanford fast ball off the fence in right-center for a double. The tying run was at the plate, in the form of Roger Maris, who had set a season home run record with 61 the previous year, 1961.

The Giants went into a shift against the pull-hitting Maris, with third baseman Davenport lining up at second, shortstop Pagan moving just to the second-base side and second baseman Hiller moving several steps toward first base. It was the perfect defense on this play. Maris hit a sharp ground ball just to the right of McCovey

Jim Davenport slides into home during 1962 World Series action at Candlestick Park, with Yogi Berra trying to apply the tag.

Felipe Alou crashes into the right field fence trying to catch a Roger Maris fly ball during Game One of the 1962 World Series.

This classic newspaper photograph shows Willie McCovey crossing the plate after hitting a solo homer in Game Two of the 1962 World Series. The Giants won 2-0.

at first base. Against a conventional defense, it would have gone into right field for a single. But Hiller was able to get to the ball and throw Maris out at first, and the San Francisco Giants had the first World Series win in their history.

The Series then went back to New York, and McCovey got a frightening experience: playing right field in Yankee Stadium.

McCovey usually played left, but Dark knew that left field in Yankee Stadium in October, with the low-lying sun right in the fielder's eyes, is murderous for experienced outfielders. McCovey would have been seriously overmatched, so Dark moved Felipe Alou from right to left. "That's the most scared I've ever been on a baseball field," said McCovey. "Roger Maris hit a fly ball to right center and my heart was in my mouth. I looked at Mays, hoping he'd come over and catch it, but Mays wasn't even moving. But after I caught that ball, I was all right."

The 35-year-old Pierce, in the last successful season of what was an outstanding career, had a two-hit shutout going into the seventh. Then, the Yankees scored three times. With Don Larsen having relieved Pierce, the third run scored on what should have been a double-play grounder by Clete Boyer. Hiller bobbled the throw from Pagan just long enough to allow Boyer to beat Hiller's throw to first, with Maris scoring from third.

Yankee starter Bill Stafford was struck in the left leg by a fearsome line drive off the bat of Alou in the eighth, but he stayed in the game and held the Giants scoreless until Bailey followed a Mays double with a home run in the eighth. His leg still burning with pain, the courageous Stafford got Davenport to fly out to left fielder Tresh for the final out, as the Yankees took a game edge in the Series with the 3-2 win.

Hiller, whose slight bobble had made him the goat in the fourth game, was the hero as he hit a grand slam, the first for a National Leaguer in a Series game, in the seventh inning, giving the Giants a 7-3 win.

The game had shaped up as a pitching duel between Ford and Marichal, but neither came close to finishing. Marichal left first, after tearing a fingernail while attempting to bunt in the fifth inning. It was not only the end of the game but the end of the season for Marichal.

Ford lasted only slightly longer. In the second, he had given up a two-run homer to Tom Haller on a breaking pitch. "Ford's control was off, so I just waited for a pitch I could hit," said Haller. After that, Ford pitched strongly after giving up two

Prior to Game Three of the World Series, Giants pitchers (left to right) Bob Garibaldi, Mike McCormick, Jim Duffalo and Juan Marichal run the Yankee Stadium outfield.

second-inning runs on a homer by Tom Haller, but the Yankees rallied for two runs to tie in the bottom of the sixth as Ford's turn at bat came up. "I'm not tired," he told Manager Ralph Houk, "but I'm losing my stuff." So Houk sent up Yogi Berra as a pinch-hitter. Berra walked, but the Yankees got no more runs.

Jim Coates relieved Ford and gave up a walk to Davenport, struck out Haller and then gave up a double to pinch-hitter Matty Alou, with Davenport stopping at third. Houk brought in Marshall Bridges, a hard-throwing left-hander, and when Dark sent up right-handed pinch-hitter Bob Neiman, Houk ordered him intentionally walked to load the bases and set up a potential double play.

Houk was playing the percentages. Hiller had come up in the same situation two innings earlier, the bases full of Giants, and had whiffed on a 3-and-2 curve from Ford. He was facing another left-hander, and Houk was hoping for another good result for the Yankees. The last thing he was expecting was a home run; Hiller had hit only three, none off left-handed pitchers, all season.

Though he was known primarily for his fastball, Bridges threw two curves to Hiller, the first for a strike on a half-swing by the fooled Hiller, the second a ball. Then he

Chuck Hiller crosses home plate after hitting the first grand slam by a National Leaguer in a World Series game.

tried to jam Hiller with a fastball inside, but the ball came out across the plate, so Hiller could get a full extension. He lashed at the pitch and sent it high to right field. Maris backed up against the 344-foot sign but had no chance as the ball sailed over his head and into the stands. Hiller, who had been running full-out after hitting the ball, slowed and went into a home-run trot he had seldom been able to utilize. After he crossed the plate, he was mobbed by teammates.

"I didn't think he could hit the ball that far," said Bridges after the game. "I didn't know he had that much power."

It was just as much a surprise to Hiller, who admitted he was just trying to get a piece of the ball and get a run across. "It was the first grand slam I've ever hit in organized baseball," said Hiller. "When I hit it, I thought it might go out but I couldn't be sure, so I just ran like hell."

Rain washed out the first attempt at the fifth game, and that extra day gave both managers the chance to come back with their second-game starters. Sanford didn't have quite the mastery he'd had in the second game, though he did strike out 10 Yankees, but the score was tied at 2-2 going into the bottom of the eighth. Then Tresh hit a three-run homer. Terry gave up a single run in the top of the ninth and then shut down the Giants, the 5-3 win giving the New Yorkers a 3-2 edge as the Series headed back to San Francisco.

A severe storm delayed the Sixth Game of the 1962 World Series for five days. Members of the Giants (left to right) Harvey Kuenn, Doc Bowman, Orlando Cepeda and John Orsino survey the conditions at Candlestick Park.

October is often the finest month of the year in San Francisco, the Indian Summer when the fog disappears, the sun shines and temperatures are in the 70s. In 1962, though, a heavy storm pounded the Bay Area, forcing postponement of the sixth game for three days and sending both teams to Modesto for workouts.

"We should have won the World Series," said Mays. "We had just as good a team as the Yankees. We had the pitching and we felt we were the better team, but when we had to go to Modesto to work out, it was kind of a letdown."

Remembering how Dark had ordered the Candlestick field watered down a month earlier, Dodgers Vice President Fresco Thompson professed to wonder why the games couldn't be played. "It was wetter than this when we played here," he said.

Even then, it took some doing to play the sixth game because the rain had sunk deep into the field at Candlestick. Helicopters were sent whirling over the park to dry out the ground. Commissioner Ford Frick, who gave permission to play the game, ordered the teams to forego batting practice and have only minimal infield drills. Even after the helicopters left, the outfield remained soggy.

The delay caused by the rain enabled both Ford and Pierce to return for their third starts of the Series. That was especially gratifying to Pierce because, when his Chicago White Sox team had played in the Series in 1959, he had not been given a chance to start, pitching only in relief. He made the most of his opportunity in this game, going the full nine innings and yielding only three hits to pick up a 5-3 victory that tied the Series again. For Ford, it was his fifth loss in World Series play to go with 10 victories; both were records.

The game also gave Cepeda a chance to redeem himself. Orlando had gone into the game at 0-for-12 in the Series, but got three hits, including a double in the three-run Giants fourth and a single when the Giants added their final two runs an inning later.

That brought on a classic matchup, Terry, 23-12 for the Yankees in the regular sea-

New York Yankees' pitcher Whitey Ford (left) and teammate John Blanchard watch a helicopter dry the Candlestick Park field prior to Game Six of the 1962 World Series.

son, against Sanford, the Giants' leading winner, though perhaps not their best pitcher. Marichal was already regarded as the Giants best in his third season, but his fifth game injury made him unavailable.

The game was exactly the type of pitchers' duel that had been expected, scoreless for the first four innings. In the fifth, Bill Skowron and Boyer singled, and Terry walked to load the bases with nobody out. If it had been a couple of innings later, the Giants probably would have played the infield in, but at this point, they stayed back and got Tony Kubek to ground into a double play. But Skowron scored, and the Yankees had a 1-0 lead.

In the eighth, the Yankees again loaded the bases with nobody out, knocking Sanford out, but O'Dell came in to get Maris to hit a ground ball to Hiller, who threw home to force Bobby Richardson. Elston Howard then hit a double-play ground ball to Davenport, and the score remained at 1-0.

In the bottom of the ninth, Matty Alou led off with a bunt single for the Giants, but Felipe Alou and Hiller struck out. The Giants were down to one out, but it was a big one—Mays. Willie knew what he wanted to do. "I was thinking home run," he said, "but I was a little behind the pitch." His drive went screaming down the right field line for a double.

Now, the rain was definitely a factor. On a dry field, Mays' drive would have been into the corner, and Alou would have scored easily, because with two outs, he was running as soon as Mays hit the ball. But the field was soggy and the ball held up long enough for Maris to come over and cut it off.

Knowing that Maris had an accurate arm, Giants third base Coach Whitey Lockman held Alou at third. It was the right decision, but ever since, those close to the Giants have played a mind game: What if Mays had been the runner on first and Alou had been the hitter?

There's no doubt in Dark's mind. "If it had been Willie Mays running, he'd have run over the catcher if he'd had to to score. There would have been a terrific collision at

Giants Manager Alvin Dark (left) and Yankees skipper Ralph Houk make small talk prior to Game Seven of the 1962 World Series.

The lone run from Game Seven of the 1962 World Series came in the fifth inning as the Yankees' Tony Kubek grounds into a double play, scoring Bill Skowron from third base.

home plate. Mays was always thinking of scoring when he was on base. Other players don't do that. They're thinking one base at a time, or maybe two, but Willie was always thinking of what he had to do to score."

There is no doubt in Mays's mind, either. "I scored many times on plays like that in the regular season," he said. "If it had been me, I'd have tried to score.

Another factor in Lockman's mind, too, was the batter coming to the plate: McCovey. In the regular season, platooned so he hit only against right-handed pitchers, McCovey had hit 20 home runs in just 229 at-bats. Terry, of course, was a right-handed pitcher.

Some interesting thoughts were going through Terry's head, too. In 1960, the Yankees had lost the World Series when Terry had surrendered a home run to Bill Mazeroski in the bottom of the ninth in Game 7. It was again the bottom of the ninth, and McCovey was a much more dangerous hitter than Mazeroski, and Willie had hit a home run off Terry in the second game of the Series.

This time, though, Terry had good fortune on his side. McCovey crushed an inside fastball but it went to the wrong spot, just up and to the left of second baseman Richardson. Though some later stories about McCovey's drive had Richardson leaping for the ball, in fact he just reached up to grab it. Except for its importance, it was an ordinary play.

And so ended the Giants' first World Series in San Francisco. Fans were disappointed that the team had lost, but thrilled by the season and certain that with players like Mays, McCovey and Cepeda, and pitchers like Sanford and Marichal, there would be many pennants to come.

The Three Alous
(left to right): Jesus,
Matty and Felipe.

But all these players would be long gone before the Giants would again reach the
World Series.

The Giants added to their reputation with two unusual firsts the next two years. On
Sept. 15, 1963, at Forbes Field, they became the first team ever to play three brothers at
the same time in the same game with Felipe, Matty and Jesus Alou. In 1964, Masanori
Murakami became the first Japanese player in the Major Leagues, compiling a 5-1 record
in relief over two years before his Japanese team recalled him. Murakami knew no
English before coming to the Giants and relied on his teammates to teach him, and they
used him to have some fun with Herman Franks, who was the Giants manager. When
Franks came to the mound, Murakami greeted him with a phrase he had been taught:
"Take a hike, Herman."

There was little hilarity in the Giants front office, though, when the club faded to third
place, 11 games behind the pennant-winning Dodgers. Dark tried to explain that his
club had had too many injuries to compete. "Injuries are part of the game, Alvin," said
Stoneham. "You have to win."

Time was clearly running out for Dark, who knew he had to win the pennant in 1964
to save his job. He had two problems with Stoneham, one of which became very public
in mid-season and another which was not publicized until well after Dark had been fired.

The public issue was Dark's attitude toward black and Latin players. He had
had several run-ins with Cepeda, particularly after a game in which Orlando did
not run-out a ground ball and Dark slammed into him verbally in the dressing
room later. Cepeda publicly criticized Dark then, and he feels even today that
Dark was overly critical. "I had always had knee problems," said Cepeda, in an

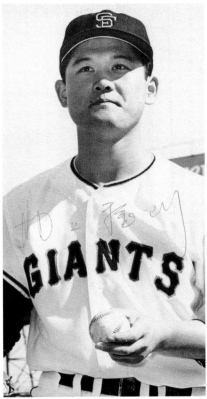

Masanori Murakami saved eight games and won four for the Giants in 1965. He returned to Japan after the season.

Murakami became the first Japanese player to pitch in a Major League Baseball game, making his debut, Sept. 1, 1964.

Despite pitching in only 19 games from 1963-64, pitcher John Pregenzer achieved cult-like status. Even a fan club was formed for the six-foot-five right hander. Gaylord Perry sits beside Pregenzer.

Ron Herbel was a middle-inning reliever in the 1960s.

The "Baby Bull," Orlando Cepeda, ranks among the San Francisco top 10 in homers (226) and RBI (767).

interview for this book. "I had an operation when I was only 15. In 1962, I hurt my knee again, but I kept playing. Dark thought I was faking it, but it got so bad that I finally had to have another operation in 1965."

McCovey alludes to some "racial things" that were going around the clubhouse. "It didn't bother me as much as some of the older players," he said. McCovey had been through much worse, playing in the largely segregated South when he was a minor leaguer. "When I played for Dallas in the Texas League, black players couldn't play in Shreveport. We had three black players, so when the team went to Shreveport, we stayed in Dallas."

Dark was from the South—he had played quarterback for Louisiana State University—and he had been warned by Feeney when he was hired as manager that he would have trouble because the Giants had several black and Latin players on the team who would assume that he was prejudiced because of his background.

In mid-season, the Giants were in New York and *Newsday* columnist Stan Isaacs stopped by to interview Dark, asking him what was wrong with his team. Dark cited injuries and "dumb base running," talking of a play the previous night on which Del Crandall had almost grounded into a triple play.

Isaacs' column quoted Dark at length. The most damaging quotes, and the most widely-circulated, were these: "We have trouble because we have so many Negro and Spanish-speaking ballplayers on this team. They are just not able to perform up to the white ballplayers when it comes to mental alertness. You can't make most Negro and Spanish players have the pride in their team that you can get from white players."

Dark pointed out that the Giants were starting seven Latins and blacks, and that three of them—Jim Ray Hart, Pagan and Jesus Alou—had replaced white players. He

Felipe Alou's .316 average was tops on the Giants in 1962. His speed helped him cut off many balls out in right field.

Willie Kirkland was the Giants' right fielder from 1958-60.

had made Mays the captain in mid-season. None of his explanations, nor the fact that he claimed to have been misquoted, had any effect. Jackie Robinson, who had played against Dark in New York, came to his defense, but that didn't seem to make any difference.

It is important to remember the atmosphere at the time. Civil rights protests were going on everywhere, and the South was still resisting integration of schools and public facilities. Dark was undeniably Southern, in his talk and his religion, and his bias was assumed.

It was not quite as simple as that. I have talked to Dark many times since he was first named Giants manager up to the present, and this is what I believe: Dark held many of the beliefs about blacks and Latins that were common to those of his background and I have little doubt that he was accurately quoted by Isaacs. Simmons, in fact, remembers Dark making similar comments later to Bay Area writers that were not written. But despite that, he tried conscientiously to treat players as individuals, not by the stereotypes, with the possible exception of Cepeda. He did not deserve the public criticism he got.

It was not the racial issue that was most bothering Giants Owner Stoneham, though, as Dark admitted in a 1980 book with John Underwood, *When in Doubt, Fire the Manager.* Dark wrote, "I became a hypocrite in Mr. Stoneham's eyes. I, a married man, had fallen in love with another woman."

Dark had met a stewardess, Jackie Rockwood, on his way back from winning the Baseball Players Golf tournament in Miami in January, 1962, and he had fallen in love. He would eventually be divorced from his first wife in 1969 and marry Jackie the following year, a marriage which has lasted ever since.

This probably wouldn't have bothered Stoneham except that he knew that Dark was a deeply religious man. The Giants owner had not expected Dark to drink with him, as other managers did, because he respected Dark's religious beliefs. Then, Dark turned out to be all too human and, as Dark suggested, a hypocrite in Stoneham's eyes.

So Dark had to win the pennant or else. Thanks to a late-season collapse by the Phillies, who blew a 6-1/2 game lead with just 10 games to go, the Giants were in the race on the final weekend, but a loss to the Chicago Cubs on the last Saturday eliminated them from the race. It was goodbye Alvin, hello Herman Franks, as the Giants manager.

Franks had been a coach for Dark, and for Rigney in the Giants' first year in San Francisco, and he was a good friend of both men, as well as Chub Feeney. He had also closed out his undistinguished playing career with one game with the Giants in 1949, so he was a natural choice.

Herman was a volatile man whose low boiling point caused him to have contentious debates with reporters who questioned his strategy after games, though his anger never

Jimmy Ray Hart's 31 homers in 1964 is the most by any San Francisco Giants' rookie.

Herman Franks with Owner Horace Stoneham. Franks managed the Giants to four consecutive second place finishes from 1965-68.

carried over to the next day. He was not the tactician that Dark was, preferring to let his players do their thing. He made no pretense of treating every player the same: There was one code for the stars, particularly Mays, and another for the lesser players. That was a successful strategy to a point, because the Giants had great players like Mays and McCovey and two great pitchers in Marichal and Gaylord Perry. "Mays used to have problems getting up in the morning because he'd stay up watching TV at night," remembered Franks, "so I'd give him an extra half hour to show up at the park. I know some players resented that, but I'd say to them, 'Look at what he's doing for us. He's carrying us on his back.'"

But Franks is best known for residing over the most frustrating period in San Francisco Giants history, managing four straight second-place teams. In 1969, the National League split into two divisions and Clyde King was the manager, but it made no difference to the Giants, who finished second in the new Western Division. "We finished second so many times, I sometimes thought we would never win again," said Mays.

There has probably never been a team with such big stars that couldn't win a pennant. Mays and McCovey are in the Hall of Fame, and Mays is usually regarded as the best player of his generation. Marichal and Perry are also in the Hall of Fame.

GREATEST GAME

On a cold (naturally) night on July 2, 1963, at Candlestick, Juan Marichal and Warren Spahn dueled in what may be the greatest baseball game ever.

Marichal had already pitched a no-hitter the previous month, 1-0 over Houston, the first no-hitter by a Giants pitcher since Carl Hubbell in 1929, and he brought a 12-3 record into the game, en route to 25-8 for the season. Spahn would win 23 games that year for the Milwaukee Braves, the last big year in his magnificent career, which would end two years later with Spahn pitching for the Giants.

Inning after inning, the two great pitchers put up zeroes on the scoreboard. After nine innings, Milwaukee Manager Bobby Bragan asked Spahn to come out of the game. Spahn refused. In the Giants dugout, Manager Alvin Dark asked Marichal if he wanted to come out. "A 42-year-old man is still pitching," the 25-year-old Marichal told Dark. "I can't come out."

So, they kept pitching and putting up zeroes until the bottom of the 16th when Willie Mays hit a home run to win the game, 1-0. "Man, I was tired," said Mays. "I just wanted to go home."

There have been great games pitched by good pitchers, most notably the 1959 game in which Harvey Haddix pitched a perfect game for 12 innings, only to lose in the 13th.

But Haddix was not a Hall of Fame pitcher. Both Spahn and Marichal are in the Hall, and so is Mays, who supplied the winning run. To have the complete story written by three Hall-of-Famers. . . . well, it doesn't get better than that.

Marichal was the better pitcher but Perry was a tremendous competitor, a man who constantly challenged hitters—and, sometimes, his own teammates, if they were so foolish as to make an error behind him or strike out in the clutch. "I always thought that Marichal would have been even better if he'd had Perry's makeup," said Franks. "Perry always wanted the ball."

Marichal was a star from the first game he pitched in the big leagues, throwing a one-hitter against the Philadelphia Phillies, and his teammates had supreme confidence in him. "I always felt that, when Juan pitched, the team expected to win," said Mike McCormick, who had two separate stints with the Giants in the 1960s. "With the rest of us, even Gaylord, it was like the hitters thought they had to get more runs to win."

It took Perry quite a bit longer than Marichal to succeed. He had signed for a big bonus at 19 in 1958 but he spent 4-1/2 years in the minors before reaching the majors in 1962. That was partly his own choosing. "I said I wanted to start in Class C (the second lowest level of minor league play at the time) because I wanted to work my way up. When I went to Spring Training that year and saw Mays and McCovey and Cepeda, as well as hitters like Leon Wagner and Willie Kirkland and Jackie Brandt, I was very glad I'd made that decision."

Perry did very little in his first two years in the majors. He was up and down in the pennant year of 1962, appearing in 13 games, with a 3-1 record and 5.23 ERA. He pitched briefly in relief in the playoffs, but because he was not on the roster on September 1, he was not eligible for the World Series. The next year he was 1-6 with a 4.03 ERA.

Mike McCormick is San Francisco's all-time leader in wins (104) and complete games (77) by a left-hander.

If Perry hadn't gotten a big bonus, the Giants probably would have cut him loose before the 1964 season. As it was, he was still on the staff but relegated to the low position on the pitching totem pole, long relief.

And, that's where he was in May, when he was summoned into the second game of a doubleheader against the Mets, with the game tied in the 13th inning. "They didn't have anybody left, so they had to pitch me," said Perry. Tom Haller was the catcher. When Gaylord came to the mound, Haller said to him, "Why don't you try out that pitch you've been experimenting with?"

That pitch was a spitball, illegal in Major League Baseball since 1920 but used occasionally by pitchers anyway. "At that time," remembered Haller, "a pitcher didn't have to wipe off his hand if he came to his mouth, and there were pitchers around the league who were using the spitter. We had one on our staff, Bob Shaw, who helped teach it to Gaylord." The spitter was an effective pitch for a pitcher with a good fastball because it was thrown with the same motion but, as the hitter was thinking fastball, broke sharply down. The split-fingered fastball, which became a big pitch in the late 1980s, acts in much the same fashion.

Perry threw 10 shutout innings, with Mays at shortstop for the last inning because the Giants had run out of players. The Giants won the second game of the longest doubleheader in baseball history in 23 innings, and a star was born.

"Gaylord had other good pitches, but he had a lot of confidence in his 'special pitch'," said Haller. "So he'd throw it a lot in critical situations. That messed with the other teams psychologically, too. When he was on the mound, guys in the other dugout would be yelling at the umpires constantly to watch what he was doing. I remember he used to drive Gene Mauch crazy.

"Gaylord was just a tremendous competitor, too. He really hated to lose. And if the guys behind him messed up, he'd let 'em have it. That seemed to work, though. I know everybody was really in the game when he was pitching."

There was a little more to Perry's sudden rise, though, than the spitter. "I had been working with (Pitching Coach) Larry Jansen on a slider, too," he remembered, "but I hadn't had much chance to show what I could do. I never wanted to pitch relief. I had a strong arm, but not the kind that can pitch 4-5 days in a row. When I pitched those 10 innings, that was like starting and pitching a whole game, so they realized that maybe I could be a starter.

"I've always liked doubleheaders, because that one gave me my chance. Now, they

Right hander Frank Linzy (1963, 1965-70) led the Giants in saves for five straight seasons (1965-69).

Bob Barton was part of the Giants catching rotation from 1965-69.

almost never play doubleheaders, and I often think about some guy who's been forgotten who never gets a chance because a team doesn't get that desperate."

When Perry became a solid member of the starting rotation, he spent as much time as he could with Marichal to further his knowledge of pitching. "He was the most complete pitcher I ever saw," said Perry. "We talked about pitching all the time, how to get different hitters out. I had never had a high leg kick, but after I saw how Juan used it, I started using that, too.

"He had such command. I remember when he'd have the bases loaded with nobody out, I'd offer to bet guys in the dugout that he'd get out of it without giving up a run. I'd say that 90 percent of the time he did.

"He had so many pitches, and so many ways of throwing those pitches, that he always had the hitters off balance. I loved to follow him in the rotation because the hitters would be all screwed up after they'd come up against him."

But even Perry's emergence as a star pitcher wasn't enough to make winners of the Giants. "Sometimes, it just seemed we weren't destined to win," said Franks. "In 1965, we had the Juan Marichal suspension. He lost three starts, and you know he would have won at least two of those, maybe three. Then he lost some time because he had a taxi door close on his finger."

Entering 1966, Gaylord Perry had a career record of 24-30. He wound up going 21-8 that year, won 23 in 1970 and eventually earned more than 300 wins and a spot in the Hall of Fame.

The taxi door incident was one of the minor mishaps that plagued Marichal throughout his career, causing him to lose starts, though he still had four seasons in which he pitched at least 300 innings, as well as 295 in the 1964 season.

The suspension was much more serious, stemming from an August game in San Francisco against the Dodgers. As usual, the two teams were battling for the pennant, and the rivalry was as bitter as ever. Marichal was dueling Koufax, and Juan had sent a couple of batters, Wills and Ron Fairly, spinning into the dirt to avoid inside fastballs. Since Marichal was known for his superb control, the Dodgers naturally assumed he was aiming at the hitters, not the plate.

Marichal had taken a Koufax pitch for a strike, and catcher John Roseboro threw the ball back, nicking Marichal's ear. Marichal turned to say something to Roseboro, who apparently made a profane remark about Juan's ancestry. Marichal swung his bat down on Roseboro, hitting him on the head.

Both benches emptied quickly. Cepeda ran to grab Marichal to keep him from swinging the bat again. Blood was streaming from Roseboro's head, and it was first feared that his eye had been damaged. Fortunately, his catcher's mask had protected him and he had only a bruise on his head.

A full-scale brawl between Giants and Dodgers players broke out, and it was several minutes before the umpires could restore peace. Marichal was ejected from the game, which the Giants eventually won. He was suspended for 10 days and fined $1,750 by National League President Warren Giles, a relatively mild punishment because Giles thought Roseboro had provoked Marichal.

When he came back, Marichal's first start was in the first game of a doubleheader against the Mets. He had had great success against the Mets, 25-8 lifetime, so Franks asked him if he would pitch both games. The idea was that he'd pitch the first game and then 6-7 innings of the second. It wasn't as astounding as it seems now because Marichal paced himself very well—he once won a 16-inning game, 1-0—and was quite capable of it. But, remembered Simmons, "For one of the few times in his career, the Mets got to Juan and knocked him out of the first game, so he didn't pitch the second game."

Even with Marichal's problems, the Giants still had a very good shot at winning the pennant, primarily because of their hitting. Mays set a personal record with 52 homers, 17 of them in August, and was the league's Most Valuable Player. Early in September, the Giants won 14 straight games and took a 2-1/2 game lead, but they were like a horse who takes the lead too early. In the stretch they folded and the Dodgers caught them, eventually winning by two games.

In 1966, Marichal held out for almost all of Spring Training and then made a mockery of those who claimed that the training period was necessary by winning his first 10 games. He finished at 25-6 and Perry at 21-8, but the Giants lost again. The key, Franks remem-

The infamous Juan Marichal-John Roseboro scuffle during the 1965 season. Sandy Koufax tries to be a cautious peace-maker.

Willie Mays was in the
Opening Day lineup
every year during his
15 seasons with the
San Francisco Giants.

Former Brooklyn-Los Angeles Dodgers great
Duke Snider came off the bench to hit .210 in 91
games for the Giants during the 1964 season.

Future Hall of Famer Warren Spahn was a late
season acquisition in 1965.

bered, was a series near the end of the season with the Dodgers and Cardinals. "We were leading, but the Cardinals came into Los Angeles and the Dodgers won three games with only four runs. They could do that in those days because they had Koufax and Drysdale and a great bullpen."

The Giants still had a shot on the last weekend, as they closed with a single game in Pittsburgh while the Dodgers played a doubleheader in Philadelphia. The Giants needed to win their game—which they did in 11 innings—and have the Dodgers lose two.

"Chub Feeney got us a room at the airport," remembered McCovey, "and we listened to the second Dodgers-Phillies game. But Koufax shut them out, so that was the end of it."

Why couldn't the Giants get over the hump in that four-year stretch? Haller thinks it was because the team spent too much time waiting for the home run that could win the game. That, of course, was typical of most Giants teams when Stoneham was the owner.

"We didn't know how to do the little things to manufacture runs," he said. "We won a lot of games with home runs because we had great hitters like Mays and McCovey, but if you look back at those seasons, there were also a lot of games we'd have been able to win if we could just have gotten a single run or two, instead of always looking for the big inning.

"When you realize that we had four Hall of Famers and for part of the time Cepeda, who should be in the Hall, you just have to think that if we'd just have played a little smarter, we could have won more pennants."

Jack Hiatt shared the catching duties from 1965-69. He is currently the Giants' director of player development.

ORLANDO CEPEDA

Nobody enjoyed the first year in San Francisco more than Orlando Cepeda, then a 20-year-old rookie just three years removed from Puerto Rico.

Cepeda was pre-destined to be a star, as the son of legendary Puerto Rican star Pedro Cepeda, nicknamed "Perucho" (The Bull) and called the "Babe Ruth of the Caribbean" for his power hitting. Orlando, naturally enough, was called the "Baby Bull."

Orlando smashed his way through a three-year minor league career, leading two leagues in hitting and finishing with a .309 average in 1957 at Minneapolis, then the Giants Triple-A team.

Yet he was not called up at the end of the 1957 season, as Major League clubs usually do with top minor leaguers, and he was a non-roster player when he came to Spring Training the next season. Not in the eyes of Manager Bill Rigney, though.

"Rigney really helped me," remembered Cepeda. "He told me from the beginning that he really wanted me. The first day, he said, 'Regulars take infield.' So, I stepped back, but he said, 'No, you take first base.' When he said that, I thought, 'Wow.' That really motivated me."

Cepeda's first hit, on Opening Day, was a home run, one of the earliest Major League home runs hit on the West Coast, and he remembers it well. "It was a changeup and I hit it to right field," he said. "That was the way I hit. Tom Sheehan used to say I reminded him of Rogers Hornsby, the way I could hit for power to the opposite field."

"He and Tony Oliva had a better ability to hit the curve ball than any other young hitters I ever saw," said Rigney.

Orlando went on to hit .312 as a rookie with 25 home runs and 96 RBI. He was named the National League's Rookie of the Year in a unanimous vote, and he was also named the Giants Most Valuable Player by San Francisco fans.

The last was a stretch. Willie Mays led the Giants that year in batting average (.347), home runs (29), triples (11), runs scored (121), stolen bases (31) and tied Cepeda for the RBI lead. It was clearly a popularity contest, and Orlando was more popular.

"I was surprised," admitted Cepeda, but he understood the fans' vote. "They (the Giants) built up Mays so much. Then, Willie would strike out, as any player would. I started doing well, I was new, I was 20 years old..."

And, he was a San Francisco Giants player. In the eyes of many fans, Mays was still a member of the New York Giants, playing in a San Francisco uniform now. Cepeda had never played in a New York uniform.

On the field, it was non-stop excitement for Cepeda. "Opening Day, when I saw the Dodgers take the field, I thought, not too long back, they were my heroes—Carl Furillo, Duke Snider, Pee Wee Reese, Don Newcombe. Wow, what a day, a dream come true. It was like that all year. We went into St. Louis and I saw Stan Musial, Ken Boyer. In Cincinnati, it was Frank Robinson, Ted Kluszewski."

Off the field, it was non-stop excitement, too. "I used to go to the Copacabana, a Latin club, every Thursday night and dance," he remembered. "Herb Caen used to call me the 'Copacabana Kid.' Charles McCabe called me the playboy, the Cha-Cha Kid. I loved the city. I always lived in the city, not San Mateo or San Bruno."

After he was traded in 1966, Cepeda lived in St. Louis and Boston, where he was playing ball, and moved back to Puerto Rico after his playing career. "But, I started thinking, San Francisco is such a great city. I wish I could move back there." In 1989, Bob Lurie hired him to work with the Giants, and he has been here since. "I hope I can live here forever," he said.

So do we, Orlando.

Reserve infielder Billy Sorrell spent one year (1967) with the Giants.

Lefty Ray Sadecki (1966-69) will forever be remembered as the man acquired from the St. Louis Cardinals for Orlando Cepeda.

Of course, the Giants were also playing at a time when the National League was probably as strong as it ever has been, with great teams and great players. "People ask me if I wish I were playing today," said Haller, "and for monetary reasons, yes, it would be nice. But to play at that time against those great teams and against players like Hank Aaron and Frank Robinson and with Willie Mays and Willie McCovey. . . well, that was just a great thrill."

Franks lays the Giants problem during that time to defense. "Our big trouble was that we had no good shortstop in that time. Forget about making the double play. We couldn't even get one out a lot of times. If we'd had Chris Speier (who joined the Giants in 1971), who knows how many pennants we might have won."

Pagan had been a great shortstop for the Giants in the pennant season of 1962, but he declined rapidly after that. Dick Scofield, Tito Fuentes and Hal Lanier followed him, and all were mediocre. Fuentes came up as a shortstop with Lanier at second. Unfortunately, both were better second basemen than shortstops. In 1967, Fuentes moved to second and did well there, while Lanier moved to shortstop and got lost.

"In 1967, I was trying to get Maury Wills after he had gone to Pittsburgh," said Franks. "That was the one time Chub Feeney and I had a disagreement. Chub didn't want Wills, but I had persuaded Horace, just before the trading deadline, to trade for Wills. We were going to give the Pirates Bobby Bolin, who always pitched great against them. But then they came into San Francisco and Wills had a great series, hitting something like .500 and stealing bases, so when we put up the deal, they wouldn't go for it."

Franks insisted that the Giants pitching was "better than people gave us credit for." But his big stars, Mays and McCovey, thought that the Giants lack of pitching behind Marichal and Perry was the killer. "It seemed like they didn't ever make that effort to get another pitcher," said Mays. "It was frustrating because we had such a good team, but we didn't have that third pitcher we needed," said McCovey. "We always had two super pitchers, but we never had that third or fourth guy we needed, and that tells on you down the stretch."

In 1966, for instance, when Marichal and Perry had great years, Bolin was the third most effective starter, with just 11 wins.

To some close to the team, that was even more galling because the Giants had passed up a chance to sign a young pitcher who would have given the team another superb starter.

"I scouted Dean Chance when he was pitching high school ball in Ohio," remembered Charlie Fox, later to be the team's manager. "He was unbelievable. Every pitch he threw was below the belt, and he was six-foot-five so the ball was coming down at a level that made it unhittable. He threw 97 no-hitters in high school!

"Tom Sheehan told me to offer him $15,000. I went in to the front office and said I couldn't get in the door unless I was prepared to offer at least $65-70,000. I told them, 'I've been watching this kid pitch for two years. You know how many hits he's given up in that time? Zero.'

"But I couldn't get the authorization to offer that kind of money, so when Bill Rigney went down to the Angels (as manager), he took my scouting reports with him and they signed Chance."

"Absolutely true," said Rigney. "Chance had the best right arm of any pitcher I'd ever seen."

In the 1960s, Chance had six seasons in which he won in double figures, even though he was often pitching for weak teams, and five seasons in which he gave up fewer than three earned runs a game. He won the Cy Young Award in 1964 when he won 20 games, 11 by shutouts, and had an ERA of 1.65. Yes, the Giants could have used him.

Meanwhile, the Giants continued to look for another starting pitcher. They especially wanted a left-hander because Candlestick, with its strong wind blowing out to right field, was made for left-handed power hitters.

"It seemed like other teams knew what we needed and they wouldn't trade with us," said Perry. "When we finally were able to make a trade for a left handed starter, (Cepeda for Ray Sadecki) we had to pay too high a price, and then Sadecki didn't do much for us."

In 1967, the Giants finally got the left-handed starter they needed, bringing back McCormick, though at the time it seemed just an exchange of bodies, because the Giants gave up only two utility players, Cap Peterson and a pitcher Bob Priddy.

McCormick had signed with the Giants in 1956, when they were still in New York, and he was one of the last players to come in under the old "bonus baby" rule, which said that players signing a bonus of more than the big league minimum, just $6,000 in those days (McCormick got $50,000) had to stay with the Major League team before they could be sent down to the minors.

"I don't think that hurt me because by my second full year, I pitched almost 100 innings (74-2/3) and after that, I was pretty much in the starting rotation," said McCormick. "There were a lot of guys, though, who just had to sit for two years."

McCormick was a steady pitcher, though unspectacular, for his first four years in San Francisco, winning 51, losing 42. But when the Giants won the pennant in 1962, he was virtually useless.

"I came up with a sore arm in Spring Training," he remembered, "and I never really was able to contribute all year (5-5, 5.38 ERA). That really hurt, to watch the team doing so well and not being a part of it. In those years, you didn't have the sports medicine that you have now. They'd send you to the trainer, and if he couldn't fix it, that was it. I probably had a rotator cuff problem. There was certainly something wrong with my shoulder."

McCormick was traded to Baltimore after that season, then to Washington two years later. In 1967, he came back to San Francisco, with a different pitching style, depending more on finesse than the fastball that had originally got him a bonus for signing. Though he started the season in the bullpen, he was made a starter by in early June and he went on to win a league-leading 22 games, earning him the Cy Young Award.

But once again, the Giants were dogged by bad luck. Marichal had a rare off-year because of injuries, winning just 14 games instead of his usual 20-plus, and Perry was just 15-17, though nine of his losses came by one run. The Giants lost by 10-1/2 games to the St. Louis Cardinals.

Marichal was back in form in 1968 with a 26-6 year. Perry pitched a no-hitter on Sept. 17—and Ray Washburn came back the next day with a no-hitter for the Cardinals, the first back-to-back no-hitters in baseball history. McCovey had 36 homers and 105 RBI. "It wasn't my best year as far as the numbers go," said McCovey, "but I think it might have been my best year when you consider how bad the hitting was that year."

But McCormick fell off sharply. In Spring Training, Franks had come up to Mike while he was running in the outfield and told him Marichal would pitch the opening game. "I think Juan would be upset if he didn't pitch the game," he said. McCormick told him, "Herman, who are you kidding? Juan doesn't care. You're the manager. He'll do whatever you say."

Marichal did pitch the opener, of course. "He won it big, something like 13-1," McCormick remembered. "I pitched the next game and lost by one run. That kind of set the tone for the whole year."

McCormick went 12-14, the Giants finished nine games behind the pennant-winning

A stunned Orlando Cepeda learns he's been traded by the Giants to St. Louis for pitcher Ray Sadecki in 1966. Juan Marichal has his arm around Cepeda, with Cap Peterson at right.

CEPEDA TRADE

"Everywhere I go," the late Chub Feeney used to say, "people ask me, 'Why did you trade Orlando Cepeda?' They never ask me about the good trades I made."

The trade of Cepeda, for St. Louis left-hander Ray Sadecki, was as traumatic for Orlando as for the fans. "It came on Mother's Day," he remembered. "My mother was crying, my wife was crying. It seemed like a funeral. It took me a couple of days to get over it."

Even so, the trade seemed logical at the time. The Giants hadn't been able to solve the dilemma of having two All-Star first basemen, Cepeda and Willie McCovey, and they needed a left-handed starter. Sadecki was a young pitcher (25) who had won 20 games two seasons earlier and seemed to have a bright future.

Though fans didn't realize it, the Giants had been after Sadecki for nearly four years. Before the 1962 season, knowing he needed a left-hander to win the pennant, Manager Alvin Dark had pleaded with owner Horace Stoneham to get Sadecki. But the Cardinals wanted either Cepeda or Willie McCovey, and Stoneham was unwilling to trade either one, because they were the power hitters he loved. Eventually, he traded for Billy Pierce, who was a big factor in the 1962 pennant race.

This time, Stoneham was willing to let Cepeda go, but the trade was a disaster for the Giants. Sadecki had a series of misfortunes. The pressure of being traded for such a popular star seemed to unnerve him, and he had problems with his eyesight, finally getting contact lenses. He had one decent season, 12-6 with a 2.78 ERA in 1967, but overall, he was just 32-39 before being traded to the Mets before the 1970 season.

Meanwhile, Cepeda went on to become Most Valuable Player for the Cardinals as they won the World Series in 1967.

And that's why Feeney got all the questions.

Outfielder Charles "Cap" Peterson (1962-66) was traded after the 1966 season to the Washington Senators, along with pitcher Bob Priddy, for pitcher Mike McCormick.

Cardinals, and Franks resigned. "I shouldn't have quit when I did," said Franks, "but you know Horace used to like to change managers every four years or so. He was such a nice guy, he didn't like to fire anybody, so I figured I hadn't won a pennant so I might as well get out of there. A couple of years later, we were drinking after a game and Horace said, 'You know, you were the best manager I ever had.' I said, 'Hell, Horace, if you'd just told me that, I'd never have quit.' But, it was too late then."

So the Giants had a new manager in 1969, Clyde King, and a new alignment, being in the six-team National League West. They got an MVP year from McCovey, who batted .320, hit 45 homers and knocked in 126 runs, despite the fact that pitchers often preferred not to pitch to him; McCovey walked 126 times, a figure which included a Major League record 45 intentional walks. Bobby Bonds, in his first full season, led the league in runs scored with 120; with 32 homers and 45 stolen bases, he joined Mays in the exclusive 30-30 club, the only players to that point to have had at least 30 home runs and 30 stolen bases in a season.

And, once again, the Giants finished second, this time to the Atlanta Braves.

McCovey had another big year in 1970, with 39 homers, another 126 RBI and a San Francisco Giants-record 137 walks. Bonds, too, set a San Francisco record with 134 runs scored, 26 homers, 48 stolen bases and a .302 average. This was all accomplished despite a league-leading 189 strikeouts (he had struck out 187 times the year before). When Bonds put the ball in play, he hit .422.

The Giants seemed to be slipping, though. When they were only 19-23 in May, Stoneham fired King and replaced him with Charlie Fox, who had had a thorough preparation for the job. A native of New York, Fox had played briefly for the Giants in 1942 before going into the service. When he came out in 1946, he became a minor league man-

Mike McCormick is the only Giants pitcher ever to win the Cy Young Award. His 22 victories in 1967 also earned him National League Comeback Player of the Year honors. Veteran baseball writer Jack Hanley (left) and Commissioner William D. Eckert present McCormick with the hardware.

MIKE MCCORMICK

Though the Giants have had two Hall of Fame pitchers in San Francisco—Juan Marichal and Gaylord Perry—their only Cy Young Award winner has been Mike McCormick, who won the award in 1967, when he was 22-10, with a 2.85 ERA.

McCormick started his career with the Giants, was traded away in 1963 and returned in a trade just before the 1967 season. He still has trouble believing what happened that year.

"I wasn't pitching much early in the season and I think I was something like 3-4 the first week of June," he remembered. "Then, Herman Franks told me he wanted to start me in the Astrodome. I started and won, so he kept pitching me and I won 11 straight. So, I had gone from the forgotten man to the leader in the rotation.

"I don't even think that was my best year. I thought I pitched better in 1960 (when he led the league with a 2.70 ERA) and 1961. In 1961, I was just 13-16, but 13 of those losses were 3-2 or less. Pitching is so much luck."

Willie McCovey made a splash in his Giants debut by going four-for-four against Robin Roberts and Philadelphia in 1959. McCovey made a splash more than once—he ended his career with 18 grand slam homers.

Clyde King replaced Herman Franks as Giants manager in 1969. He was relieved of his duties midway through the 1970 season.

ager in the Giants system for the next 12 years, then a scout, then a third base coach for Franks. He was also the most extroverted manager the Giants had had since Rigney. He was a genial Irishman who enjoyed the long-time baseball custom of swapping stories, some of which may even have been true.

The team he inherited was one whose big stars were losing their touch. "I thought the team would win in '69," he said, "because the big players, McCovey, Mays, Marichal, all had big years. By the time I took over in '70, it was obvious that we were going to have to start re-building, and we had some good young players coming up. The farm system was still producing. For a long period, any time the Giants needed a player, they could dip down into the farm system and bring up a player who would fill the hole. Hell, we supplied the whole National League with outfielders for awhile, guys who could hit, run like deer, field, throw."

Fox knew he had to start resting his aging stars, particularly Mays and McCovey, who was almost seven years younger but had long been plagued by knee problems. The first day Fox took over, May 24, 1970, Perry gave him an idea. "We were playing a double header, and I'd figured I'd rest Mays and McCovey in the second game," said Fox. "We had a big lead going into the sixth inning of the first game, so Gaylord said to me, 'If you take Mays out now, he could probably play the second game. So, I went to Willie and told him I wanted to do that, and he said OK. McCovey heard me, so he volunteered to come out and play the second game, too. I thought, 'Way to go, Gaylord!'"

Fans knew Juan Marichal would be special when he tossed a one-hit shutout against Philadelphia during his Major League debut in 1960. Opposing hitters never knew what to expect from Marichal. His high-leg kick and command of five pitches—thrown from three different motions—propelled him to a San Francisco club-record 238 career wins and the Hall of Fame.

Second baseman Ron Hunt (1968-70) holds the San Francisco franchise record for being hit by pitches the most times in a season (26 in 1970).

Bobby Bolin's 1.98 ERA in 1968 is a San Francisco franchise record.

The "Mule," Dick Dietz, was the last Giants catcher to play in an All-Star Game (1970) until Bob Brenly in 1984.

Rookie shortstop Chris Speier (left) played a big role in the Giants' 1971 National League Western Division Championship season, named "The Year of the Fox," after Manager Charlie Fox (right).

The team improved under Fox but still could not climb out of third place in the division. The next year, though, the Giants got the type of shortstop Franks had yearned for in rookie Chris Speier. His arrival was too late to do Herman any good, but the addition of Speier was enough finally to get the Giants a first place finish in 1971.

A native of Alameda, Speier had come to camp as a non-roster player after playing in the Double-A Texas League at Amarillo the year before. "I don't know if the Giants expected me to make the club," he said. "I certainly didn't. I had grown up watching the Giants, and I was thrilled just to be in camp with them. When I started my first game, in San Diego, I looked across the diamond and saw Willie McCovey. I looked at the mound and saw Juan Marichal. I knew that Willie Mays was behind me in center field. Then I looked up in the stands and saw 40,000 people, and, I thought to myself, 'What am I doing here?'"

There was no question in the minds of those who saw him that he belonged. Only 20, Speier had excellent range and a very strong throwing arm, which enabled him to go deep into the hole and throw out runners. He and second baseman Fuentes quickly developed into an excellent double play combination. He would spend only six years in a Giants uniform before being traded, but in that period he was probably the best shortstop to play in a San Francisco. If he'd come along half a dozen years earlier, the Giants would probably have had a couple more National League pennants flying.

"He hit more than Hal Lanier," said Fox, "and he had that fire. He always questioned everything. He'd ask why, why, why. But once you explained it to him, he'd go out and do it."

Nicknamed "The Alameda Rifle," Chris Speier provided the Giants with solid play at shortstop from 1971-76.

Speier and Fuentes also fit well in personality, as well as performance. Fuentes was a vibrant personality. "He kept the clubhouse loose," said Fox. "I could always tell when he came in. I'd be back in my office, but all of a sudden, I'd hear everybody laughing. I knew Tito had done something."

Speier wasn't so outgoing in the clubhouse, but on the field, he and Tito would occasionally clown around. "They'd flip the ball over their heads, behind their backs," remembered Fox. "Horace used to ask me, 'What are they doing down there?' I'd say, 'I don't know. I'm not watching.'"

Once, Johnny Bench hit a grounder to Fuentes at second. Though there was nobody on base, Tito punched the ball to Speier with his glove and Speier grabbed it, touched second and then fired to first. Bench said to Fox, "Didn't they know nobody was on first?" "I don't know," said Fox, "but you're out."

For Speier, as well as his teammates, it was a magical year. "Everybody was so good to me," he remembered. "I basically took Hal Lanier's job, but he was my roommate on the road and he gave me a lot of advice. Bobby Bonds helped, everybody helped teach me not just about hitting or playing in the field but how to act in the big leagues, which was sure a lot different than what I'd been used to."

The Giants got off to a very fast start that year, winning 18 of their first 23 games. It was far more than just Speier, of course. The big stars of the past were contributing in a big way. In his third start of the year, Marichal had a no-hitter going into the ninth against the Chicago Cubs, before yielding two hits in that inning. Mays hit four home runs in his first four games, one of them a grand slam, and, at 40, seemed to be turning the clock back to his youth. Mays, who always kept himself in great physical condition, continued his spurt through June, setting a National League career record for runs scored that month.

"Everybody played fantastic that year," said Fox. "Marichal and Perry were great. We had great relief pitching with Jerry Johnson and Don McMahon."

Johnson was a very pleasant surprise for the Giants. He had done little prior to that season and, though he lasted 10 years in the majors, he did little after 1971, finishing with a career mark of 48-51. But in 1971 he was terrific, winning 12 games, all in relief, and saving another 18.

"He had a good fastball, a good hard slider, he came right at you," said Fox, "but he was a fellow you had to know, know his character to get a lot out of him. He was a wild kid. He liked to get on horses and break them. That was his father's trade. You had to try to con him out of that; otherwise, he might have come in with a broken leg."

There was a blip on the screen in May, though, when the Giants traded promising young outfielder George Foster to the Cincinnati Reds for a backup shortstop, Frank Duffy, and pitcher Vern Geishert.

The trade especially upset Bonds since Foster was living with him at the time. Bonds

From 1970-74, Tito Fuentes snared nearly every ground ball hit to the right side of the infield. He handled 861 chances at second base in 1971, the second-highest total in the National League. Fuentes and shortstop Chris Speier formed one of the Senior Circuit's dynamic double play duos in the 1970s.

At the age of 40 in 1971, Willie Mays stole 23 bases—his best in more than a decade.

1973 was a memorable year for Bobby Bonds. He scored a league-leading 131 runs, his 11 lead-off homers tied a National League record, and was named MVP of the All-Star Game. Bonds was a Giants coach from 1993-96 and is the father of current Giants left fielder Barry Bonds.

took Foster to the airport and then came to the clubhouse early. When Fox arrived, Bonds said, "Skip, how could you do that?" Fox didn't know what he was talking about, and when he called upstairs to get the bad news, he was as upset as Bonds. "I thought he was going to be a great player," he said. "Every time I put him in the lineup, it seemed he hit a home run. I wasn't anxious to go looking for another guy who could play as well as he did."

Several Giants players were very upset and told writers that in the clubhouse. Many years later, Mays remembered, "He was like our favorite kid. He was young but we felt if he was brought along slowly, he could develop into a good player."

Mays's judgment was better than that of the Giants front office. It took Foster time to develop but in 1977 he exploded, with 52 homers and 149 RBI. He wound up hitting 348 home runs in his career.

At the time, the Giants felt he was expendable because they had what seemed a glut of young outfielders. Garry Maddox and Gary Mathews were just a year away, Dave Kingman was on the club and was capable of playing the outfield. Bernie Williams had been up the year before briefly, and the Giants thought Williams had more potential than Foster.

As it happened, though, the first three had their most productive years with other clubs, and Williams did almost nothing, playing only 104 major league games spread out over four years and ending his career 344 home runs short of Foster.

Yet, although the Foster trade caused a momentary ripple in the clubhouse, it didn't slow the Giants drive. By the All-Star game, they were up by six games. By the end of August, they had an 8-1/2 game edge.

Then, in September, they virtually collapsed. By the middle of the month, their lead was down to one game. "I remember that last month. We were in Houston and Willie Mays called a meeting," said Speier. "He reminded us of how we got there and what we needed to do the rest of the way. From that point on, we thought we were going to win, though we had to win on the last day of the season to accomplish that."

"We were trying to milk two pitchers, Marichal and Perry, and it started to catch up to us," said Fox. "No question, we got tired, too. I tried to rest Mays and McCovey as much as I could. We had to play them on Sunday, because that's when families come out and the kids wanted to see them. We'd have Mondays off, so I'd try to keep them out on Tuesday, too, to give them a couple of days.

"I had to rest Al Gallagher (the third baseman) every 30 days or so, because he played

Bobby Bonds led the Giants in steals for seven straight seasons (1968-74).

Charlie Fox took over the managerial duties in 1970. He piloted the Giants until 1974.

so hard. Basically, though, we had the same lineup day after day. You came to the ball park, you didn't have any question who was going to be in the lineup."

Injuries to Mays, McCovey, Marichal and Bonds were also a part of the slump, but the biggest problem was probably that age had finally caught up with Mays, who had been the team's driving force for so long.

Mays's slide had actually begun after the 1966 season, in which he hit 37 home runs and knocked in 103 runs. That was the last of an incredible 13-year run in which he scored more than 100 runs for 12 straight seasons (and missed the century mark by a single run in the 13th), knocked in at least 100 runs in 10 seasons, hit at least 34 home runs in 11 seasons, hit 40 or more home runs in six seasons and more than 50 in two, and hit over .300 in nine seasons.

Fireballing Jerry Johnson saved 18 games and won 12 in helping the Giants win the 1971 National League Western Division crown.

Wes Westrum was a reserve catcher for the New York Giants from 1947-57. He had two terms as a San Francisco Giants coach (1958-63 and 1968-71) and was owner Horace Stoneham's last manager (1974-75).

Before making his mark with the Cincinnati Reds, outfielder George Foster started his Major League career with the Giants. Foster was traded to the Reds in 1971.

Willie Mays is congratulated by Alan Gallagher (10) and Jimmy Rosario (43) during a 1971 game.

Dave Marshall was a reserve outfielder from 1967-69.

After that, he never again hit more than 30 home runs in a season or scored or knocked in more than 100. He was still feared for his ability to hit in the clutch—he led the league in walks with 112 in 1971—but he no longer had the power to hit home runs consistently, nor the reactions to hit for a high average.

As the 1971 season wound down, Mays's physical problems became even more apparent. Without Willie as a big offensive force, the Giants won only eight of their final 24 games, and Marichal won four of those. The Giants went into the weekend in San Diego with a chance to clinch the division with a win on Saturday, but they lost. With the division title on the line on the last day, their aging stars reached back to past glory. Marichal ignored a sore hip to win a five-hitter, Mays crashed a three-run homer and the Giants beat the Padres in San Diego, 5-1. That put the Giants into the National League Championship Series against the Pirates, but it also meant that in what was then a best-of-five series, Marichal could be used only once.

The Giants actually won the first game of the NLCS, as McCovey and Fuentes both hit two-run homers in the fifth inning off Steve Blass. Perry got the win on a 5-4 decision. It was a typical Perry performance. He got stronger as the game went on and battled the Pirates so relentlessly that Fox didn't think of going to his bullpen. With two outs in the

Outfielder Frank Johnson (left) and third baseman Alan Gallagher (right) help promote Cap Day during the 1971 season.

ninth, the Pirates had a runner on first with Willie Stargell, who had led the National League with 48 homers that season, at bat. Perry had intended to pitch around Stargell, but when Stargell swung and missed at two pitches outside the strike zone, Gaylord challenged him and got Stargell to ground out for the final out.

The Pirates evened the series with a 9-4 win the next day, and the difference was Pittsburgh first baseman Bob Robertson, who hit three homers and drove in five runs.

Marichal finally got his shot when the series moved to Pittsburgh and he gave up just four hits, but two of them were home runs in a 2-1 Pirates win. The big story, though, was a Willie Mays bunt. In the sixth inning, the score was tied, 1-1, and Tito Fuentes was on second with nobody out. Everybody expected Mays to be swinging away, but on the first pitch, he squared away to bunt against Pirates righthander Bob Johnson and fouled the pitch off. He took the next pitch and then bunted, in play this time, but was thrown out at first. The startled Fuentes never moved off second, and the Giants did not score in the inning.

After the game, Mays explained that he wanted to get Fuentes to third, where he could

Part of "The Young Giants" from 1973: left fielder Gary Matthews (top) and center fielder Garry Maddox.

The Giants celebrate winning the National League Western Division title after beating the Padres, 5-1, in San Diego on Sept. 30, 1971.

Big Dave Kingman joined the Giants late in 1971 and contributed six homers in 115 at bats.

Don Carrithers (1970-73) split time between the starting rotation and the bullpen.

score on a fly, a wild pitch, an infield grounder. It was a sad moment because Mays, the greatest player anybody on the field had ever seen, was tacitly admitting that he didn't think he could get a hit to drive in Fuentes.

Perry, a 16-game winner during the season, was the Giants starter in the fourth game, but Gaylord didn't have his best stuff on this day, as seen as early in the second inning, when Richie Hebner hit a three-run homer for the Pirates. McCovey responded with another three-run homer and the game was tied, 5-5, after five innings, but the Pirates scored four times in the sixth to win the game, 9-5, and advance to the World Series.

"We probably lost our chance by having to win that last game against San Diego," Fox said years later, the subject obviously still foremost in his mind. "Even then, though, if we could have won that third game that Juan pitched, we might still have done it. When you win two of the first three in a best-of-five, you've got a great shot. I could have saved Gaylord for the fifth game, and he'd have been sharper. I don't know how we would have done in the World Series, but I sure would have liked to have had a shot."

Though it wasn't obvious that year because the Giants had played well, it was the end of an era, for the players and the owner. Stoneham would own the Giants just four more seasons, and only one of those was a winning one, an 88-74 finish in 1973 that earned the Giants third place in their division.

The first move was a blockbuster trade that sent Perry and Duffy to Cleveland for "Sudden Sam" McDowell. For years, the story has been that the trade was made because Fox had scouted McDowell as a high school pitcher and had wanted to sign him then. Perry himself believed it for a time, though not now.

"That was what bothered me the most," said Fox, "was that Gaylord thought I was the guy who traded him. I was only the manager. Nobody told Horace and his buddy, Tom Sheehan, what to do. I was very close to Gaylord in those days. He would do anything he had to do to win, and that's my kind of guy."

Fox says now that, if anybody had asked him about the trade before it was made, he would have said no. "I believe you look at what you have and what you don't have, and then you try to get what you don't have," he said. "You don't give away what you've got. I knew Gaylord could win in this league. I didn't know what the other guy could do."

But Stoneham had long since stopped listening to Fox, probably because Fox had been so outspoken in his beliefs earlier. "I got into trouble because of that," he admitted.

Coach Hank Sauer spends time during Spring Training in 1972 with outfielders Garry Maddox (center) and Jim Howarth (right).

Why did the Giants trade Perry? Fox believes it was because Stoneham and Sheehan thought that the umpires wouldn't leave Perry alone, because of his use of the spitball. Umpires were constantly stopping the game to examine the ball, trying unsuccessfully to catch Perry using the illegal pitch. Fox said, "I don't care how much they bother him if he keeps winning 18-20 games a year." But Stoneham wasn't listening.

"I wasn't surprised by the trade, but I was disappointed," remembered Perry. "I had always been with the Giants. Tom Sheehan had scouted me and signed me, and I had come up through the organization. I thought a lot of Horace Stoneham, and I had really hoped to play my whole career in San Francisco.

"It was a bad time for me, too, because we had four kids in school, and suddenly, we had to find a new home in Cleveland. But, in those days, players didn't have any choice in where they played, so we coped."

WILLIE MAYS

Everybody who saw him play has the same opinion: Willie Mays was the greatest player they ever saw. "Willie Mays is the standard for ballplayers," said former Giants Manager Alvin Dark.

Mays could do it all. As a hitter, he hit for average, as high as .347, and for power, twice hitting over 50 home runs in a season. He adjusted his hitting according to the park or pitcher.

At the Polo Grounds, with its short distances down the line, he pulled the ball. At Candlestick, with the wind blowing in from left field, he hit with power to the opposite field. When he first started hitting home runs with frequency, pitchers started pitching him low and away, so Mays learned to hit balls through the right side of the infield, and his average soared. "In the majors, you can't just consistently hit home runs," he said. "Pitchers are going to knock you down and pitch you outside. I felt like if I got a base hit, it's like a double because I can steal second base."

And, great as his statistics are, including a career mark of 660 home runs, Mays's record could have been even better, if he'd cared about his numbers. "He just cared about winning," said former Manager Herman Franks. "If he saw we had the game won, he'd take it easy."

As a fielder, he was best known for his catch of a Vic Wertz drive in the 1954 World Series, but he has always insisted he made many others at least as good. "That got all the attention because it happened in the World Series," he said. Former Giants Manager Bill Rigney has another favorite, against the Pirates in long-gone Forbes Field in Pittsburgh. "We always waited for Willie to tap his glove because that was a sign that he had it," said Rigney. "This time we waited and waited and waited. Willie just kept running and running, and at the last moment, he reached out his hand and caught it barehanded! When he came back to the bench, he told me, 'Sorry, Skip, but I couldn't reach it with my glove.'"

He was also quite a showman, with his famous basket catch. "When I was in the Army (in 1952 and 1953), I decided the fans needed something different when I came out," he said. "I played around with it and found that I could catch the ball real easy that way. I didn't know if Leo (Durocher) would let me do it differently but Leo said, 'Hey, if he catches the ball, I don't have a problem.'"

What many people remember most about Mays, though, is his baserunning. He seemed to be able to do anything he wanted on the bases. Announcer Lon Simmons remembered a time when Mays was halfway between second and third with Don Demeter in left field. "Demeter faked a throw to third but he didn't believe Mays was going there, so he threw to second. Mays just kept going and scored on the play."

When Mays was ahead of runners, he'd often coach them even as he was running. He had an unerring instinct in going for the extra base and almost never got thrown out at third. "I remember Roberto Clemente did it one time," he said. "He had a great arm and I didn't pick up the ball right away, and I was out on a bang-bang play."

He and Willie McCovey used to change positions in the batting order, depending on whether a right- or left-handed pitcher was going. "I'd have to prod Willie Mac a little because, with his knees, he didn't run real well," said Mays. "One time, I was so close behind him coming in to home plate that I had to slide so he could tag home first."

There were times he would score on passed balls that went only a few feet away. "I always anticipated that when I was on third base," he said. "I could tell by the angle of the pitch that it would be wide of the plate and I'd just take off. One time I remember against the Mets, when Choo Choo Coleman was catching, the ball bounced off him and in front of the plate, but as he started to go after it, he saw me coming and couldn't move. So, the ball just laid there. He didn't get it, the pitcher couldn't get it, and I scored.

"I used to amaze myself sometimes, the things I could do. People would ask me, 'How do you do that?' I didn't know. I just felt I could do what I wanted to on the ball field, with no problems."

Part of it, Mays thought, was his football training in high school, where he was a quarterback on offense and a safety on defense. "I could visualize the whole field," he said. "You can't teach that. You can't tell another guy what's happening because he's not going to understand it. I did things on the spur of the moment and I did it very quickly. I couldn't tell anyone what I was going to do before I did it, because I didn't know."

Without any fanfare, Mays also helped other players, especially those who weren't well known. He would give away the money or merchandise he got for appearing on radio and television interviews to other players, as well as other gifts. "Sporting goods dealers used to hate to see him come in their stores," said Simmons, "because he'd ask them for five sets of golf clubs and then give them to his teammates."

"I used to get a real kick out of helping guys out," said Mays. "It was important to me to make the other guy feel he was important to the club. If I did something for the 25th player, it would make the guy very proud to have a star like me helping him out."

Willie Mays, a true original.

What..? Mays at Short!

24

MEL OTT MEMORIAL AWARD
HOME RUN CHAMPIONSHIP
NATIONAL LEAGUE

AWARD TO
WILLIE MAYS
SAN FRANCISCO GIANTS
52 HOME RUNS - 1965

Mays Will Sign
Contract Today

Mays Wins MVP; Kou

YEAR BOOK
SAN FRANCISCO
GIANTS
1958

Fairfield Industrial High School

1962
WORLD SERIES

The many accomplishments of Willie Mays are artisically displayed in this commemorative assemblage by Ray Ward.

#512

WILLIE HITS 4 HOMERS

NATIONAL LEAGUE
Giants 14, Braves 4
SAN FRANCISCO

Snider, Slaughter Fall Short

Mays Voted Into Hall

SAN FRANCISCO
Giants
We're #1

RAY WARD

Infielder Ozzie Virgil played parts of two seasons
(1966 and 1969) and was the Giants' third base
coach from 1969-72 and 1974-75.

McDowell was an exciting pitcher, a power pitcher reminiscent of Koufax in his prime. His fast ball exploded, and the pop it made when it hit the catcher's glove could be heard throughout the ball park. He was the kind of pitcher other players went out of their way to see. "I remember going to a game in Oakland when we were off and seeing him strike out 17 A's," said Speier.

McDowell had twice gone over 300 strikeouts in a season, and in his career had averaged more than a strikeout an inning. In 1968, the Year of the Pitcher, he had an ERA of 1.81. In 1965, a more normal year, he had an ERA of 2.18, had struck out 325 batters and given up just 178 hits in 273 innings. He was, at that time and for five years after, when his often shaky control allowed, a dominating pitcher comparable to Randy Johnson today.

Unfortunately, by the time the Giants traded for him, his arm was not what it had been. Fox asked Sheehan, "Is the guy healthy? I hear he's taking the needle, taking a shot in his arm." Fox's information was correct. Only occasionally in his short time with the Giants did McDowell ever flash that powering fast ball.

McDowell was also undisciplined in his private life, which no doubt led to his downfall on the field. "He got drunk on the plane coming out here," remembered Fox. "I had to go to the airport to get him so he didn't have to go to jail." McDowell's drinking habits were a throwback to earlier years in baseball, where hard drinking was almost a badge of honor, and he had the body of a middle-aged man. "You could fine him, threaten him," said Fox. "Nothing worked."

McDowell won 10 games for the Giants in 1972 and just one the next season before he was traded to the Yankees. He was out of baseball after the 1975 season.

Meanwhile, Perry won 24 games for the Indians in 1972 and won the Cy Young Award. He won 170 games after leaving the Giants, for a career total of 314. "It worked out well for Gaylord," said Fox. "What he did in the American League is what got him into the Hall of Fame. I just wish he could have done it here."

Next to go was Mays, who was traded on May 11, 1972 to the New York Mets for pitcher Charlie Williams and $50,000. "That was such a shock to everybody," said Speier. "It seemed to just knock the heart out of the club."

Stoneham harbored no illusions that the trade would greatly benefit the Giants. Williams was a pitcher who defined mediocrity; in seven years with the Giants, as a reliever and spot starter, he was 18-18 with four saves. The trade was made for financial and sentimental reasons. In that era, star players often were not paid what they were worth earlier in their careers, but it was understood that they would stay at a high salary level in their later years, even though their abilities were declining. Stoneham would certainly have preferred to continue paying Mays a high salary, but he could not afford to.

The Mets, on their way to their fourth straight year of more than two million attendance, had the money to pay Mays a high salary, even if he was no longer the player he had been. Equally important to Stoneham was the thought that he would be giving Mays a chance to return to New York, where he had started his career and been idolized.

Because Mays so seldom spoke publicly about himself, everybody, including Stoneham, assumed that he still preferred New York to San Francisco. In fact, Mays had become very comfortable in the Bay Area. He went back to New York and played 2-1/2 years for the Mets, getting into one more World Series, but he kept the home in Atherton which he had bought in 1969 and returned to it in the off-season and when he retired. He still lives in it today.

After the 1973 season, both Marichal and McCovey were traded, Marichal to the Red Sox for cash and McCovey to the San Diego Padres for Mike Caldwell, who won 14 games for the Giants in 1974. Marichal was clearly at the end of the line. McCovey still had some good years left, probably more than the Giants realized at the time.

"That was disappointing," said McCovey. "I don't like change. I don't like the unknown. But ironically, it was something Horace and I had talked about for 2-3 years. We'd go to his home or a hotel suite and we'd talk about teams and ballparks. I remember we talked

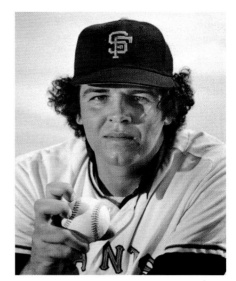

Pitcher Charlie Williams' claim to fame is that he was acquired from the New York Mets for Willie Mays on May 11, 1972.

"Sudden Sam" McDowell came to the Giants from Cleveland after the 1971 season for Gaylord Perry and Frank Duffy. Even though he led the American League in strikeouts five times and was a five-time All-Star, McDowell seldom showed that form during his one-and-a-half seasons with the Giants (1972-73).

"Dirty Al" strikes again. Alan Gallagher slides into first base during a 1971 game with the New York Mets. This native San Franciscan and Mission High School graduate manned third base for the Giants from 1970-73.

about Detroit, because that was a good park for left-handed hitters, but I told him I didn't want to go to the American League. I was always a National League guy. When San Diego was one of the teams that came up, I thought, well, I'll still be in California and in the National League. But even though we talked about it, in the back of my mind I always hoped I wouldn't be traded."

There was one big trade left in the Stoneham era: Before the 1975 season, Bobby Bonds was traded to the New York Yankees for Bobby Murcer. It was an interesting trade because each player had suffered by comparison with a great star. Bonds had been billed as "the next Willie Mays." Murcer's comparison had been with Mickey Mantle, who rivaled Mays as an all-around star. Neither player had lived up to that billing, of course, because no player could, and it was thought by both clubs that the players would both benefit from a change of scenery.

Bonds was always a blunt, outspoken man, and that did not make him popular with

JUAN MARICHAL

The San Francisco Giants have never had a pitcher the equal of Juan Marichal, and the odds are high that they never will.

Even as a rookie, Marichal had remarkable command on the mound, seeming almost to toy with hitters. He had such a variety of pitches that it didn't matter who was hitting or from which side of the plate he swung; in fact, left-handed hitters seemed to have even more problems with Juan because he threw a wicked screwball that broke away from them.

Most important, he had control of every pitch he threw—in one year, he walked only 36 batters in 307 innings—which meant he could throw any pitch on any count and be confident that he could get it over.

Announcer Lon Simmons heard a story about Marichal in the minors that demonstrated what kind of pitcher he was even then. "The bases were loaded," said Lon. "The shortstop came in to talk to him—he was an interpreter because Juan didn't speak English very well at that point—and then went to the manager and said, 'He wants to know how you think he should pitch to the next three hitters.' The manager said, 'Well, low and outside might be a good idea.' Nine low and outside pitches later, the inning was over. Juan had struck out the side."

His distinctive high-leg kick was a further distraction to hitters, who always seemed off balance. Marichal had a very good fastball and he had as many as 248 strikeouts in a season, but he didn't try for strikeouts except in situations where one was necessary.

Winning the game was what mattered to Marichal, not statistics. If he had a big lead, he would relax and give up three or four or five runs, not worrying about his earned run average. If he had less than his best stuff, he might give up several hits, but he would bear down to get the outs he needed and still get the win.

A pitcher as good as Marichal, even when he isn't concentrating on statistics, still has some outstanding ones. Beyond wins and earned run average, baseball people regard a good pitcher as one who allows about as many hits as innings pitched and who has more strikeouts than walks. In his first 10 seasons with the Giants, before he started having back problems, Marichal never allowed as many hits as innings pitched; in four seasons, he had fewer hits and walks combined than innings pitched. In his career, he struck out more than three times as many hitters as he walked. That's mastery.

Because he was considered the Giants' ace from his second season on (though Jack Sanford won more games in the pennant year of 1962), his managers always made certain the rotation fell so Marichal would pitch against the top teams. He had, for instance, 15 more decisions against the Dodgers than any other team and had an excellent 37-18 mark against them. In the key years of 1962 through 1966, when the two teams were always in contention for the pennant, Marichal was 17-5 against the Dodgers.

Marichal also has a distinction he didn't want: the best pitcher never to win a Cy Young Award. Looking at his record in the 1963-69 period, that seems incredible. He won 26 games one season, 25 in two seasons, 22 in another and 21 in two more. He allowed fewer than 2-1/2 earned runs a game in six of those seasons and only 2.76 in the seventh. He pitched as many as 325 innings in a season, had as many as 30 complete games in a season, had one year in which he pitched 10 shutouts and another in which he pitched eight.

Unfortunately for Marichal, he came along at a time when there were other great pitchers. Sandy Koufax won three Cy Young Awards in that time, and Koufax was as dominating in that span as any pitcher in baseball history. Bob Gibson set an ERA record of 1.12 in 1968, the Year of the Pitcher. Until 1968, there was only one Cy Young Award, and Dean Chance of the California Angels won it in 1964. The one year Marichal had the best shot, 1967, when Koufax had retired, he had a rare off-year, winning only 14 games, due to an injury. Teammate Mike McCormick won it.

But baseball historian Bill James did some research on Marichal's career and determined that, if you combine his 1963, 1964, 1966 and 1968 seasons, he had a four-year record of 97-31, while the award winners in those years (Koufax, Chance, Koufax again and Gibson) had a combined record of 94-32.

As great as Marichal's career was, it would have been even better if he could have stayed healthy. Before his 32nd birthday, Marichal had 191 wins and seemed to have a serious shot at 300 wins (at age 32, Warren Spahn had 145 wins, and he finished his career with 363).

Plagued by a bad reaction to a penicillin injection, Juan fell off to 12 wins in 1970. He bounced back to win 18 games the next season, but constant back problems reduced him to an ordinary pitcher after that, and he ended his Giants career with an 11-15 record in 1973. He pitched just 57 innings for the Boston Red Sox in 1974 and another six for the Dodgers in 1975 before calling an end to his glorious career with 243 wins.

Marichal was elected to the Baseball Hall of Fame in 1983.

From 1972. Former San Francisco Giants players turned coaches. Left to right: Joey Amalfitano, Hank Sauer and Jim Davenport.

Manager Charlie Fox takes the long walk in the tunnel between the Giants dugout and the clubhouse after a 1974 game at Candlestick Park.

Bobby Murcer, long touted as Mickey Mantle's replacement with the Yankees, came to the Giants in 1975 for Bobby Bonds (top), who was earmarked as Willie Mays' successor. Murcer's time with the Giants was productive as he had at least 90 RBI in each of his two seasons (1975-76).

Giants managers and executives, nor with the managers and executives of the other clubs with which he played. The Giants were also bothered by his high strikeout totals. But he was also an outstanding player, an excellent defensive outfielder in right field and a great leadoff hitter because he was always a threat to hit a home run, and there's nothing more disconcerting to a pitcher than to have a hitter begin the game by hitting a home run. Despite his strikeout totals, Bonds was a very productive hitter, both scoring and knocking in runs. He had twice led the National League in scoring as a Giant, and in his two seasons prior to being traded, he scored 228 runs and knocked in 167.

Murcer was a good player but inferior to Bonds both as a fielder and a hitter. In his two years with the Giants, batting lower in the order than Bonds, he knocked in 14 more runs than Bonds had in his previous two seasons but scored 75 fewer. He constantly complained of the cold weather at Candlestick, and the Giants granted him his wish by trading him after two seasons.

The pattern was clear: The Giants were consistently getting less back in trades than they were giving up. That hadn't been true in earlier years. There had been some mistakes—the Cepeda trade being the most obvious—but most of their trades had been good ones.

What had happened? Many close to the club traced the Giants' problems to the fact that Feeney had left in 1970 to become National League president. "Horace didn't have anybody left who would say no to him," noted Simmons. Stoneham's advisors after Feeney left tended to be his old-time friends, such as Sheehan and Ryan, and they were all growing old together, their judgment probably lessened by age. Fox, who was fired as manager in 1974, to be replaced by another ex-Giant, Wes Westrum, thought many decisions were based on whether Sheehan or Ryan liked or disliked players.

There was another problem that Stoneham didn't like to acknowledge publicly: He didn't have much money. Only in the Mays trade was it acknowledged that money was involved, but a Giants executive at the time, speaking under the cloak of anonymity, revealed that the Giants had gotten money back in most of the trades they made under Stoneham in the 1970s.

The coming of the A's to Oakland in 1968 had been a body blow to Stoneham. At a time when an attendance of one million was considered good in baseball, the Giants had easily surpassed that total every year in San Francisco. But in 1968, when they suddenly shared the market with the A's, attendance dropped to 833,594. Attendance rose to nearly

Dave Kingman doing what he did best for the Giants: swing for the fences.

Long before he was "The Sarge," Gary Matthews patrolled left field from 1972-76. He was named National League Rookie of the Year in 1973.

After Willie Mays was traded in 1972, Garry Maddox became the starting center fielder for the next three years. Maddox enjoyed his best season in 1973, when he finished third in the NL with a .319 batting average.

Infielder Ed Goodson takes a swing at a wiffle ball during some clubhouse hi-jinx prior to a 1975 game. Pitchers Charlie Williams (playing catcher) and John D'Acquisto (umpire) are part of the "action." In the background, pitcher Jim Barr chats with a reporter.

Don McMahon joined the Giants in 1969 and finished his 18-year Major League career with San Francisco in 1974—at the age of 44—as a player/coach. He saved 19 games in 1970 and won 10 in 1971.

John D'Acquisto won 12 games in 1974—the most by a first-year Giants pitcher since Ruben Gomez won 13 in 1953. D'Acquisto led the team with 167 strikeouts. His stellar season earned him 1974 National League Rookie Pitcher of the Year honors.

1.1 million in 1971, when the Giants won the division, but that was the only year attendance exceeded a million for the rest of Stoneham's time.

It dropped almost to half a million twice in the mid-1970s, lower than the attendance which had driven Stoneham out of New York. Speier remembered coming out of the dugout for a late September game in 1974. "We looked up in the stands and we could count the people," he said. An exaggeration, but not by much: The Giants drew only 748 people that night.

The lack of money also affected what could be spent on the farm system, which had been the lifeblood of the franchise. The system was no longer producing the great players like Mays, McCovey and Cepeda. There were still some good prospects, but they weren't being developed at the major league level.

Dave Kingman was probably the best example. Kingman was a great raw talent. He had been a pitcher at USC, but he had speed, power and a good arm. It seemed to make sense to try him as an outfielder in the minors, since McCovey was at first, but the Giants played him at first in the minors and then switched him to the outfield when they brought him up. Then, when Davenport got hurt, Fox tried him at third base, and he couldn't handle that position at all.

Kingman was a moody, introspective young man, and the constant shifting seemed to damage his confidence seriously. "He could have been a guy who hit a lot of homers for them, year after year, and he was a good all-around athlete when he came up," said

Rob Dressler made his Giants debut in 1975.

First baseman Willie Montanez spent most of one season (1975) in a Giants uniform after coming from Philadelphia for Garry Maddox. Montanez hit .305, second on the club behind Von Joshua's .318 mark.

Rally Time! The Giants turned their caps inside-out to see if they could score some runs during a 1973 contest. Sitting on the bench (right to left): Steve Ontiveros, Gary Thomasson, Tom Bradley, Randy Moffitt, Dave Kingman, Juan Marichal, and Don McMahon.

Pitcher Ron "Bear" Bryant and his friend, who kept him company throughout the 1973 season. The stuffed bear brought Bryant good luck as he led the National League with 24 wins.

Shortly after Ed Halicki pitched a no-hitter against the New York Mets in 1975, he posed for a picture with two Giants greats who also tossed no-hitters: Carl Hubbell (left) and Juan Marichal (right).

Giants fans didn't receive a "Croix de Candlestick" when they attended this fog-shrouded game against the Atlanta Braves on Sept. 17, 1974. Only 1,347 die-hard fans witnessed this contest.

Simmons. "But they really messed with his head with those changes. He just couldn't handle that."

Kingman went on to hit more than 400 homers in his career, most of them for other teams, but he became a one-dimensional player, usually hitting for a low average, and was a defensive liability.

Garry Maddox came up in 1972 and quickly established himself as an outstanding defensive center fielder and a timely hitter, but he was traded in 1975 for first baseman Willie Montanez, who was in turn traded the next year. Meanwhile, Maddox had a fine 15-year career and was a key player for the 1980 World Series champion Philadelphia Phillies.

Gary Matthews was one player who did develop with the Giants, a solid hitter and a decent defensive outfielder in left field, but the Giants lost him after the 1976 season in the first year of free agency.

"What an outfield that could have been, with Bonds, Maddox and Matthews," said Fox. "They were at the stage of their careers where you knew they had at least 4-5 years ahead of them, more with Maddox because he was younger. He was a great defensive player, a decent hitter, a greyhound on the bases. Matthews was a leader, a good man in the clubhouse."

There were some individual high marks in those years. Ron Bryant won 24 games in 1973 and was named Pitcher of the Year by *The Sporting News*. Ed Halicki threw a no-hit game in 1975. But overall, the last years of the Stoneham era were a down cycle.

The worst news was yet to come. In January, 1976, Stoneham announced he had sold the Giants to the Labatt's Brewery and the club would be moved to Toronto.

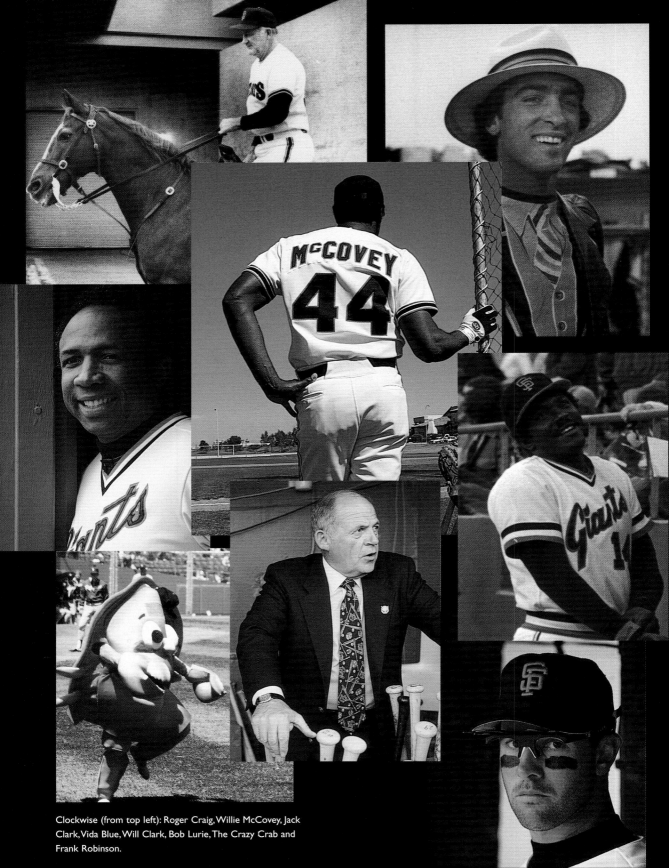

Clockwise (from top left): Roger Craig, Willie McCovey, Jack Clark, Vida Blue, Will Clark, Bob Lurie, The Crazy Crab and Frank Robinson.

II

HUMM–BABY

• THE BOB LURIE ERA •
1976-1992

D uring the San Francisco mayoral campaign in the fall of 1975, there were occasional questions asked of George Moscone about the future of the Giants. "We didn't take it seriously," said Corey Busch, then an aide to Moscone. "It wasn't a big deal."

After Moscone was elected, though, it quickly became a big deal. A few days after he was sworn in, he called Busch into his office to tell him the Giants had been sold to Labatt's Brewery, which would move the team to Toronto. "That's a helluva way to start your administration," remembered Busch, "by losing your Major League Baseball team."

Horace Stoneham had decided to sell the Giants because he could not compete financially. There was an eerie similarity to what had happened in 1957, when falling attendance in New York had caused Stoneham to move the team to San Francisco. In 1974 and 1975, the Giants had barely exceeded 500,000 in attendance, less than half of what had been their normal attendance before the A's came to Oakland.

Moscone immediately had the city file a lawsuit to force the Giants to honor their contract at Candlestick and stay in San Francisco. An injunction was issued, but the judge warned Moscone that, if he couldn't find local buyers for the team, it would be lifted.

There was only one potential buyer: Bob Lurie, who had been a member of the board since the late 1950s, when Stoneham had sought out local businessmen. Lurie was a big fan; he had gone to every World Series since 1961 with Chub Feeney, who had been a Giants vice president until he was named National League president in 1970. Lurie resigned after the board voted to approve the move to Toronto, and he was contemplating the idea of buying the club.

Arizona businessman Bud Herseth (right) and Bob Lurie formed a partnership in 1976 to purchase the Giants from Horace Stoneham. Listening to Herseth in the Giants Spring Training locker room are (left to right) Randy Moffitt, Mike Sadek and Gary Lavelle.

"Bob's second greatest passion, behind golf, is baseball," said Busch. "He viewed the Giants purchase in those terms, not as an investment." Lurie met with Moscone and Busch in the mayor's office and said, "I'm here. I'll pay half of it."

Nobody in San Francisco seemed willing to share the risk, though, so Moscone made calls around the country and found a possible partner, Bob Short, who had owned both a basketball team (the Minneapolis Lakers, before they moved to Los Angeles) and a baseball team, the Washington Senators, who had moved to Texas to become the Rangers.

"I made four trips to Minneapolis," remembered Lurie. "Short was in a hospital because he'd broken his hip. We even interviewed potential managers, because we were getting close to Spring Training. He wanted to hire Alvin Dark. I wanted Bill Rigney."

Lurie and Short could not agree on a manager, but they did come to a tentative agreement to buy the club and then talked to league owners on a conference call. Only one owner could vote in league meetings. The other National League owners, aware that both of Short's previous teams had moved to other cities, wanted Lurie to have that vote, and Lurie wanted that, too.

Short had a much different idea. He told Lurie he had to have control of the team. Lurie told him, "You want my money, but you want control? I don't think it's going to work." With that, Short bowed out.

Lurie returned to San Francisco, and Feeney set up another conference call with league owners. "There were some people in the league who thought Toronto would be a better place," said Lurie. "Candlestick hadn't worked out, and they liked the idea of new ownership, Labatt's. I said I'd like 48 hours to find a new owner. They wanted a decision right then; they wanted to say no. Then, Walter O'Malley made a big speech, because he didn't want to lose the rivalry, so they gave me five hours."

It was a frantic five hours. Several men in the San Francisco business community had told Lurie before that they were behind him and that if he needed help, to give them a call. "Now, all of these people who had indicated great support seemed to be out to lunch, all out of touch, not available," said Lurie.

In the mayor's office, Busch was calling everyone who had ever shown an interest in the Giants. Nothing worked. "I was getting a ton of calls and trying to return them all," remembered Busch, "but it was getting ridiculous. Kids from the Richmond district were calling and saying, 'I've got $46 in my piggy bank.'"

A call came in from an Arizona cattleman, Bud Herseth. When Busch was told about it, he thought it was another false alarm, but his secretary urged him to return it. When Busch called, Herseth told him, "I'm a cattle rancher in Arizona, God has been good to me, I've got $4 million in CDs in the bank. Here's my lawyer's number. Check me out."

A frantic round of telephone calls followed. Busch called Lurie and told him to check out Herseth; Lurie called back and said everything Herseth had said was true. Moscone talked to Herseth and, while he was talking, gave the thumbs up signal to Busch, who then put Lurie and Herseth together on the phone. Lurie and Herseth agreed to a deal. Minutes before the deadline imposed by the National League owners, Lurie called to tell them he and Herseth would buy the Giants.

The next day, Herseth came to San Francisco and met with Lurie and Feeney. He told Feeney, "I've always liked baseball and I love betting on the World Series." Whoops! thought Feeney, who told him, "You're not going to be betting on baseball any more."

After Lurie and Herseth had worked out the deal, they went into court with Moscone and told the court they had the buyers to keep the team in San Francisco. Asked by television reporter Jan Hutchins how he felt, Moscone said, "Bobby Thomson lives!"

National League owners still had to approve the deal, so Lurie, Moscone and Busch went back to Chicago to meet with the owners.

An aerial photograph of the Giants' Casa Grande Spring Training facility.

The viewing tower overlooking the four practice diamonds at the Giants' Spring Training headquarters in Casa Grande, AZ. Team executives, coaches and scouts would stay in the tower to analyze the players. The complex, which was used during the Horace Stoneham era, also included a hotel.

A look from inside the viewing tower.

Alameda native Bill Rigney, who was Giants manager from 1958-60, was new Owner Bob Lurie's choice to manage in 1976.

While Lurie got Rigney to manage, he couldn't convince National League President Chub Feeney to return to the Giants as general manager.

H.B. "Spec" Richardson served as Giants' general manager from 1976-81. He reached his zenith as Giants' GM in 1978 when he acquired Vida Blue from the Oakland A's for seven players. Richardson's shrewdness at the trading table earned him 1978 National League Executive of the Year honors.

Herseth didn't make the trip, though his contribution had been crucial. "He was a strange individual," said Lurie. "When he made the deal, his wife didn't even know about it, and I gather that caused some problems later. He enjoyed the spotlight when he had it. He liked going around saying he was the owner of the Giants. When we first talked, I told him I had to have management control, even though we had a 50-50 split in the ownership, and he agreed. I told him I wasn't used to having a lot of partners but I would certainly keep him informed. But it was often difficult, because he just didn't understand how baseball worked."

After two years, Lurie bought out Herseth, but the Arizonan remains a very important footnote in Giants history. "We got very lucky with Herseth," said Busch. "Nobody else was willing to come forward. Without him, the club wouldn't have stayed in San Francisco."

That was the start of a wild first year for Lurie, who had to make some very quick decisions. The first was an easy one, hiring Rigney as manager. "We had been friends for a long time," he said. "I had always respected Rig's baseball ability, just a helluva guy, and I thought he would bring continuity to the operation, which was important." Rigney, though, would last only one year, and Lurie has one theory about that. "I think Rigney was in such shock at the attitude of new players. They would worry more about the costs of race horses or their new cars. They wouldn't come in just thinking about the ball game."

Rigney wasn't the same person he'd been in his earlier managerial stints, either. "I didn't have the fire in my belly any more," he admitted. "I was always the first guy at the park because I could hardly wait for the game to begin, but I wasn't that way any more."

Many thought Lurie would bring back another long-time friend, Feeney, as his general manager, but Feeney had other ideas. "Chub wanted to stay with the league," said Lurie. "He enjoyed that. When he first got that, it was a tough decision, but he liked the challenge."

Owner Bob Lurie, son of San Francisco financier Louis Lurie, was a Giants board member during Horace Stoneham's reign as San Francisco Giants owner.

The late San Francisco Mayor George Moscone, who was instrumental in preventing the Giants move to Toronto in 1976, throws out the first pitch on Opening Day in 1978.

Before he was seen throughout America as one of the voices of the Chicago Cubs on WGN-TV, Steve Stone made his Major League debut with the Giants in 1971.

Catcher Dave Rader was named 1972 National League Rookie of the Year by *The Sporting News*.

The league had installed Spec Richardson to run the franchise during the period in which it was for sale. When Lurie took control, he kept Richardson on as his general manager. That was a mistake, but an understandable one in retrospect. When Lurie asked the baseball men he had met during his years on the Giants board, many of them recommended Richardson. Lurie had no way of knowing at the time that the advice wasn't intended to help him.

"When you come in as a new owner, they look at you as just another opponent, which is one of the major problems in baseball," Lurie said. "I understand that there's competition on the field, but I think there should be cooperation off the field. We need to have a course for new owners in how to run a franchise. There are just so many people who have retired from baseball, like Al Rosen, who have such a great knowledge and wealth of experience, it doesn't make sense that the commissioner's office wouldn't use them.

"Instead. . . well, I remember the suggestions I got. In retrospect, a lot of that advice was detrimental on purpose. It didn't make sense."

Richardson was almost a caricature of a Texan, from his cowboy hat to his boots to his big belly to the cigar sticking out of his mouth. That and his pronounced Texas accent—fellow southerner Vida Blue quipped that he often had to translate Spec's speech for players from other areas of the country—made him appear stupid. He wasn't, but neither was he the kind of imaginative general manager the Giants needed at the time, to work out of the morass into which they had fallen in the last years of the Stoneham ownership.

Ed Goodson (left) and pitcher Pete Falcone were teammates at the start of the 1975 season. Goodson was dealt later in the season to the Atlanta Braves for infielder Craig Robinson.

Ed Halicki had his finest year in 1977, leading the Giants in wins (16), ERA (3.31), innings pitched (258), strikeouts (168) and complete games (seven).

Dave Heaverlo, known as "Kojak" for his shaved head like the television detective played by Telly Savalas, was a middle-inning reliever from 1975-77.

Richardson was an old-style baseball man. He knew everybody in the game, and he worked the telephone relentlessly, always looking for a deal. His deals, though, usually solved one problem by opening up another. For instance, in 1977, he made a trade in which the key players were Bill Madlock, whom the Giants got, and Bobby Murcer, whom they gave up. Madlock was a good player and helped the Giants at third, but trading Murcer meant they needed another outfielder. Two years later, he traded Madlock for pitchers Ed Whitson, Fred Breining and Al Holland. Holland had a good, though brief, run as a relief pitcher, but the trade left the Giants short at third base.

These Richardson moves left the Giants basically where they were, but another move was devastating: For economic reasons, Spec cut the scouting staff and put his reliance on the Central Scouting Bureau which had been established by Major League Baseball. The scouting staff that Jack Schwarz had put together painfully had been the basis for the Giants success in San Francisco, though bad trades and bad management had kept the Giants from capitalizing on that in the 1970s. Now, the cutback on the scouting staff meant that the farm system would wither for the next few years, and that drought would mean that the Giants would make only two serious runs at a pennant until Al Rosen replaced Tom Haller in the mid-1980s.

There seemed to be a black cloud hovering over the team. Even when they seemed to be making progress, it was illusory. In 1977, for instance, they had what appeared to be the nucleus of a good young pitching staff in righthanders Ed Halicki and John Montefusco and lefthander Bob Knepper. Halicki, a 6-foot-7-inch fastballer who could be overpowering, had thrown a no-hitter in 1975 and he won 16 games in 1977. Montefusco had been

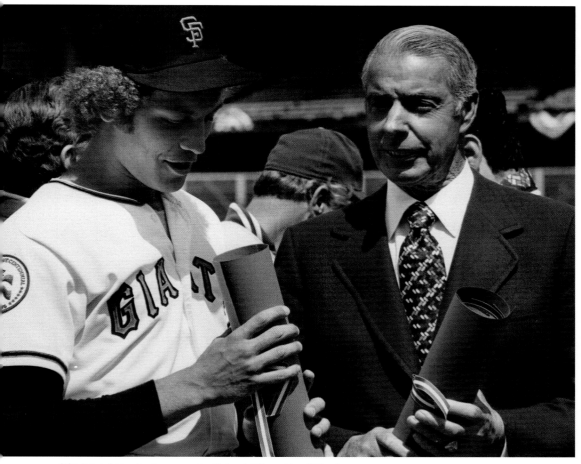

John Montefusco shares a moment with baseball legend Joe DiMaggio.

Catcher Dennis Littlejohn spent parts of three seasons (1978-80) with the Giants.

Jim Barr was one of the National League's top control pitchers during his time in a Giants uniform (1971-78 and 1982-83). "J.B." set a Major League record by retiring 41 consecutive batters over two consecutive games in 1972.

Lefty Mike Caldwell, who was acquired from the San Diego Padres for Willie McCovey and outfielder Bernie Williams after the 1973 season, led the Giants with 14 wins in 1974.

the NL Rookie of the Year in 1975, and in 1976 he, too, threw a no-hitter. Knepper had great stuff and appeared capable of winning 20 games more than once. But in each case, after a short period of success, they flamed out and were soon gone.

Montefusco was probably the most disappointing because he was a colorful character who had given himself the nickname of "Count" and was a good gate attraction for a time. He loved the attention he got as a big league pitcher, and he liked to boast of what he would do against the next team he faced. He backed up his claims with strong seasons, winning 31 games in his first two years as a Giant. But then he dropped to seven wins in 1977 and was never a top-level pitcher again.

The disappointment over Montefusco, though, was largely forgotten in 1977 because the Giants made an important connection with their more illustrious past, bringing back Willie McCovey. It seemed merely a sentimental move, because McCovey had hit a combined .204 in 71 games with the San Diego Padres and 11 games with the Oakland A's in 1976, but McCovey knew what he could do better than anybody else. In his first year back in San Francisco, he hit a solid .280, with 28 home runs and 86 RBI in 141 games.

"I didn't surprise myself," McCovey said, "and I don't think players who knew me were that surprised. I didn't play much that last year in San Diego. The first two years there, I led them in home runs and RBI, and then they decided they didn't want to play me. I'm just not a part-time player, and that's the reason I didn't have a good year in San Diego."

McCovey had a point. With his knee problems, when he didn't play regularly, he would stiffen up. He also had a big swing, and his timing could be messed up when he wasn't in the lineup every day. "They tried to make me a Manny Mota (a notable pinch-hitter of the day) and I wasn't Manny Mota," he said.

Practically speaking, it didn't make a lot of sense for McCovey, with his knee problems, to come back to the Giants and Candlestick. His doctor advised him against it, telling McCovey that the 'Stick was the worst possible place for him.

But nobody ever had much success in telling Willie Mac what to do, and considering the bad advice he got from the supposed baseball experts, from Alvin Dark to Lefty O'Doul, that was probably a good thing. He had learned in his previous stint with the Giants how

Gary Lavelle appeared in two All-Star Games (1977 and 1983) for the Giants.

Derrel Thomas came from San Diego in 1975 to be the starting second baseman. By the time he was traded back to the Padres three years later, he had played all four infield positions and the outfield.

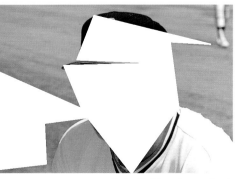

Spring Training phenom Randy Elliott was invaluable as a pinch hitter in 1977.

to deal with Candlestick, and he was ready to come back to the scene of his great triumphs.

"What I liked about Candlestick," he said, "was that you could stay strong there. When you'd go on a long road trip in the east, with 90-degree temperatures and 100 percent humidity, when you came back to Candlestick and cool weather, you could feel your body rejuvenating.

"I put that hot stuff on my joints. Even on hot days, I had to have long underwear to cover my knees. We used to have that sauna in the clubhouse. When we were coming up to hit, we'd go into that sauna for a couple of minutes and get warm, and we'd be ready to hit.

"You have to get ready. You can't just sit there in the corner of the dugout and go up and hit. You have to do your stretches. You can't let it beat you mentally. You know the other team isn't liking it. Those guys would come out of the right field bullpen, cursing the wind, and I always thought, psychologically, we had them. We had that attitude— it's bothering them more than it's bothering us."

McCovey's return wasn't enough to make the Giants a winner. It took an uncharacteristically bold trade by Richardson before the 1978 season: Vida Blue from the Oakland A's for seven players—Gary Alexander, Gary Thomasson, Dave Heaverlo, Alan Wirth, John Henry Johnson, Phil Huffman and Mario Guerrero—and $390,000.

In one of the team's biggest trades during the 1970s, Darrell Evans was acquired from Atlanta in 1976, along with infielder Marty Perez, for first baseman Willie Montanez, infielder Craig Robinson, outfielder Jake Brown and minor leaguer Mike Eden.

Willie Montanez making one of his trademark wrist-flicking backhand catches at first base.

An opposing hitter's view of Vida Blue.

Bill Madlock (left) is introduced to the San Francisco media. He came to the Giants in a five-player deal with the Chicago Cubs before the 1977 season.
"Mad Dog" spent three years with the Giants (1977-80). Owner Bob Lurie and General Manager Spec Richardson are to Madlock's left.

With Blue added, the Giants had a well-balanced staff, with Blue and Knepper the left-handers, Montefusco and Halicki as right-handed starters. "We kind of pushed each other, too," said Blue. "Montefusco would challenge me about who could get the most wins, the most strikeouts, the best ERA, that kind of thing. And, by the way, he didn't beat me in any of those categories."

In fact, it was no contest. Blue had an excellent year, 18-10 with a 2.79 ERA, and finished second in the Cy Young voting to Gaylord Perry, who was still reminding the Giants what a disastrous trade they'd made in 1972. Perry became the first pitcher to win the Cy Young in both leagues, an honor that would have been Blue's if he'd won.

Vida's attitude was as important as his performance. He was an instant fan favorite at Candlestick, often stepping out of the dugout to wave a towel and lead cheers. "I remember saying, 'Free, free, free at last,'" he said, in reference to his years under Finley's thumb.

His experience with the A's also helped Blue in the heat of the pennant race. "I was almost the only player on the team who had been involved in a pennant race," he said. (McCovey had played in a World Series and a National League Championship Series, but he was not a factor when the race got down to the critical last month.)

"We had a very good team that year. We had a young outfield of Terry Whitfield, Larry Herndon and Jack Clark that looked like it was really coming together. I don't think Clark ever really knew how good he could be. He had that sweet swing, and he was really tough in the clutch."

From the time he had hit the Giants farm system, Clark had been labeled a "can't miss" prospect, a young player who had all the tools, good speed, a great throwing arm and, above all, great hitting form.

Bill Madlock ices his left ankle after being hit by a Nolan Ryan pitch during 1978 Spring Training action.

Terry Whitfield was the Giants' left fielder from 1977-80.

Shortstop Johnnie LeMaster spent 10 years with the Giants (1975-85). Although he wasn't spectacular at the plate, he more than made up for it with his glove.

Clark was probably the best prospect to come up through the Giants organization since McCovey in 1959, but his Giants career became bogged down in controversy and disappointment. He became a butt of jokes because of the times when he lost track of the outs in an inning, starting to trot in from right field when there were only two outs. He was fiercely dedicated to winning, and he could not understand why the Giants could not make the trades to develop a winner. When he vented his anger publicly, he got the reputation of being a malcontent, though his complaints were legitimate ones, often the same ones being made in columns at the time.

He was an average fielder at best, and he was not a base stealing threat, but he was always a very dangerous hitter. He could absolutely crush a fastball, sending searing line drives through the infield, off the fences and sometimes over them. Best of all, as

Jack Clark, "The Ripper," tied Keith Hernandez for the NL's game-winning RBI lead in 1982 with 21.

You can count on "The Count." John Montefusco would never be described as being modest or shy. The cocky right-hander earned 1975 National League Rookie of the Year honors and tossed a no-hitter in 1976. But after winning 34 games in his first three years, Montefusco lost 37 over his last four years with the Giants and wound up being traded to Atlanta after the 1980 season.

Infielder Rob Andrews joined the Giants in a trade with the Houston Astros before the 1977 season.

Hector "Heity" Cruz, brother of Houston Astros' star Jose Cruz, spent parts of 1978 and 1979 with the Giants.

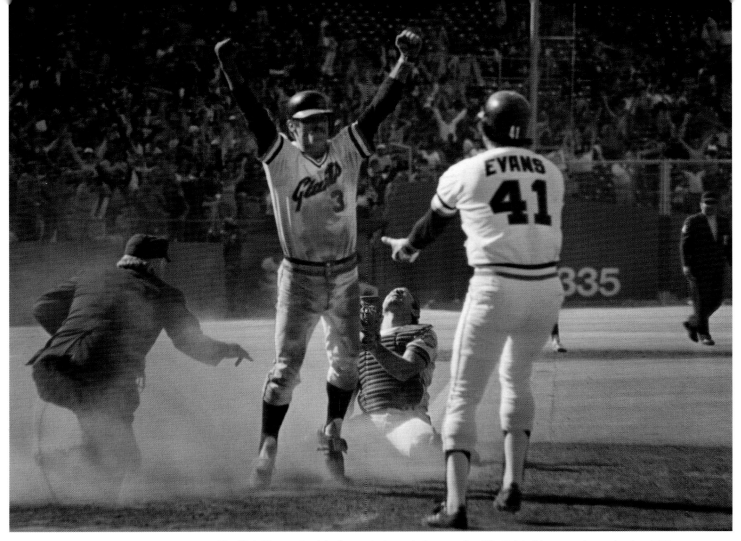

New York Mets catcher John Stearns looks to the heavens after Mike Sadek slides across home plate in a 1978 game. Darrell Evans waits to congratulate Sadek.

Joe Altobelli's managerial skills kept the Giants in the thick of the 1978 National League Western Division race for most of the season. His reward: being voted National League Manager of the Year.

Blue noted, he was an even better hitter in clutch situations. "There are hitters who can get their hits in the early innings but they don't want to be up in the ninth inning with the game on the line," said Joe Morgan, his teammate for two years in the 1980s. "Jack loves to be up there in those situations. That's what he lives for." In 1982, Clark set a club record with 21 game-winning RBI.

Throughout his Giants career, Clark was dogged by injuries. One year, 1984, a knee injury resulted in a surgery which ended his season before the halfway mark, but usually, Jack just played through his injuries. He never used them as an excuse, belying his reputation as a complainer.

In 1978, though, Clark was healthy and not yet well known enough for pitchers to take extra caution against him, and he had the kind of year everybody was expecting: .306 with 25 home runs, 46 doubles and 98 RBI. He also set a San Francisco club record with a 26-game hitting streak in June and July.

Manager Joe Altobelli was in his second year. "He was probably the best kind of manager for that team," thought Blue, "because he was kind of laid back, easy going. He didn't get on the young players. He was certainly different than Frank Robinson. Wooee, I still remember Frank getting on Jack Clark. Frank was always challenging you, trying to make you prove that you were as tough as he was. The way he played the game, he just went all-out, and he wanted you to play the game the same way."

At mid-season, though, Altobelli made a decision to use Mike Ivie as a full-time player. It seemed a sound move at the time, but it soon took the wind out of the Giants sails.

Ivie had started his professional career as a catcher in San Diego, getting a big bonus for signing, but developed a psychological block against catching, which manifested itself in a tendency to throw the ball into center field when he was only trying to get it back to the pitcher.

Ivie was shifted to first base but had little success there with the Padres and was traded to the Giants for infielder Derrel Thomas before the 1978 season.

He seemed to find himself with the Giants and had some dramatic hits as a pinch-hitter in the first half of the 1978 season. In a critical Memorial Day weekend series against the Dodgers, Ivie beat Don Sutton with a grand-slam pinch-hit home run. In June, Ivie hit another grand-slam in a pinch-hitting role, though this one came in a losing game against Atlanta.

Putting Ivie in the starting lineup, though, meant that McCovey became a part-time player and, as Stretch had noted before, he was not a good part-time player. The move effectively ended his career, though he didn't officially retire until mid-season in 1980. He hit only 12 home runs in 1978.

Ivie? He was a good player in 1978 and had a career year in 1979 with a .286 batting average and 27 home runs, but that was his last good season.

The Giants were a Cinderella story for the first four months of the 1978 season, during which they led by as much as half a dozen games.

The Giants had no finishing kick, though, and Blue thinks that the team's lack of experience with a pennant race was critical. "Maybe if I'd been an everyday player, I could have done something to help everybody get the feeling of what they had to do," he said, "but as a pitcher, I just wasn't involved every day."

Outfielder Larry Herndon (1976-81) had speed to burn. He led the Giants in triples three times.

Vida Blue's charm made him an instant favorite with Giants fans. Winning 18 games in his first season (1978) didn't hurt, either.

Guy "G-Man" Sularz was a reserve infielder from 1980-83.

Mike "Poison" Ivie. He hit four home runs as a pinch-hitter in 1978—two were grand slams. Ivie came from San Diego prior to the season for Derrel Thomas.

The signature follow-through of a Willie McCovey swing.

Jack Clark always made things exciting when he stepped to the plate. Clark's best year as a Giant was in 1982 when he led the team with 27 homers and 103 RBI.

KNBR replaced KSFO as the Giants' flagship radio station in 1979. The team's new voices were Hank Greenwald (left) and former New York Mets announcer Lindsay Nelson (right).

When the Giants collapsed in September, winning just 12 of 29 games, they slipped to third, with the Dodgers winning the pennant and the Reds moving into second. Altobelli was named Manager of the Year, Richardson Executive of the Year, and the Giants finished with their second highest attendance, 1,740,000. Nice, but none of that erased the bitter disappointment of their weak finish.

It also was a harbinger of what was to come, as the Giants fell to 71-91 the next year. Altobelli was replaced in the last month of the season by Dave Bristol.

Blue thought part of the problem was religion in the clubhouse. It was an era when Born Again Christians were becoming very public in baseball, and nowhere more than in the Giants clubhouse. "We always had our Sunday morning chapel," said Blue, "but now, some of these guys were wanting to have meetings during the week. I've got nothing against religion and I believe everybody has the right to worship whatever God he wants to in his home or in his church, but doing this in the clubhouse created cliques. You can't have one group of guys in one corner of the clubhouse and another group in another. It just doesn't work."

"It also got to the point where guys were saying it was God's will. If a pitcher lost a game, it was because that was what God wanted. If a hitter struck out with the bases loaded, same thing. That's bull. The pitcher didn't make his pitches, the hitter couldn't hit that hard slider on the outside corner. You can't make excuses. You have to do the job."

On July 6, 1980, McCovey took his last at-bat as a Giant, in a game in Los Angeles, driving in a run with an eighth inning sacrifice fly in a game eventually won by the Giants in extra innings. It was an emotional moment, as McCovey came out of the game, with the Dodgers fans putting aside their partisanship to recognize one of the all-time greats, rising to give him a long standing ovation. Busch had gone down to the dugout for the special moment. McCovey told him, "I don't know what I'm going to do. I can't remember a time in my life when I didn't play baseball." Remembering it today Busch thinks of that as an area where baseball has failed its players. "There just isn't enough thought given to what happens to players after they leave the game, or any preparation for that moment while they're still playing."

In the off-season, Lurie fired Bristol and brought in Frank Robinson. It was a bold move by Lurie. Robinson had been baseball's first black manager in Cleveland, but he had eventually been fired by the Indians and he had the reputation of being a manager who was very hard on his players, expecting them to play the same way he did.

Robinson seemed to carry his bitterness over his firing in Cleveland with him in the first half of the 1981 season. He was harsh and demanding with the players, and the Giants were just 27-32 in their first 59 games, at which point all of baseball was stopped by a strike.

There was an interesting dynamic developing during that time, though, with Robinson and the newly-acquired Joe Morgan, whom the Giants had signed for his leadership qualities as well as his playing ability. Eventually, Robinson and Morgan would both be named to the Hall of Fame, so they could talk as equals, but their relationship got off to a bad start when Robinson pinch-hit for Joe in the second game of the season.

"I would never do anything during a game that would embarrass a manager," said Morgan, "but I went into Frank's office after the game to talk about that. I told him that he couldn't expect me to be a leader if he was going to do that so early in the season. It wasn't like this was a game we had to win or our season would be ruined."

In Cleveland, Robinson's problems had been mostly with the black players, who seemed to expect that he would be more lenient with them, which he wasn't. "Maybe Frank was expecting me to be like that, too, and he had to make his point early," said .

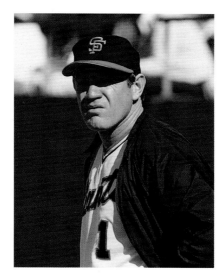

Dave Bristol relieved Joe Altobelli as Giants manager during the 1979 season. Bristol was replaced after the 1980 season by Frank Robinson.

Willie McCovey waiting in the on-deck circle during his last game, July 6, 1980, at Dodger Stadium.

The four decades of Willie McCovey's Hall of Fame career are captured in this assemblage by Ray Ward.

McCovey, Seaver On All-Star Team

"Without a doubt," says Willie McCovey of the San Francisco Giants, "it's the high point of my career. But if I could make a straight trade, I'd take a pennant."

That was the first baseman's reaction today when told that he had been voted the National League's most valuable player for the first time.

"It's the highest individual award a player can win," McCovey said. "I was hoping for it and I think every ball player has secret dreams of winning the award.

McCovey, Bonds Sizzle

MAC 44

GO GIANTS GO

GIANTS NOTES
THE GIANTS HAVE ANNOUNCED THAT SEPTEMBER 21 WILL BE DESIGNATED AS WILLIE MC COVEY DAY TO HONOR SAN FRANCISCO'S ALL-TIME FAVORITE GIANT IN PRE-GAME CEREMONIES.

#411

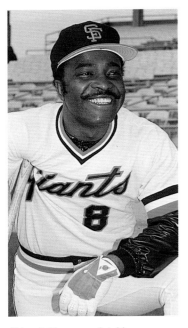

Although his stay was brief, Joe Morgan's (1981-82) presence was clearly felt. He led the Giants with a .289 average in 1982 while earning National League Comeback Player of the Year honors.

Frank Robinson and Bob Lurie. Robinson managed the Giants from 1981-84, earning National League Manager of the Year honors in 1982. Robinson was also named manager of the Giants' 25th Anniversary Dream Team.

Morgan. "But. truthfully, I never looked at him as a black manager. He was just my manager, period."

That session in Robinson's office seemed to clear the air, and he and Morgan had a great working relationship for the rest of the season. Morgan would come into Robinson's office frequently with ideas; sometimes they would agree, sometimes not, but there was a mutual respect.

Whether it was Morgan's influence or his own maturation as a manager or, most likely, a combination of both, Robinson gradually changed as a manager.

"Sparky Anderson (Morgan's manager in Cincinnati) was the best I ever knew at working with players," said Morgan, "but Frank became much more like Sparky the rest of the time I was with the Giants. He and Gene Mauch are also the two best managers I've known at knowing every aspect of the game. There are guys who know pitching or who know hitters, but these two knew everything. because they'd taken the time to talk to the guys who really knew about specific parts of the game."

Robinson was still intense, still determined to win, but now he would talk more to players, explain more to them, try to get them thinking as he was. The difference showed on the field: When the strike ended and play resumed, the Giants went 29-23

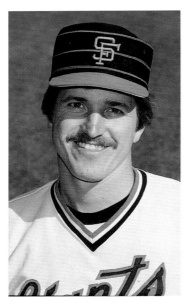

Pitcher Alan Hargesheimer poses with the rarely seen "Bicentennial" pillbox hat from 1980. These hats were not worn in games.

Marc "Boot" Hill caught for the Giants from 1975-80.

Roger Metzger shared the shortstop position with Johnnie LeMaster from 1978-80.

Darrell Evans sliding home against the Cubs in 1978. Former Giants catcher Dave Rader tries to apply the tag.

Catcher Milt May (1980-83) provided a solid bat from the left side.

Keeping warm, with the help of a bonfire, in the tunnel from the Giants bullpen (left to right): John Montefusco, Dave Heaverlo, Ed Halicki and Randy Moffitt.

DAVE BRISTOL

Dave Bristol managed only 183 games for the Giants, taking over for Joe Altobelli late in the 1979 season and lasting through the next season, but his time was a memorable one.

There was always something going on with Bristol. He even got into a fight with a player, pitcher John Montefusco, in the dressing room during the 1979 season. Reportedly, he decked Montefusco, who showed up the next day with a black eye.

Though Owner Bob Lurie and General Manager Spec Richardson weren't happy with that, Bristol survived it, but an outburst during the 1980 World Series sealed his doom.

At the time, the Giants were trying to trade Mike Ivie, who had worn out his welcome. Bristol apparently thought he'd speed up the process. Before the third game of the Series in Philadelphia, Bristol called this writer and said he wanted to talk.

Over coffee in the dining room, Bristol told me, "We've got to get rid of the cancer (Ivie) on this club. When he cut his hand in the off-season and the doctor told him it would take a year to fully heal, that's all Mike had to hear. He was ready to accept it.

"I told him that he had as much ability as Johnny Bench, Tony Perez and Lee May, three great right-handed hitters I had when I was managing at Cincinnati. But they have something inside that he doesn't have. They wanted it."

Bristol's comments effectively ended his Giants career. Lurie was livid, because Ivie trade talks had to be put on hold; it's difficult to get much for a player who has been labeled a "cancer" by his manager. Lurie didn't fire Bristol until December, but the decision was made as soon as Bristol's comments were printed.

Infielder Joe Strain and outfielder Terry Whitfield were teammates during the late 1970s.

The classic high leg kick of Vida Blue.

Al Holland (1979-82) served as set-up man for Gary Lavelle and Greg Minton.

Billy North's 58 stolen bases in 1979 is still a San Francisco franchise record.

Second baseman Rennie Stennett was one of three free agents signed by the Giants prior to the 1980 season.

Doyle Alexander pitched just one season (1981) for the Giants, but won a team-leading 11 games.

Johnny Rabb was a reserve catcher from 1982-84.

for the rest of the season, finishing with an overall mark of 56-55 and setting the stage for the next season.

During the strike, Robinson took a trip to Phoenix, primarily to look at Bob Brenly, whom he had been wondering about for some time. "I kept looking at the stats of this young man down at Phoenix and wondering why he wasn't up here," said Robinson. "It wasn't like we had much at catcher, but nobody was blowing his horn. They kept telling me he didn't have a position. I went down and took a look at him and I liked what I saw, so we got him up here when the strike was over. He always worked hard, gave you everything he had, and he knew how to play the game."

"There had been many times when I thought I'd have to quit and get a real job," remembered Brenly, who was to become a key member of the Giants in the 1980s. "For a time, I was a substitute teacher in Fresno in the off-season, and in 1978, they offered me a full-time job, teaching and coaching in high school. I was ready to take it, but my wife talked me out of it."

Though at 27 he was much older than a typical rookie, Brenly was still in awe of everybody and everything when the Giants brought him up after the strike.

"The team had a lot of veterans at the time," said Brenly, "guys like Joe Morgan, Darrell Evans, Reggie Smith, Johnnie LeMaster, so they kind of ran the team. I was just along for the ride.

"There wasn't anything I could tell the veteran pitchers. I remember Doyle Alexander came up to me before one game and said, 'We'll use the 2-5 rotation and just keep sliding up and down on the signs.' I had no idea what he was talking about. I tried to ask some of the other players to help me, but most of the time that day, I was just guessing right along with the hitters because I had no idea what the signs I was giving him meant."

Gary Lavelle was the main stopper in the Giants' bullpen from 1977-79.

Fred Breining, who graduated from San Francisco's Lincoln High School, pitched for the Giants from 1980-83.

Rich Murray, brother of future Hall of Famer Eddie Murray, played parts of two seasons (1980, 1983) with the Giants.

Champ Summers hit .322 as a pinch hitter in 1982.

Pedro Borbon was a mid-season acquisition by the Giants in 1979.

Bill Laskey came to the Giants in the Vida Blue trade with Kansas City shortly before the 1982 season. That was also his best year in a Giants uniform, as he led the club in wins (13), ERA (3.14) and innings pitched (189).

The mainstays (firemen) in the Giants' 1982 bullpen were (left to right): Jim Barr, Gary Lavelle (top), Al Holland (bottom) and Fred Breining.

Tom O'Malley was popular with the fans during his short stint with the Giants (1982-84).

Brenly thought Robinson was still pretty tough. "Frank was hard on rookies," he said, "and I was in his doghouse a lot. I think I'd have been a great player for him later in my career, but at the time, I really didn't know very much and Frank expected a lot of his players, even rookies. If you didn't do the right thing, it drove him crazy. Like, if there was a runner on third base with less than two out and you pulled the ball to third base, he would really get upset."

"I just wanted them to be the best that they could be," Robinson said. "I tried to tell players how to play. Some of them got it, some didn't."

Bill Laskey, who joined the Giants in 1982 after being traded from Kansas City, had an easier time dealing with Robinson. "He gave me an opportunity," said Laskey. "I appreciated that because when I was with the Royals, I was 10-2 in the minors and didn't get a sniff. If you were pitching well, he'd give you the ball. I had 36 starts that first year.

Manager Frank Robinson (right) and umpire Bruce Froemming share a light moment while watching Atlee Hammaker warm up.

Al Holland was valuable as a spot starter and reliever in 1982. He also struck out 97 in 129.2 innings.

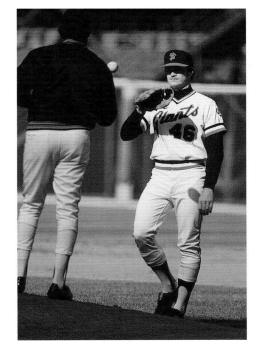

An example of why reliever Greg Minton was nicknamed "Moonie."

Frank Robinson (left) relied on Gary Lavelle's bullpen expertise 68 times in 1982—second to Greg Minton's team leading 78 appearances. "Pudge" account-ed for 10 wins and eight saves.

"Overall, he was a good motivator. He managed like he wanted to play. He was such an aggressive hitter, if hitters didn't show that aggressiveness, he would bitch and moan. But some players have that intensity, and you don't get it from others."

Laskey also remembered a playful side of Robinson that would surprise many. "In 1984, we lost our first six games after tearing up the Cactus League (18-9). Frank called a team meeting and said, 'I've brought in a woman psychologist to talk to you to see if she can loosen you up.' When she came in, she had glasses on, a straight-back hairdo, wearing a suit, very business-like. We were all wondering what this was all about. Then, she opened up her briefcase and pulled out a blaster and started strip-ping, right down to nothing! Well, I guarantee you, that loosened up the entire team. We won that game to end our losing streak."

The best season of Robinson's time was 1982, when he was named Manager of the Year. That team had a solid lineup and a re-made pitching staff. Between seasons, General Manager Tom Haller had traded for Laskey, Atlee Hammaker and Renie Martin. The rookies, Laskey and Hammaker, who won 13 and 12, respectively, were their lead-ing starters. The real strength of the staff, though, was the bullpen. Greg Minton had

Joe Morgan was traded to Philadelphia, along with Al Holland, for Mark Davis, Mike Krukow and C.L. Penigar after the 1982 season. Morgan's .289 average led the team in 1982.

Shunned by the Dodgers, Reggie Smith signed just before the 1982 season. Smith played the entire season at first base.

Chili Davis (1981-87) paced the Giants in batting three times— including a .315 average that earned him an invitation to the 1984 All-Star Game.

30 saves from the right side, and Gary Lavelle and Al Holland were a great left-handed combination. "Nobody could hit our left-handers," remembered Laskey. "Gary would drop his arm down and come sidearm, and Al would just overpower guys."

Though Brenly was only in his first full year, he had taken control behind the plate, particularly with the younger pitchers. At Robinson's urging, he had his pitchers throwing inside, keeping batters from digging in at the plate.

The team also had great leadership from Reggie Smith and Joe Morgan. Smith's leadership was more of the quiet type, because younger players could see how hard he worked and what a fierce competitor he was. Morgan was all of that, too, but he was also a very analytical player, not just about his own play but that of others. Over the years, many players got a baseball education from Morgan. "You'd just be listening to him talk in the clubhouse," said Brenly, "and all of a sudden, he'd point out something you'd never thought of that could make you a better player."

Morgan also became a great liaison between Robinson and the players; Joe could tell Robinson what the players wanted, and he could also get Frank's message to the players.

"I always told players they had to learn how to lose," said Robinson. "A lot of people wondered what I was talking about because they thought the idea was to learn how to win. What I meant was that when a team was losing and going through a bad time, you don't want to have players pointing fingers and blaming others for losing. If you can keep from doing that when you're losing, you can build a team attitude, and that sets the stage to win. Joe and Reggie had been on winning teams and knew what I was talking about, so they could get that message across."

From his second base position, Morgan was always in the middle of the action, and he would come in and talk to pitchers when they got in trouble.

"He used to come up to the mound between hitters," said Laskey, "and kind of test me. 'What are you going to throw this guy, how are you going to set him up? Remember, you've got a runner on first base.' Basically, he'd stop the game to see what you were doing. He wanted to know your strategy because it helped him position himself in the field. He educated me. It made me think before I made a pitch. That's what made him a leader."

Morgan wasn't quite the player he'd been when he'd won back-to-back Most Valuable Player awards in 1975 and 1976 with the Cincinnati Reds, but he was still productive. In the field, he used his knowledge to position himself to make the plays, and he turned the double play quicker than any second baseman since Bill

Right-handed reliever Randy Moffitt doing an impression of a left-hander.

Greg Minton led the Giants in saves for five straight seasons (1980-84). His 30 saves in 1982 were a San Francisco franchise record until Rod Beck earned 48 in 1993.

BILL LASKEY

In the middle of a fine first year in 1982, during which he would win 13 games for the Giants, Bill Laskey appeared headed for a spot on the National League pitching staff for the All-Star Game.

Then, he was called into Manager Frank Robinson's office. Robinson told him NL All-Star Manager Tommy Lasorda wanted to take Phil Niekro instead. Laskey said he still wanted to go, but Robinson said, "You're going to be around a few years. Why not let Phil go?"

"I knew what Tommy was doing," said Laskey. "He always

wanted to have his guys around and he hated to have Giants players. One time, I remember he took out Greg Minton after Minton had pitched to one guy and got him out. But I agreed, so Niekro went."

Niekro, a knuckleballer, pitched five more years in the Majors. Laskey lasted only one year beyond him, and he never got another shot at the All-Star Game.

"Phil lives down in Arizona, and he's a collector," said Laskey. "I told him, he's got my All-Star ring."

An occasional double play combination in 1982: Shortstop Johnnie LeMaster and second baseman Duane Kuiper.

Mazeroski. He was also an effective hitter, at .289 with 14 home runs. Laskey remembered how Morgan almost willed himself to do things. "He used to go out and say, 'I'm going to go to right center' or 'I'm going to go to left,' and sure enough, he'd go out there and hold up on his swing and hit everything to left. But the best thing he did was to educate the young players."

The Giants started slowly that season. In the first half, they were at .500 only once, at 5-5, and they were 42-46 at the All-Star break.

There had also been some anxious moments. After one game, won by Jack Clark with a home run, Robinson had criticized the players for sloppy play. "I think we'd had three or four physical errors and just as many mental ones," said Robinson. "I wasn't yelling at them, but I told them I wanted them to go home and think about how they had played, because if they played the same way the next day, they'd lose."

Clark had gone on the radio after the game and missed Robinson's talk, but he heard about it, somewhat inaccurately, when he came into the dressing room. When writers came by his cubicle, he told them Robinson was wrong for criticizing players after a win.

"Jack was an outspoken guy, but he didn't always understand what he was complaining about," said Robinson.

"But I never had a feud with Jack. He always played hard for me, and he was a great clutch hitter."

The Giants' malaise lasted for a couple of weeks after the All-Star Game, as they fell as much as 13-1/2 games out of first place. Then, in early August, they went on a 10-game winning streak that catapulted them into contention. In late September, they won three straight against the Dodgers in Los Angeles to pull within a game of division-leading Atlanta.

"I've always said that I was more proud of that team than any I'd played for," said Morgan. "In Cincinnati, we had great players, so we should have won. We didn't have the best team in 1982, but everybody was playing hard and totally focused on winning.

"The thing that has always bothered me was that (General Manager) Tom Haller didn't go out and get us another pitcher down the stretch. We were just one pitcher short of winning. Don Sutton was available, for instance, but Milwaukee grabbed him (and Sutton won four of five down the stretch, helping the Brewers get to the World Series).

Going into the final weekend, the Giants trailed by a game, with the Dodgers at Candlestick for the final three games of the season, which would be watched by more than 147,000 fans.

Before the first game, Robinson held a very unusual meeting with his team leaders, Morgan, Smith, Clark and Darrell Evans. At that point, the Giants starters were all exhausted, as much mentally from the pressure of the stretch drive as physically. They also had no clear-cut staff leader, no pitcher who could be counted on to pitch a game in the series opener that would set the tone for the weekend.

Robinson told the four players, "I know how hard you've played all season, and I'm proud of you. Now, I want you to tell me what you think the pitching rotation should be for this weekend. I can make the decision myself, but I want your input because of what you've done."

The consensus was that it should be Fred Breining, Renie Martin and Bill Laskey. Breining, who had won 11 games that year, and Dodger starter Jerry Reuss pitched seven scoreless innings in the opener. In the eighth, the Dodgers loaded the bases. Though Al Holland was ready to go in the bullpen, Robinson stayed with Breining, who surrendered a grand slam home run to Rick Monday.

"That's one of the few moves I ever made that I've second-guessed myself on." said Robinson. "At the time, I was thinking that Breining had pitched a good game and he was a forkballer, so he might be able to get the ground ball that would get us

Reggie Smith hit .284 in 106 games during 1982, the final season of his 17-year career. His presence was very valuable during the Giants run at the NL Western Division pennant.

the double play. He didn't give up many home runs. But he was tiring, and thinking about it now, I should have brought in Holland against Monday. The Dodgers would probably have brought up Pedro Guerrero to hit for Monday, but Guerrero had a bad leg, so we would have had a better chance for the double play. I've thought about that one a lot over the years."

That ended the Giants' hopes, and they succumbed to the Dodgers, 15-2, the next day.

Going into the final day, the pressure was now on the Dodgers to win and force a one-game playoff with Atlanta. Because the Dodgers had already won a coin flip, the game would have been played in Los Angeles. But Morgan hit a dramatic three-run homer off Terry Forster to beat the Dodgers, 5-3, and make the Braves the champion.

"That was one of my biggest thrills in baseball," said Morgan, "but not because we had beaten the Dodgers and knocked them out. Going into that game, I wanted the team to play well for our fans, so they'd remember something more than the fact that we'd lost our chance to win the division. I didn't want us to be swept. So when I hit that home run, I really felt good for the team and for our fans, and the way they responded made me feel all the better. At that point, I was already looking forward to the next season, because I thought we would have a real good chance to win in '83."

It didn't work out that way. After the season, Reggie Smith left for Japan and Morgan and Holland were traded to Philadelphia for Mike Krukow. The official

One of the most memorable moments in San Francisco Giants history was Joe Morgan's home run off the Dodgers' Terry Forster on the last day of the 1982 season. Morgan's homer helped the Giants defeat the Dodgers and prevented Los Angeles from winning the National League Western Division title.

The Giants celebrate the end of the 1982 season with a 5-3 win over their arch-rivals from Los Angeles.

FRANK ROBINSON

Frank Robinson was a tough man as a manager, and he intimidated many players, and writers as well. One player who understood him, though, was Duane Kuiper, then a second baseman for the Giants and now part of the broadcast team.

"I called him the Ayatollah," said Kuiper, "but I called him that to his face, not behind his back. He always seemed to take more from me, maybe because we had started out as rookies in Cleveland, him as a manager and me as a player.

"If we were on the bench, something might come up, like it was an obvious bunt situation and Frank wasn't going to bunt. Players would look at each other on the bench like, 'What's going on here?' but they wouldn't say anything, because they didn't want Frank to hear. So, I'd ask him—always prefacing it by saying I might want to manage some day and I wanted to know why things were done—what he was thinking of. So, he'd tell me and everybody on the bench would know. They might not agree with his thinking, but at least it was out in the open.

"Frank always had a way of making his point with sarcasm. If you could react the same way, then he respected you. He was the same way with reporters.

"As a player, if you went into his office and said your piece forthrightly, he'd listen to you. If you went in there with your tail between your legs, you were going to come out the same

way. He wanted a man to come in there. I think his feeling was that, if he could intimidate you, then so could the guy on the mound.

"I think Frank got more into studying the game when he was with the Orioles. When he was with the Reds, he was a young player and just doing his thing. By the time he got to the Orioles, he was more experienced, and he started looking at the game the way a manager would.

"The Orioles manager was Earl Weaver, and he was of the old school: 'I don't have to explain to you what I'm doing.' I think Frank pretty much managed in the same way.

"Frank was very demanding, but I think he helped young players like Chili Davis and Dan Gladden because he wasn't easy on them, just as he hadn't been easy on me, Dennis Eckersley and Rick Manning with the Indians. He made us all come up to a certain level, and it helped us.

"I've talked to players who played for Vince Lombardi and how they weren't sure they liked him when they were playing but when they got out of football, all their comparisons were to the way Lombardi did it. I think players who played for Frank have a lot of the same kind of reaction. They might not have liked him when they played for him, but after they were through playing, they understood what he had done for them."

Skipper Frank Robinson and his coaching staff in 1983. From left to right: Don Buford, Herm Starrette, Robinson, Tommy McCraw, John VanOrnum and Danny Ozark.

Mike Krukow accompanies Academy Award winning actor Yul Brynner to the mound for the ceremonial first pitch on Opening Day, 1983.

reason for the trade was that the Giants couldn't work out a salary agreement with Morgan, but he insisted that was not true.

"I let them put out that story because I didn't want to bad-mouth the team, but I was always willing to take less money to stay here. I had grown up in the Bay Area and I rooted for the Giants when I was a kid. My home is here (then in Oakland, now in Contra Costa County). I was just about at the end of my career and I wanted to help bring a World Series to San Francisco.

"The real reason I was traded was that Haller thought Duane Kuiper could play second base. Kuiper's knees were already shot. You know how it is in baseball: If a guy doesn't play much, he can look good, but when he has to play every day, he can't do it."

Before he left for Philadelphia, Morgan had lunch with Giants owner Bob Lurie at Trader Vic's in Emeryville. Joe wanted to leave on good terms, and he thanked Lurie for giving him the chance to play for the Giants, but Morgan has always been a man who speaks his mind. He told Lurie, "You're going to finish last. I'm so sure of that, I'll bet my Philadelphia salary, $1 million."

Lurie laughed and the bet was never made. Morgan would have lost—barely. The Giants finished a game ahead of cellar-dweller Cincinnati in the NL West in 1983, with a 79-83 record. Meanwhile, Morgan was in the World Series again with Philadelphia, while Mike Krukow had to deal with the fallout of the trade in San Francisco.

"The day before I was traded," said Krukow, "there was a story in the *Philadelphia Inquirer* saying I was one of the four untouchables on the Phillies

Joel Youngblood came to the Giants as a free agent in 1983. During his six seasons (1983-88), he played left field, second and third base.

Equipment Manager Mike Murphy (left) started as a bat boy in 1958, became visiting clubhouse manager in 1960 and took over as Giants equipment manager from long-time Giants equipment boss Eddie Logan (right) in 1980.

Duane Kuiper (1982-85) was popular with the fans and the media during his time in a Giants uniform. His eloquence earned him a spot on the Giants' broadcast team after he retired as an active player.

Duane Kuiper turning two.

roster. But, I kept hearing that Tom Haller was holding out for me in a trade for Joe Morgan. The Phillies needed a second baseman because they'd sent Manny Trillo to Cleveland, so the day after that story appeared, I was traded to the Giants.

"I wasn't happy because I knew what kind of team we had in Philadelphia. That year we'd just missed winning the pennant when Mike Schmidt got hurt and the next year the Phillies were in the World Series.

"When I got to San Francisco, I read stories that were critical of the trade. When I went into the press conference, frankly, I was pissed. If I'd been younger, I probably wouldn't have been able to handle it, but I went in there and said all the generic bullshit about how I was happy to be there, and I got through that.

"In the spring, my elbow was on fire, but I couldn't say anything about it because we were negotiating an extension in my contract. I'd had that trouble before and it had worked out OK, but this time it didn't. Frank Robinson seemed to enjoy putting me out there, like he was getting back at Haller for making that trade. Frank hadn't wanted to make the trade, and I couldn't blame him, because he was losing Morgan and Al Holland, who had been a real force in the bullpen. It was a pretty grim spring for me."

"Tom and I never worked well together," said Robinson. "I don't know what it was. Some people thought he was upset because he'd wanted to be the manager when I got the job. I thought he wanted to put his stamp on the team. He very rarely took my advice about what players to get. Before he traded Morgan and Holland, I pleaded with him not to make that trade. I didn't want to lose Reggie Smith either. With Reggie and Joe gone, the team went back to what it was before I came there, a lot of guys pointing fingers at one another."

Jeffrey Leonard, better known as "Hac Man" or "Penitentiary Face," had a scowl and a temperament better suited for a football field. He led the Giants in RBI three times (1983-85).

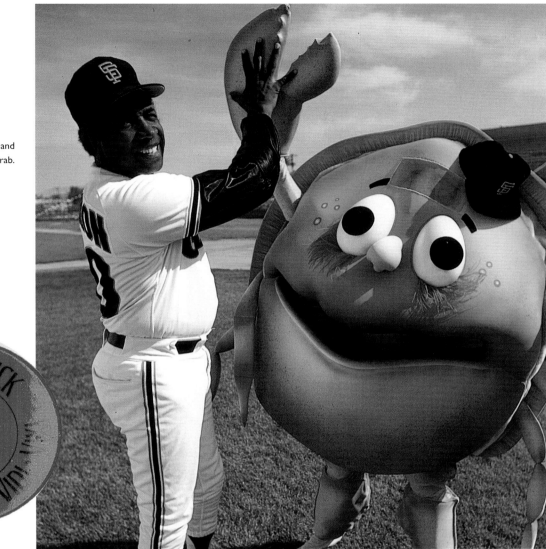

Manager Frank Robinson and The Crazy Crab.

PROMOTIONS

Innovative promotions added spice to the Giants seasons in 1983 and 1984.

"We wanted to have a promotion that would show Giants fans were different," said Giants Senior Vice President Pat Gallagher, who had become baseball's first marketing director when he was hired by Bob Lurie in 1976. Gallagher knew it took a special breed to brave the weather at Candlestick, especially at night games, when fans had to dress as if they were going to the Arctic, in heavy jackets and caps, leaving as little skin as possible exposed to the cold wind that swept into the park from the Pacific.

The result: The Croix de Candlestick, a badge awarded to people who stayed for extra-inning night games. The inscription read, "I came, I saw, I survived."

The promotion was the idea of John Crawford, who also came up with next year's idea: The Crazy Crab.

"That was a time when other teams were going for mascots, like the San Diego Chicken and the Phillie Fanatic," remembered Gallagher. "We wanted to come up with some-

thing that would poke fun at the mascots, so we had The Crazy Crab."

The promotion started with television commercials, with Crawford as the voice of the Crab, that had Giants Manager Frank Robinson attacking the supposed mascot. When he was brought out at games, with actor Wayne Doba inside the costume, fans would boo and hiss, just as planned.

But not everybody got the joke—or wanted to. Chili Davis threw a soft drink in the Crab's eyehole. Greg Minton put mint-flavored chewing tobacco in his costume, creating a terrible stink. Doba even filed suit against the San Diego Padres because one of their players blindsided him, throwing his back out.

When the 1984 season went down the drain—the Giants lost 96 games that season—the fans got nastier, throwing things onto the field. Before the last day of the season, as Gallagher stood next to the mascot on the field, Doba said, "I hope there's nobody up there with a gun."

That was the exit line for The Crazy Crab.

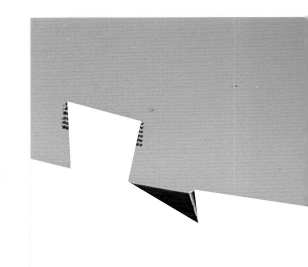

Southpaw Atlee Hammaker (1982-90) led the Giants in ERA twice—including a league-best 2.25 in 1983.

From 1982: "Kuip," "Doody," and "Wolfie." Duane Kuiper's (left) 14 pinch hits set a then-San Francisco franchise record. Darrell Evans (center) picked up 32 of his 61 RBI in the last two months. Jim Wohlford (right) provided outfield depth and a strong glove.

The three-four-five spots of the Giants
batting order in 1983: Chili Davis (batting),
Jack Clark (center) and Jeffrey Leonard.

One player made 1983 noteworthy: Atlee Hammaker. In his second season with
the Giants, Hammaker was the best pitcher in the league in the first half of the season,
going 9-4 with a 1.70 earned run average.

"There's no telling how good he would have been if he hadn't had arm trouble,"
said Robinson. "He wouldn't admit to it at first, but I knew it. I told him, 'You don't
have the same stuff on the ball that you had.' But he didn't want to admit he was
having shoulder problems until the All-Star Game. He was never the same pitcher
after that."

Hammaker was battered in the All-Star Game. "He couldn't get a third strike past
anybody," said Robinson. When he came back, teammates plastered newspaper stories about his disastrous showing in the clubhouse. That's typical of baseball players,
especially in that era; sensitivity training was not an issue. Whether it was physical or
psychological, nobody will ever know, but Hammaker was never again a dominating
pitcher. Because of his great first half, he still won the league ERA title with a 2.25
mark, but he went on the disabled list with his injured shoulder after the All-Star Game
and then lost six of his last seven decisions when he returned.

Though 1983 was a disappointment, the 1984 season was much worse. Two-thirds
of the way through, with the record at 42-64, Haller fired Robinson, and the team fin-

San Francisco played host to two All-Star Games. The first was in 1961 when Stu Miller was "blown off" the pitcher's mound by a gust of the infamous Candlestick Park winds. This photograph was taken prior to the 1984 contest.

The Giants had two representatives for the 1984 All-Star Game at Candlestick Park. Wearing their All-Star rings: Bob Brenly (left) and Chili Davis.

After throwing out the first pitch before the 1984 All-Star Game, Giants Hall of Famer Carl Hubbell is greeted by future San Francisco Giants catcher Gary Carter, then with the Montreal Expos.

ished with 96 losses. For the 1985 season, Haller named his former teammate and friend, Jimmy Davenport, as manager, but then traded the one player Davenport was depending on, Jack Clark, for first baseman David Green, pitcher Dave LaPoint, utility player Gary Rajsich and shortstop Jose Uribe. Because the first three players did little for the Giants, it was essentially Clark for Uribe. Though Uribe played a very good shortstop for the Giants through the latter part of the 1980s, it was a lopsided trade.

The 1985 Giants became the first in franchise history to lose 100 games. Haller had won his personal battle with Robinson, but he had lost the war; both he and Davenport were fired in September by Owner Bob Lurie, who knew he had to make a drastic change in the way the team was run.

Lurie had made friends with Al Rosen, who had represented first the New York Yankees and then the Houston Astros at league meetings. Rosen was general manager for the Astros, but Owner John McMullen wanted to make changes. Lurie talked first to McMullen, then to Rosen and hired Rosen in September of 1985.

"Bob had told me he was going to resign as president of the club and I would have full authority," said Rosen. "A lot of owners don't want to give that up, but I've always felt it was unfair to a general manager to have responsibility without having full authority. I always had the ability to talk to another general manager and say I could make a deal, without having to say, 'I'll get back to you on that.' If you have to do that, a lot of times the other guy will start thinking about the deal and change his mind."

Rosen had been an outstanding third baseman as a player, hitting a then-American League rookie record 37 homers in 1950 and hitting .336 with 43 homers and 145 RBI in his MVP season of 1953. He was a fiery, courageous player, and he had lost none of his intensity as a baseball executive. He was very demanding of

Manny Trillo was signed prior to the 1984 season to fill a void at second base.

Chili Davis acknowleges the crowd after hitting a pinch-hit grand slam in 1984 against Cincinnati.

Mike Krukow earned a reputation as a competitor during his six years (1983-89) with the Giants. Krukow's best year was 1986 when he won 20 games and pitched a scoreless inning in the All-Star Game.

He was first known as Jose Gonzales. Then he changed his name to Uribe Gonzales. Eventually, he settled for Jose Uribe and settled in as the Giants shortstop for seven years (1985-92).

Seven-time All-Star and 1982 National League Batting Champion Al Oliver joined the Giants prior to the 1984 season. He hit .298 in 91 games before being traded to Philadelphia in mid-season.

players, often in their face in the clubhouse after Giants losses. He wanted results, not excuses, and those who did not produce often found themselves on what became known as the San Francisco-Phoenix shuttle until they showed they belonged.

His first job was to find the right manager. "I was looking for a strong manager who knew pitching. I'd heard good things about Roger Craig. He'd done great things with the Detroit champion in '84 because Sparky Anderson gave him a lot of things to do, not just being the pitching coach." While he was still in Houston, Rosen gave Craig a call and asked him if he would be interested in returning to managing.

Craig had managed the San Diego Padres for two years, 1978 and 1979. Fired after his second season, he had gone to Detroit and spent five years as the Tigers pitching coach. At the time Rosen called, though, he had been retired for a year on his ranch in the hills near San Diego.

"At the time," remembered Craig, "there was a lot of talk about Bob Lillis losing his job with the Astros and I thought that was what Al was calling about. Bob was a friend of mine, and I told Al I wouldn't want to take his job. He said, no, no, there's a chance that I might go with the San Francisco Giants and I want to talk to you about that job. Well, I wasn't sure. I liked San Francisco, but the team was on its way to losing 100 games, and I wasn't sure I could turn the team around. But Al told me that the Giants were coming into Houston and Bob Lurie would be along, so why didn't I hop on a plane and come down there."

Rosen, Lurie and Craig met one afternoon in the Astros office and then had breakfast together the next day. That was all Rosen needed to make his decision.

Vida Blue attempted a comeback with the Giants in 1985. After being out of the game for nearly two years, Vida was 8-8 in 33 games, 20 of them starts.

Jim Davenport has been associated with the Giants for five decades. First, as a slick-fielding third baseman, three stints as a coach and as manager in 1985. He is currently a roving instructor in the minor league system.

Bob Brenly came up as a 27-year-old rookie in 1981.

GREG MINTON

Greg Minton was a superb reliever for the Giants, notching 111 saves in the 1980-84 period, but he's best known for his off-beat behavior, which earned him the nickname of "Moonman."

Part of Minton's behavior was simply the typical joking of ballplayers, giving a player a hot-foot or putting itching powder in his shorts. Baseball humor has seldom extended beyond the sophomoric level.

He ventured beyond that on occasion, the most notorious being his bus escapade in Houston during the 1982 season. He came out of the hotel at 3:45 and got on the bus, which was supposed to leave after 4 for the ball park. Somehow, he convinced the bus driver that it was time to

leave, so when his teammates came out at 4, there was no bus, so they all had to take cabs to the stadium.

His teammates, though, were more amazed by his lifestyle. Minton was a throwback to an earlier era in baseball when players, from Babe Ruth to Mickey Mantle, sometimes came to the park after all-night parties but somehow managed to play effectively.

"Minton was known to party in those days," said Bill Laskey, a fellow pitcher on the Giants at the time. "He'd be out late with women, carousing. After BP (batting practice) he'd come in and go to sleep on the training table. He'd wake up about the fifth inning, get dressed, come out and then save the game. Nobody could figure how he did it."

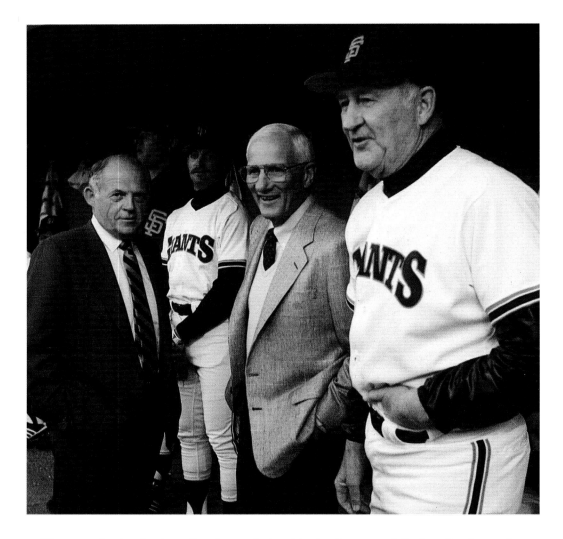

After the Giants lost 100 games for the first time ever in 1985, Bob Lurie (left) made two major hires: Al Rosen (center) as team president and Roger Craig (right) as manager.

That was the beginning of a close relationship for Rosen and Craig. On the surface, it seemed an odd pairing. Rosen was the sophisticated urban dweller, Craig the country boy, but they hit it off on a personal level as well as a professional one from the start.

"Al and I always had a great relationship," said Craig. "It wasn't that we always agreed because we didn't, but when we had differences of opinion on players, we could always talk it out. He never made a move without asking me about it first.

"Our wives hit it off, too. The four of us used to go out to dinner when we weren't playing a night game, and I remember one time Al told a reporter that he'd be happy to go out to dinner with Roger Craig and his wife 365 days a year."

"When I met him for the first time and we talked about the job, I just had the feeling that he was the right guy, and time proved that to be true," said Rosen. "There are times when it's right for a certain kind of man, and he was absolutely the right man for this time. The players really need to buy into our program because they were so beat down, and they bought into the 'Humm Baby' stuff from the start."

Though some were puzzled by Craig's constant use of the "Humm Baby" phrase, there was nothing mysterious about it; it was simply the baseball mantra uttered frequently by infielders to encourage their pitcher. Craig, though, used it as a symbol of never giving up, and his early Giants teams were known for their ability to rally to turn seeming defeat into victory.

Craig was a more complex man than his Southern drawl and mannerisms suggested. He was a student of the game, but when he was interviewed, he gave reporters only cliches and empty phrases, giving no real clue to his thinking or planning, because he knew that quotes or sound bites were enough to satisfy most, even if they were meaningless. He was portrayed as a grandfatherly figure, but players knew that he could have a very rough edge to his tongue if they did not do what he wanted.

He was a daring manager, willing to take both offensive and defensive risks. He called pitchouts from the dugout when he thought a runner would be trying to steal,

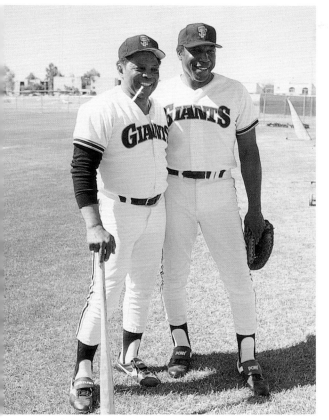

Al Rosen pledged to restore pride in the Giants uniform when he was hired. To that end, he invited the two Willies, Mays and McCovey, to 1986 Spring Training.

Will "The Thrill" Clark never failed to live up to his nickname. He homered in his first Major League at bat off Nolan Ryan on Opening Day in 1986.

From 1986: Rookie Robby Thompson was part of the "You Gotta Like These Kids" movement.

Outfielder Dan Gladden led the Giants in stolen bases for three straight seasons (1984-86).

Pitcher Jim Gott is holding a bat for a good reason: he hit three home runs in 1985–a rare feat for a pitcher.

and he made great use of the suicide squeeze his first couple of seasons, though other teams caught up with that strategy after that.

It was his attitude, though, that was most obvious at the start, and the confidence he radiated was, as Rosen said, the best thing for the Giants at that time.

Veterans like Bob Brenly and Mike Krukow understood that better than younger players.

"When Roger Craig and Al Rosen came in, it was just the right time and place," said Brenly. "The organization really needed something like that. There was no focus. Players were pretty much doing what they wanted to do. Roger came in with that 'Humm Baby' attitude and everybody bought into that, and Al came in with his roster-cutting and trades. They let it be known that they were going to change the attitude of the team and everybody that couldn't get with the program was going to be gone. That made a big difference to everybody."

Krukow saw the same thing. "Young players are always looking for a reason to fail," said Krukow, now a Giants announcer. "If they've got an injury, they blame it on that. Roger Craig and Al Rosen came in and basically said there were no excuses, there was no reason to fail. And that made a big difference in attitude."

Neither Rosen nor Craig were so sure in September of 1985, though. "When I first walked into the clubhouse," Craig said, "I didn't like the country club atmosphere there. Everybody just wanted to get the season over and get out of there. Of course, that happens with a team that loses so many games. I told Al we really had a lot of work to do to change that attitude."

Rosen started housecleaning almost immediately with a series of off-season trades for fringe players, although one trade—catcher Alex Trevino to the Dodgers for Candy Maldonado—turned out to be a steal. Maldonado did not play much with the Dodgers but he blossomed that year with the Giants, first as a pinch hitter (.420 with four home runs and 20 RBI) and then as a regular in August when Jeffrey Leonard was hurt. Maldonado finished with 20 homers and 85 RBI.

The guru of the split-fingered fastball,
Roger Craig.

SPLIT–FINGERED FASTBALL

One of Roger Craig's trademarks as a Giants manager was his evangelical preaching of the virtues of the split-fingered fastball. Craig would even teach it to pitchers on other teams, at least at first. "Al Rosen found out I was doing that and he told me to stop it and just teach it to our pitchers," said Craig.

The split-finger gets its name from the fact that a pitcher spreads (splits) his fingers in gripping the ball. Because the pitch is thrown with the same motion as a fastball, the hitter thinks fastball as the pitch approaches the plate and is unprepared for its sharp drop. Bruce Sutter first popularized the pitch when he led the National League in saves for five of six seasons with the Chicago Cubs and St. Louis Cardinals in the 1979-84 period.

Craig actually used the pitch near the end of his own pitching career, which spanned 12 seasons, 1955-66, after learning it from Fred Martin, who pitched for the St. Louis Browns in the late 1940s.

"I had arm trouble since my second year up, so I was always looking for something that was easy to throw and not hard on the arm," said Craig. "A lot of people compare it to the forkball, but it's different. The forkball is more of a change of pace, because you put the ball in the back of your hand. When Elroy Face was pitching, his fastball might have been 85-86 miles an hour and his forkball was like 40 or 50.

With the split finger, you can throw it almost as fast as the fastball. Scotty Garretts used to throw it almost 90 miles an hour. He had the best one; it was almost unhittable when he was on."

Craig had started teaching the pitch during the five years he was pitching coach for the Detroit Tigers. The pitcher who probably got the most benefit from it was Jack Morris, though Morris originally resisted learning the pitch.

"When I first met with the Giants pitchers," said Craig, "I told them I'd teach it to anyone who wanted to learn it but I wouldn't force it on anybody. I said I wanted somebody who had never thrown one to demonstrate, and Mark Davis volunteered. Pretty soon, he was throwing a real good one, and everybody was amazed, because if he could do that without ever having thrown one before, anybody could learn it.

"Mike Krukow was another one who threw a good split-finger. Mike was a guy who was always willing to try anything if he thought it would help him."

Not everybody could learn the pitch, though. When the Giants picked up Steve Carlton near the end of his great career in 1986, Carlton surprised Craig by asking to learn it, but he couldn't. "He had small hands for such a big guy, and he couldn't get a good grip on it," said Craig. "He even tried taping his fingers apart to get them to spread out, but it didn't work."

Candy Maldonado came off the bench to stroke four pinch hit homers in 1986—tying a San Francisco franchise record.

Jeffrey Leonard changed his uniform number three times during his seven Giants seasons. First, it was 26, followed by 20 and then 00.

Craig managed the Giants for the last 18 games of the wretched 1985 season, but he was mostly just watching and evaluating. His real work began in Arizona the next spring, as he worked hard to get the attitude change he knew would be essential to a team turnaround. He especially remembers one particular meeting.

"I had told the players that I wanted everybody to do things the same way, wear the same things. After the meeting, Jeffrey Leonard came up to me and said, 'Don't you know that wearing my cap backwards is my trademark?' Well, I didn't know, but I told Jeffrey I thought it was important that everybody did things the same way.

"The word spread pretty quickly about our meeting. There were a lot of reporters there, and they were waiting to see what happened. Jeffrey came out with his cap on backwards and he went through the warmups with the cap the same way. Then, he went over to the batting cage. Just before he stepped in to hit—I'll never forget this— he looked over at me and turned his cap the right way.

"From that time on, I had a great relationship with Jeffrey. He would challenge you from time to time, but he was a great leader for us, a great example for the younger players. He was a very important cog in our winning that first year."

It takes more than attitude to win, of course. It also takes players, and one that Craig and Rosen watched intently was Will Clark, the club's No. 1 draft pick in 1985,

Chili Davis and then-Giants television analyst Joe Morgan in 1986.

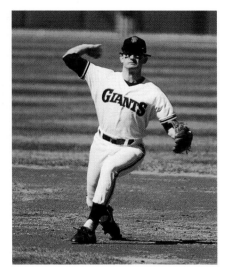

Second baseman Robby Thompson went to two All-Star Games and won a Gold Glove during his 10-year Giants career.

Will Clark led the National League with 109 RBI in 1988.

now in his first Major League training camp after playing 65 games for Fresno in the Class A California League the previous season.

"We knew Will was a good one," said Craig, "but we didn't know how quickly he would make it. When I saw him that first time in Spring Training, I thought he had one of the most natural swings I'd ever seen."

Craig was hardly alone in that evaluation. Nobody who saw Clark that spring, with that sweet left-handed swing and the confidence of a much more experienced player, had any doubts that he would have a long and productive career. The only question was how soon it would start.

"Al and I would talk every day about not wanting to rush him, but he just kept getting hits," Craig said. "I'd look up at Al in the stands after every hit, and we'd both nod our heads. Finally, we agreed that, with that swing, he was ready to hit Major League pitching."

Clark was destined to be a star almost from the time he put on long pants. He was an All-Star on every level, from youth leagues to college ball. He played on the 1984 U.S. Olympic team, and Rosen had seen him when the team came through Houston during its 35-game pre-Olympic tour. "You know how you just look at a guy in batting practice and say, 'I'd sure like to have him,'" said Rosen. "That's what I thought when I first saw Will." Clark hit .393 on that tour, and .429 in the Games, as the U.S. team won a silver medal. The next year at Mississippi State, he hit .420 with 25 homers in 65 games and was named the nation's top player. The Giants made him their No. 1 draft pick. At Fresno, he hit a home run in his first at-bat and went on to hit .309 for the rest of the season. Clearly, this was a young man accustomed to success.

"He was very mature for his age, very professional," said Rosen. "He had that great swing, and he was such a tough competitor. He always worked very hard because he wanted to win so badly. I later signed him to that four-year, $15 million contract which a lot of people criticized, but I felt it was important to sign him up before he became a free agent, because I knew there were a lot of clubs who could use a player like Will."

So Clark was no surprise, but another player, Robby Thompson, was. The Giants needed a second baseman, but Thompson seemed at least a year away. In 287 minor

'86 GIANTS.
YOU GOTTA
LIKE THESE
KIDS.

Promotional signage from the
1986 season.

league games, none above double-A, Thompson had averaged just .257, including an unremarkable .261 at Shreveport the year before. In the first week of Spring Training, he seemed overwhelmed, and it was expected that he would soon be sent back to the minors.

Meanwhile, Rosen was on the telephone so much that spring that it seemed the receiver might become implanted in his ear. Mostly, he was working to make a trade with Seattle for young second baseman Harold Reynolds, who hadn't hit much in parts of three seasons with the Mariners but seemed to have the potential to be a solid player. Rosen was right about Reynolds, who would go on to have a good career, but the Mariners were equally high on him and wouldn't make a deal.

Frustrated with his inability to make a trade, Rosen started listening to Bob Lillis, who had been his manager in Houston and was now an infield coach for the Giants. Lillis insisted that Thompson could make the jump from double-A. Rosen took a longer look at Thompson, both in the field and at bat, and the more he watched, the more excited he got.

"Robby was a late bloomer, but he was ready that spring," remembered Rosen. "We always felt he could do the job in the field, but what surprised us was the pop he had at the plate. He didn't show that in the minors, but it seemed that, once he got up against Major League pitching, he was determined to raise his game to that level, and he did.

"We were very fortunate to come up with two players like Will and Robby for the right side of our infield because they were not only good players but gave us great leadership as well."

So far, so good, but making over a team that had just come off a 100-loss season wasn't going to be easy. Nobody knew that better than Krukow, who had been through more downs than ups in his nine-year Major League career.

"We had to open that season with two tough series on the road, in Houston and Los Angeles. I was pitching that first game in Houston and I looked around and saw that we basically had the same nucleus we'd had the year before. We had Will Clark and Robby Thompson, but they were just rookies. When I compared our lineup to Houston's, I thought, we don't have a chance. It reminded me of some of the bad years with the Cubs.

"But then we won that first game. Will hit a home run off Nolan Ryan in his first at-bat. He didn't have a great year as a rookie, but to see him do that in his first game kind of energized the club. The same with Robby. When Bob Lillis had said after the first couple of games in Spring Training that Robby could do the job, we didn't believe him because we (pitchers) were knocking the bat out of his hands. But Robby just kept looking better and better. Not only did he make it, but our opinion of 'Flea' (Lillis) went up.

"We won that first game in Houston and won the series, 2-1. Then, we went to L.A. and won that series, 2-1, so we were 4-2 going into our home opener. At that point, we looked around and said, 'Hey, maybe Roger is right, we can be a good team.' But I honestly believe that if we'd lost those first two series, it would have been a long year. That's how fragile our confidence was."

Thompson would hit .271 that year, 10 points higher than his best minor league average, leading the club with 73 runs. He finished second in the Rookie of the Year balloting to St. Louis pitcher Todd Worrell.

The more celebrated Clark had a rockier season, missing 47 games in mid-season with a hyper-extended left elbow. He wound up with a .287 average (.310 in 64 games after his return from injury) but struggled with the length of the season.

"That first year was tough, psychologically more than physically," he said. "It was the first time I had to play every day. In college, you play three, four times a week, but now I was having to play every day, and having to deal with the travel and the fatigue. I could deal with it physically, but it was really tough mentally. That's the tough thing about baseball, that you have to go out there every day. There are some

Former Stanford University star Mike Aldrete was a member of the 1987 National League Western Division Champions team.

Bob Melvin (left) and Robby Thompson (right) meet actress Jane Fonda in 1986.

YOU GOTTA LIKE THESE OLD KIDS TOO!

A total of 13 rookies brought new life to the Giants in 1986. The slogan, "You Gotta Like These Kids," was developed with players such as Will Clark and Robby Thompson in mind. But there were veterans around to guide the "kids." Pictured on the classic 1968 Mustang convertible with the Golden Gate Bridge in the background are (left to right): Jeffrey Leonard, Bob Brenly, Chili Davis and Mike Krukow.

On Sept. 14, 1986, catcher Bob Brenly filled in at third base and made four errors in the fourth inning against Atlanta. Instead of being the goat, Brenly came back to drive home four runs, including a game-winning solo homer with two outs in the ninth.

days you might not feel very good or you might have some personal problems that are bothering you, but you have to put all that behind you and play."

Incredibly, the Giants were in first place as late as the 92nd game of the season (tied with Houston). They started to slide at that point and eventually finished third, 13 games out of first, but their 83-79 record represented a 21-game improvement over the previous season.

It helped that Krukow put together his first (and only) 20-win season, finishing at 20-9.

"A lot of people thought it was a Joe Hardy year, but it really wasn't like that," said Krukow. "It had actually started in 1984, when I lost three feet on my fastball and had to learn something else. I started throwing the split-fingered fastball, and by 1985, I had it under control. I actually pitched about as well in 1985 as I did the next year, but in 1985, I didn't have any run support. To win 20 games, you have to be able to pitch strong into the seventh, eighth and ninth innings, but you also need some runs behind you. They scored three runs a game for me in 1985 and five runs a game in 1986. That was the difference."

"The next year," said Clark. "I put it all together. I was hitting in the seventh spot most of the year, because we had such a great hitting team that year. I remember we hit 205 home runs. Maybe the pitchers didn't worry so much about me. I saw a lot of fast balls that year, more than I saw in the next few years." That helped Clark to hit 35 home runs, his high in a Giants uniform, along with a .308 average.

Clark's improvement, though, was not mirrored by the rest of the team in the first half of the 1987 season. The Giants started off strongly with a 21-10 record through early May but then started to slide. By July 4, just before the halfway mark, they were 39-40 and 5-1/2 games out of first. Rosen knew changes had to be made. He was looking especially for left-handed pitching, and the San Diego Padres had two pitchers he coveted, starter Dave Dravecky and reliever Craig Lefferts.

"I knew the Padres liked (third baseman) Chris Brown, and he was the key to the

Hall of Famer Steve Carlton made a brief stop in San Francisco during the 1986 season.

Kevin Mitchell, Craig Lefferts and Dave Dravecky (opposite page), came from San Diego in a mid-1987 season trade. Dravecky won seven in 18 starts, Lefferts stabilized the bullpen, while Mitchell took over at third and hit 15 homers in 69 games.

Mike Krukow works on another masterpiece, this time a painting for a magazine cover shot, at San Francisco's Palace of Fine Arts.

trade from their side," said Rosen. "He had great ability but he just didn't seem to want to play. The day before he'd said he couldn't play, and I was just fed up with him.

"I was talking to Chub Feeney, who was president of the Padres by then, and I could tell he wanted to put his stamp on the club. You can tell when a guy's ready to make a deal. For me, the key was the pitching, Dravecky and Lefferts. I thought Kevin Mitchell had a lot of potential, too, and I certainly liked him better than Brown."

Feeney mentioned Keith Comstock, a lefthander the Giants had picked up as a free agent. "Is it a deal if I include Comstock?" asked Rosen. When Feeney said yes, Rosen said, "You've got it."

The deal was Brown, pitchers Mark Davis, Mark Grant and Comstock to the Padres for Dravecky, Lefferts and Mitchell.

Davis, a talented pitcher who had lost his confidence, probably as a result of a disastrous 5-17 year as a starter in 1984, bounced back in San Diego and won a Cy Young Award in 1989 as a reliever, with a league-leading 44 saves.

Dravecky, the pitcher Rosen wanted most, was 7-5 the rest of the season for the Giants and probably would have done much more but for a cancer which struck him the following season and eventually caused the amputation of his left arm. Lefferts became a solid set-up man in the Giants bullpen, appearing in 43 games.

Mitchell was an improvement over Brown, hitting 15 home runs for the Giants in the second half of the season, and two years later he turned the trade into a real plus for the Giants when he had a monster 47-home run season.

The Giants had made a slight improvement, to 52-50, by the end of the month, when Rosen swung another deal, this time sending catcher Mackey Sasser to the Pirates for pitcher Don Robinson and $50,000.

"I had always liked Don Robinson because he was not only a good pitcher but he gave us some hitting punch, too," said Rosen. "Roger used him as a pinch hitter."

With Robinson in the bullpen, the Giants made their move, improving to 64-59 and moving into first place in the National League West. At that point, Rosen went to Craig

"Big Daddy" Rick Reuschel won 36 games over two seasons (1988-89) for the Giants, earning him a spot on the NL All-Star team each year.

Bob Brenly acknowledges the cheers from Giants fans at the end of the 1987 season—which resulted in the Giants second National League Western Division title.

Mike LaCoss won at least 10 games in three of his first four seasons with the Giants.

Don Zimmer, a veteran of many baseball wars, was Roger Craig's third base coach in 1987.

and asked his manager if he thought he could win, which was a question that answered itself. Then, he asked Craig if there was one player who might make the difference.

"At the time," remembered Craig, "there was a lot of talk that the Pirates would trade Rick Reuschel. I told Al that if he could get Reuschel, I'd guarantee him we would win the division. So he made the trade (Reuschel for young pitchers Jeff Robinson and Scott Medvin). I hated to give up Robinson, who had done a good job for us, but Reuschel was just what we needed."

Rosen agreed. "I thought Rick Reuschel would be great for us because he was a sinkerball pitcher and we had a good defensive infield, plus the turf at Candlestick always helped."

Reuschel was 5-3 the rest of the way that season. The next two seasons, he was the ace of the pitching staff, with 19 and 17 wins. He was a most improbable star. His decidedly unathletic build, with a sizeable paunch hanging over his belt, inspired the nickname "Big Daddy." He did not have an overwhelming fastball nor any other pitch which other pitchers would envy, but he had good control and knew how to move the ball around to keep hitters off balance.

The strengthened Giants swept to the pennant—Robinson won the clincher in relief and also hit the game-winning home run—and into the NLCS against the St. Louis Cardinals. The Cardinals' season record, 95-67, was three games better than the Giants' finish, but St. Louis was without ex-Giant Jack Clark, who had hit 35 home runs and knocked in 105 runs in only 419 at-bats. Clark was sidelined with a foot injury and would make only one brief appearance in the series, striking out in a pinch-hitting role.

The Cardinals took an immediate lead by winning the first game in St. Louis, 5-3, despite a home run by Jeffrey Leonard, but Dave Dravecky pitched brilliantly in the second game, allowing only two hits in a 5-0 Giants win. "That was the best game I've ever pitched," said Dravecky, who seldom praised himself, after the game. Will Clark hit a two-run homer and Leonard had three hits, including a solo homer.

Along the way, Leonard also enraged St. Louis fans by running with one flap down on his batting helmet after hitting his home run and, more important, circling the bases in a pace barely faster than a walk.

That was part of the "Hac-Man's" style. He lived for confrontations, whether it be with players, fans or reporters. He would sit in the clubhouse with a scowl on his

Giants General Manager
Al Rosen (left) and Mike Krukow
enjoy the afterglow of the Giants
pennant-clinching win.

Eddie Milner scores a run against the Padres on Sept. 28, 1987, the day the Giants clinched the
National League Western Division pennant.

Jeffrey Leonard had his 15
minutes of fame during
the 1987 National League
Championship Series. He
homered in four consecu-
tive games, hit .417, and
was named Most Valuable
Player of the series—in a
losing cause.

The signature swing of Will Clark.

WILL CLARK

Will Clark came to Spring Training in 1986 and won the first base job, and what everybody remembers most about that year was his first at-bat, against Nolan Ryan, who pitched four no-hitters in his Major League career and whose fastball was timed at more than 100 miles an hour.

Watching from the dugout and then the on-deck circle, Clark was properly awed. "I had never seen anybody throw so hard," he remembered. "My teammates were telling me just to relax up there, not get too tight, because nobody looked good against Nolan."

They needn't have worried; from the start, Clark didn't back down from anybody, not even Nolan Ryan. "When I got up there," he said, "the first pitch he threw me was a curve! I backed out of the box and kind of giggled. I mean,

here's a guy throwing 100 miles an hour and he throws me a curve, first thing. I couldn't believe it. Then, I stepped back in there and I saw a couple of fastballs."

Clark swung on the second one and sent it screaming to straight-away center field. "I knew I'd hit it pretty good, but I didn't necessarily think I'd hit it out," he said. "I mean, nobody goes up there thinking they're going to hit a home run on their first at-bat in the Major Leagues, and especially not against Nolan Ryan."

But that indeed was what he'd done, a home run over the center field fence. "When I saw that the ball was out of the park, I just kind of floated around the bases," said Clark. "I don't remember even touching them. After that, I felt I belonged. If you can hit Nolan Ryan, you know you can hit anyone."

face, seemingly daring anybody to approach him. It was mostly bluff, though. A reporter who braved his challenge (not many did) would get an articulate, insightful interview. As for his teammates, as Bill Laskey said, "When you needed support, he was always the first one there." And on the field, he was always there, a solid hitter and fielder who always gave his best.

In this series, Leonard was at his very best. He hit another homer in the third game and, with that and run-scoring doubles by Clark and Bob Brenly, the Giants had a 4-0 lead going into the sixth. Everything seemed to be going the Giants' way. Clark was already out and Cardinal third baseman Terry Pendelton, who had 96 RBI in the regular season, had to be scratched because of a bad ankle after taking batting practice. The Cardinals were fielding what they later called their "B" team.

Yet, in his private box at Candlestick, Al Rosen was worried. "We had so many opportunities in those first five innings that we didn't take advantage of," he remembered. "We should have had twice as many runs, but we kept leaving runners on base. I've seen so many games like that where you fail to take advantage of opportunities and eventually lose the game."

Rosen's concern was legitimate. In the sixth inning, Giants starter Atlee Hammaker gave up a two-run homer to Jim Lindeman, who had taken Clark's place in the lineup. In the seventh, the Cardinals scored four times on five straight hits, and they went on to win the game, 6-5.

The Giants bounced back to even the series with a 4-2 win behind Mike Krukow in the next game, as Leonard became the first player to homer in four consecutive NLCS games with a two-run blast in the fifth.

Reuschel had another bad start in the fifth game, allowing three runs in four innings, but Joe Price saved the Giants with a five-inning relief stint in which he allowed only one hit, shutting out the Cards. Meanwhile, Mitchell hit a home run in the third and the Giants scored four times in the fourth en route to a 6-3 win.

But the shadow of that third game loss still hung over the club. "We should have won that game," said Rosen, "and if we had, we'd have won the series in five games."

Still, as the teams went back to St. Louis, the Giants seemed in good position to win, with a 3-2 lead and Dravecky, who had been their best pitcher

Candy Maldonado was the starting right fielder for three consecutive Opening Days (1987-89).

Chili Davis led the Giants in hitting from 1984-86.

Joe Price had a memorable 1987—striking out 42 in 35 innings during the regular season and fanning seven over 5.2 innings in the NLCS.

down the stretch, ready to go. And, in fact, Dravecky pitched another brilliant game, allowing only one tainted run. In the second inning, Tony Pena hit a line drive to short right field. Giants right fielder Candy Maldonado charged the ball but then suddenly went into a slide and threw his arm up. The ball hit his arm and bounced far away for a triple. "I saw the ball go off the bat," Maldonado would say after the game, "but then I lost it in the lights. I would have caught it otherwise."

Dravecky got the next batter, Willie McGee, to ground out, with Pena holding at third. Jose Oquendo then lofted a short fly down the right field line. Maldonado caught the ball, no more than 200 feet from home plate, but he had to turn and plant himself to throw, as Pena broke for the plate. Maldonado's throw was a weak one, a three-hopper up the line, and Pena scored what was to be the only run of the game as John Tudor and relievers Todd Worrell and Ken Dayley shut out the Giants.

That tied the series at 3-3 and brought up a very difficult pitching decision for Craig. Krukow, who had won the fourth game, wanted to pitch, which was no surprise. "I wish I'd had a staff of pitchers like Krukow," said Craig. "He was such a great competitor. He always wanted the ball, and he never wanted to come out of a game. Sometimes I'd come out to the mound and he thought I was going to take him out, so he'd come off the mound and meet me halfway to argue that he should stay in the game." But Krukow had battled shoulder problems that year, going on the disabled list at one point, so Craig decided to start Hammaker instead.

Hammaker had missed the entire 1986 season because of his second rotator cuff surgery but he'd pitched well in 1987, with a 10-10 record and 3.58 ERA. His won-loss record would have been better if he'd had more run support; the Giants scored only 19 runs in his 10 losses.

But on the road that season, Hammaker was a dismal 1-8, and he was rocked in this game, giving up four runs in the second inning. Oquendo, who had hit only nine home runs in five years, hit a three-run shot in that inning, the best indication that Hammaker had nothing.

It hardly mattered who was pitching for the Giants, though, because they got shut

Atlee Hammaker recovered from his second rotator cuff operation to go 10-10 with a 3.58 ERA in 1987.

Mike Krukow tossed a complete game win in the 1987 NLCS.

Relief ace Steve Bedrosian joined the Giants during the 1989 season. He saved 17 games during the regular season and three in the playoffs.

Two of the most successful managers in San Francisco Giants history: Roger Craig (left) and Herman Franks.

Southpaw Terry Mulholland has been with the Giants on four different occasions: 1986, 1988-89, 1995 and 1997.

Utility infielder Ernest Riles hit the 10,000th home run in Giants history on July 8, 1988 off St. Louis pitcher Steve Peters.

out for the second straight game, Danny Cox getting the win for St. Louis, 6-0. The Cardinals would go on to the World Series.

Leonard was named the MVP of the series, which was scant consolation for him or his teammates.

The next year was a transitional one as the Giants traded Leonard and Chili Davis and moved Kevin Mitchell from third base to the outfield. At either position, Mitchell was a player who was obviously in the lineup because of his bat, but he thrilled fans with one memorable play, catching a foul fly to left field in his bare hand as he crossed the foul line.

Injuries to the pitching staff reduced the Giants to an 83-79 record, but the team was basically a sound one, and Rosen felt they had a chance to win with just one big change. "We needed a reliever, and Steve Bedrosian had some good years in Philadelphia," said Rosen. "He always wanted the ball and he was a strikeout pitcher."

So, on June 18, 1989, Rosen sent promising young pitchers Dennis Cook and Terry Mulholland along with infielder Charlie Hayes to Philadelphia for Bedrosian. "We gave up a lot," said Rosen, "but I'm a great believer in making a move if you think you can win. In this game, you never know when you'll get another chance. There are a lot of teams who missed their chance and never got another one."

Bedrosian was an immediate hit with the Giants, picking up five saves in five games in the first week. He tailed off some after that, eventually finishing with 17 saves for the Giants in 22 chances, but there was a reason: His son, Cody, was ill. "It's hard for players to put that out of their minds," said Rosen, "but he was still good enough to win for us. We couldn't have done it without him."

That 1989 team was clearly the best of the Rosen-Craig regime. The pitching staff was a solid one, though age was rapidly become a concern: The staff ace, at 17-8, was 40-year-old Rick Reuschel. Don Robinson (12-11) was 32 but frequent injuries, aggravated by a weight problem, made it obvious he would not be able to pitch effectively much longer. Mike LaCoss (10-2) was 33.

Kevin Mitchell, posing here on Diamond Heights in San Francisco for a magazine cover, started for the National League in the 1989 and 1990 All-Star Games.

Rich "Goose" Gossage saved four games in 31 appearances during the memorable 1989 season.

Even though he didn't play much, utility infielder Tony Perezchica (1988, 1990-91) was a fan favorite.

In 1989, Kevin Mitchell became the Giants' first Most Valuable Player award recipient since Willie McCovey won the honor 20 years before. "Mitch" led the National League with 47 homers and 127 RBI.

The only relative youngster was 28-year-old Scott Garrelts, who was 14-5 with a league-leading 2.28 ERA. Garrelts was the type of pitcher who drives managers mad. He had tremendous ability, a fastball which he could throw in the high 90s, and a split-fingered pitch which came in at close to the same speed before dipping like a hummingbird looking for honey. At his best, he was almost unhittable, but his career was marred by inconsistency and injuries. In 1989, he had his best year and seemed finally to be fulfilling his potential, but it was his last good year. Beset by arm injuries, he ended his career just two years later.

The biggest difference between 1988 and 1989, though, was the dramatic blossoming of Kevin Mitchell.

Mitchell was something of a mystery man, which was apparently the way he liked it because he told different stories to different reporters. He claimed to have been a linebacker on the football team in high school and an outfielder on the baseball team, but reporters who investigated his story found that he had apparently not played either sport in school, though he had played sandlot baseball. His parents were divorced, and he had been raised by his grandmother, with whom he still had a close relationship.

Mitchell had been productive for the Giants, hitting 15 homers and driving in 44 runs in 69 games in 1987 and hitting 19 homers and knocking in 80 runs in 1988. Those 19 homers were the most he had hit in any season in his career, including his minor league years.

In 1989, though, he had a tremendous season, hitting 47 homers and knocking in 125 runs, both league highs, as he won the Most Valuable Player award. His homers were meaningful, too, because 23 of them either tied the game or gave the Giants a lead. He also led the league in total bases (345), slugging percentage (.635) and extra-base hits (87). Fifty-five percent of his hits went for extra bases, a mark exceeded only by Babe Ruth (twice), Reggie Jackson and Willie McCovey.

With solid pitching and the one-two hitting punch of Mitchell and Will Clark, who

Three of Roger Craig's coaches in 1989 (left to right): Bob Lillis, Norm Sherry and Bill Fahey.

Infielder Ken Oberkfell hit .319 in 83 games down the stretch to help the Giants win the 1989 National League pennant.

Outfielder Donell Nixon stole the 10,000th base in Giants history on May 14, 1989 in Montreal.

Giants alumni from the 1970s are reunited in 1989 (left to right): Bill Madlock, Bob Knepper and Gary Lavelle.

Bill Bathe became the 21st player to homer in his first World Series at bat. He belted a three-run pinch hit home run off Oakland's Gene Nelson in Game Three of the 1989 World Series.

The radiation treatments took their toll on Dave Dravecky as his left arm snapped when he delivered a pitch in a game at Montreal on Aug. 15, 1989—just five days after his triumphant return in San Francisco. Dravecky won the game against the Expos, but his career was over. His teammates elected him recipient of the Willie Mac Award toward the end of the season.

Few people thought Dave Dravecky would ever pitch again after having a cancerous tumor removed from his left shoulder following the 1988 season. He came back on Aug. 10, 1989 and won his first start of the season, a 4-3 victory over Cincinnati.

DAVE DRAVECKY

Dave Dravecky was the player Al Rosen believed was the key to the big 1987 trade with the San Diego Padres, a very talented left-handed pitcher but one who had a series of arm and shoulder problems.

Dravecky pitched well for the Giants after the trade, going 7-5 and then giving up only one run in two games in the National League Championship Series.

That earned him a start on Opening Day in 1988, and he responded with a three-hit, 5-1 win over the Dodgers and Fernando Valenzuela. But then his injury problems re-surfaced. He had two separate stints on the disabled list in May and June before underoing arthroscopic surgery on his left shoulder to repair a partially detached bicep tendon. He was sent to Phoenix on injury rehab but pitched only one game, allowing 11 hits and five runs in 2-2/3 innings.

His injury problems went beyond the normal. On Oct. 7, he had surgery to remove a cancerous tumor from the deltoid muscle in his upper left arm.

To everyone but Dravecky, his baseball career seemed over, but he determinedly set out on a rehabilitation program. He began throwing again in May, 1989, and pitched in two simulated games in early July. He went to Stockton in the Class A California League and threw three complete game wins.

On Aug. 10, he returned to the mound at Candlestick Park. It was a joyous occasion, covered almost like a World Series game, with representatives from *Sports Illustrated, The Sporting News, People, Entertainment Tonight,* the *Today Show, CBS Morning News* and the *Christian Science Monitor,* among others. The scoreboard flashed, "Welcome Back, Dave," and the 34,810 fans gave him a standing ovation when he came

on the field. In the dugout, players were quiet, caught up in the drama, until Dravecky yelled his traditional pre-game saying, "Remember, everyone on your bellies," baseball talk for "Dive for balls and play your hearts out." The players laughed and got ready to play.

Dravecky pitched a marvelous game, allowing only one hit in his first seven innings. He yielded three runs in the eighth, after which he left the game, but won, 4-3.

That was the last good news for Dravecky. Five days later in Montreal, as the Giants were on their way to a 3-2 win over the Expos, Dravecky threw a pitch in the bottom of the sixth to Tim Raines. A terrible loud crack could be heard throughout the stadium, and Dravecky fell to the ground in pain, the ball sailing over the on-deck circle, about 20 feet to the right of home plate. He had broken his left humerus, the long bone in the arm that leads from the shoulder to the elbow.

The entire Giants infield rushed to the mound. Dravecky told Will Clark, the first to reach him, "I'm in terrible pain. It just hurts so much." Clark noted that Dravecky's eyes were rolling back in his head, his pupils almost out of sight, with the pain. "He was sweating up a storm, and all he could do was sit there and shake," said Clark.

During his operation of the previous October, Dravecky's humerus had been frozen to facilitate removal of the tumor. Doctors had warned him that freezing the bone might weaken it, and that apparently was a factor in this break.

The courageous Dravecky tried valiantly to rehabilitate his arm after another surgery, but it eventually had to be amputated.

The eternal optimist, Roger Craig, during the 1989

Kevin Mitchell contributed seven RBI during the 1989 NLCS.

finished second to his teammate in the MVP voting after hitting .333 with 29 homers, 104 runs and 111 RBI, it seemed the Giants might win easily. In September, they had a seven-game lead. But then, San Diego started to make a move and the Giants went into a mini-slump. With four games to go, their lead was at four, and then they lost their third straight game to the Dodgers in Los Angeles. The Padres, playing Cincinnati in San Diego, could cut the Giants lead to three games with a win.

"We were going to close the season with a series in San Diego," remembered Krukow, "and, to be honest, I'm not sure we could have won it down there if it had come down to that. After we lost that third game to the Dodgers, we were listening in the dressing room to the Padres game against Cincinnati. When (Cincinnati reliever) Norm Charlton got the last out on a three-pitch strikeout, we drowned out the 'strike three' call with our cheers. We did our celebrating under the stands at Dodger Stadium. We had wanted to do it on the field, but that was all right."

The Giants ended their season by losing two of the now meaningless three games in San Diego, but there was no sign of their slump when they hit the NLCS against the Chicago Cubs. Probably no San Francisco Giants team has ever had a better stretch against quality opposition. "We just played great the whole time, making all the plays," said Clark, who would have perhaps his most significant clutch hit ever in the fifth game of the series.

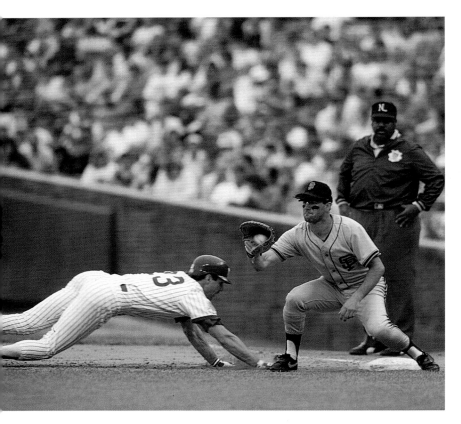

Will Clark hit .650 against the NL Eastern Division Champion Chicago Cubs and was named MVP of the NLCS.

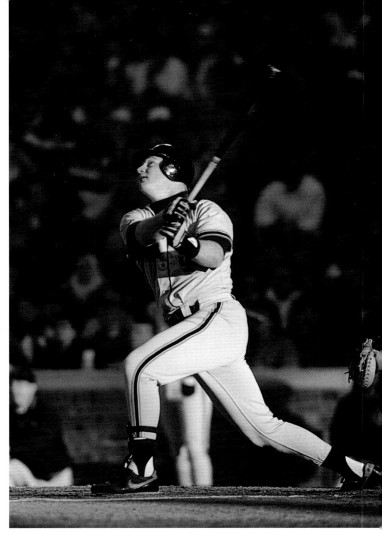

Matt Williams hit two home runs during the 1989 National League Championship Series.

In the series opener in Chicago, Clark hit two homers and Mitchell one as Garrelts cruised to an 11-3 win. The Cubs knocked out Reuschel early in the second game, the Giants' only bad one of the series, and home runs by Mitchell, Matt Williams and Robby Thompson weren't enough in a 9-5 loss.

The Giants came from behind twice in the third game at Candlestick. After a two-run first inning by the Cubs, the Giants scored three in the bottom half of the inning; in the seventh inning, after the Cubs had gone ahead, 4-3, the Giants came back with two runs for a 5-4 win. In the fourth game, Williams got his second homer of the series in a 6-4 Giants win.

So, going into the fifth game, the Giants led the series, 3-1. They were mindful of their 1987 collapse in St. Louis, though, and they knew it was vital to win the series at home. They didn't want to have to go back to Chicago.

In the eighth, the score was tied at 1-1 with two outs and Giants runners on first and second. It was a classic matchup. Clark, who had become known as "Will the Thrill" for obvious reasons, against ace Cubs reliever Mitch Williams, who had earned the nickname of "Wild Thing" because of his unpredictability; Williams was capable of walking the bases loaded but then striking out the side.

"I pretty much knew what I was going to see, because I'd hit against Mitch often enough," said Clark, "but it doesn't always matter that you know what's coming if it's a 92-93 mile an hour fastball. I got in the hole right away at 0-2. Then, Mitch came in with a high fastball and I just got a little piece of it, fouling it off. I think he was trying to throw me another ball like that, maybe just a little higher to see if I'd go after it, but instead of getting it higher, he came in lower. I got a good swing at it and hit it into center field."

His single scored the go-ahead run in what was to become a 3-2 Giants win, and that was the capper for Clark, who hit .650 in the NLCS, a record for a five-game series, as were his 13 hits, eight runs and 1.200 slugging average.

The Giants were in the World Series, and the Bay Area was buzzing with excitement

The 27-year wait ended Oct. 9, 1989. The San Francisco Giants had won the 1989 National League pennant by beating the Chicago Cubs in the NLCS.

Scott Garrelts got
the nod to start
Game One.

Giants Manager Roger Craig and A's skipper
Tony LaRussa meet at home plate prior to
Game One.

Will Clark had four
hits in the 1989
World Series.

Terry Kennedy tries to break up a
double play in Game Two.

Former teammates Robby Thompson and
Dave Henderson exchange greetings prior to
Game One of the 1989 World Series.

over the first Bay Bridge World Series, but a natural disaster soon overwhelmed the baseball.

The A's won the first two games of the Series in Oakland, 5-0 and 5-1, but the Giants were still confident the tide would turn at Candlestick. They had been overwhelming on their home field that year, 53-28, the best record in the National League.

Then, half an hour before the game was scheduled to start, the Loma Prieta 7.1 earthquake hit, causing extensive damage throughout the Bay Area, though the epicenter was 80 miles south of San Francisco, near Santa Cruz.

The Candlestick crowd was buzzing after it hit, but it wasn't immediately apparent how much damage had been caused because Candlestick itself withstood the shock with little structural damage. At first, it seemed that this was simply another of the jolts that pass through the area on a regular basis. In the Giants dugouts, players had the same thought.

"We'd all been through earthquakes before and we didn't think too much about it," said Clark, "but then we started hearing stories in the dugout about fires in the Marina and the Bay Bridge collapsing, and all of a sudden, we realized that there was something happening that was a lot more important than the World Series."

Players quickly gathered in the middle of the field, as far as they could get from structures, and their families came out of the stands to join them. The power was out at Candlestick, even a backup generator. There would be no third game that night. Those at the park slowly made their way home, journeys which took hours because

The destruction on the Bay Bridge, fire in San Francisco's Marina District and concerns about recovery, not the World Series, are on the minds of everyone in the Bay Area.

San Francisco Police Chief and future Mayor Frank Jordan (top left) discusses the situation with his aides.

Baseball Commissioner Fay Vincent reacting seconds after the earthquake prior to game three of the 1989 World Series.

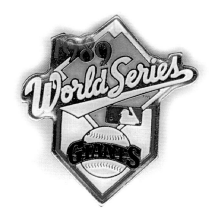

Anticipation turns to fear after a 7.1 earthquake rumbles at 5:04 p.m., Oct. 17, throughout the Bay Area.

Oakland Mayor Lionel Wilson, Baseball Commissioner Fay Vincent and San Francisco Mayor Art Agnos meet the press.

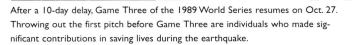

After a 10-day delay, Game Three of the 1989 World Series resumes on Oct. 27. Throwing out the first pitch before Game Three are individuals who made significant contributions in saving lives during the earthquake.

San Franciscans showing their sense of humor prior to Game Three. That's comedian Will Durst in shirt sleeves to the right.

Matt Williams hit a solo home run in Game Three.

Don Robinson got the start in the make-or-break Game Four.

The day after Game Four at Candlestick Park.

extensive damage had been done to freeways and a portion of the Bay Bridge had collapsed.

Then began a waiting game. Baseball Commissioner Fay Vincent came out to survey the damage at Candlestick, which was minimal, and to confer with San Francisco Mayor Art Agnos. For a time, the possibility of simply calling off the rest of the Series was discussed. Moving the remainder of the Series to the Oakland Coliseum, which had not been damaged, was also considered. Finally, after a 10-day delay, Vincent ruled that Candlestick could be used for its scheduled games, and the Series resumed.

"That delay was really hard," said Clark. "You never have 10 days off during the season. By the time we started playing again, the idea was, well, we want to win, but mostly, we just wanted to get it over. We were just beat down, exhausted."

There was another problem for the Giants. "That delay allowed Tony LaRussa to come back with Dave Stewart and Mike Moore," said Dusty Baker, then the hitting coach and later team manager. "Not that Bob Welch (who had been scheduled to pitch the third game, prior to the earthquake) was a day at the beach. But at that time, in a big game, Stew was just unbeatable, and Moore was almost as tough that year."

As it turned out, neither Stewart nor Moore pitched well, but it made no difference because the A's hitters were awesome as the Oaklanders won the third and fourth games, 13-7 and 9-6, to sweep the Series.

"Even though we lost the first two games of the World Series in Oakland," said Craig, "I felt we could turn it around at Candlestick because we'd been so tough at home that year. But after the earthquake, our pitching just fell apart. We just weren't thinking baseball any more. I remember Brett Butler saying that maybe we shouldn't even play the rest of the Series. When your players start talking like that, you've got real trouble."

It's a truism in sports that it's much harder to repeat than to win the first time, and the Giants proved that in the next two seasons, as they slipped to 85-77 in 1990 and even further down to 75-87 in 1991.

There were some individual highlights. Matt Williams finally turned potential into performance as he had back-to-back years with 33 and 34 home runs, driving in a league-leading 122 runs in 1990. Will Clark led the league in slugging percentage in 1991, also hitting .302 with 29 homers. But the pitching staff was falling apart because of age and injury—it had a collective 4.03 ERA in 1991—and Kevin Mitchell was declining precipitously from his great 1989 season. In two years, Mitchell's seasonal totals had declined from 47 home runs to 27 and from 125 RBI to 69.

Mitchell had always had to fight a weight problem, and he was obviously losing the battle. Nobody knew exactly what his weight was, but he was thought to be as much as 50 pounds heavier than he had been earlier in his career. In baseball terminology,

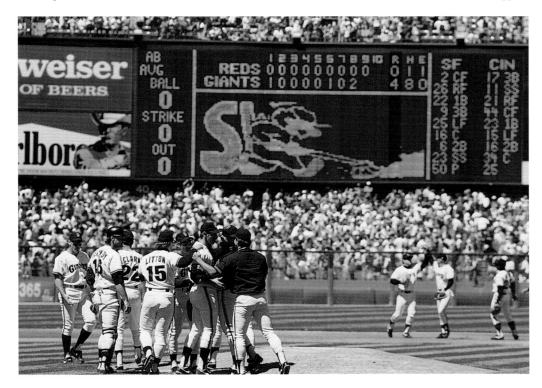

The Giants celebrate a four-game series sweep in 1990 over eventual World Series Champion Cincinnati.

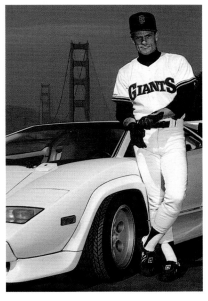

Speed is what Brett Butler brought to the Giants in 1988. He led the Giants in steals three times—including 51 in 1990. Here he poses with a Lamborghini for a magazine cover.

Matt Williams led the National League with 122 RBI in 1990.

Matt Williams wearing a "Turn Back the Clock" 1925 Giants uniform and doing his impression of Babe Ruth.

Mitchell was a load, and that expression referred to more than high weight. He was a very likeable person, smiling and amiable no matter what was happening, but he was always unpredictable. He showed up late for Spring Training, usually with a creative excuse. He missed workouts and planes. He was injured more and more frequently, playing in only 113 games in 1991.

Yet, the memory of Mitchell's sensational season in 1989 lingered, and when Rosen sent Mitchell and pitcher Mike Remlinger to Seattle for pitchers Bill Swift, Mike Jackson and Dave Burba on Dec. 11, 1991, the Giants president got a firestorm of criticism.

"You know how some guys wear out their welcome?" said Rosen. "They might have two years, four years, but then, their time is up. It was like that with Kevin. Roger never knew when he was going to be in the lineup, and we didn't know whether he was really hurt or his injuries were in his mind."

Rosen also knew the Giants needed pitching, because the Giants starters were growing old. He had very good reports on all three pitchers. "We figured we had a good starter in Bill Swift, and a guy who could pitch the seventh and eighth innings in Mike Jackson. Dave Burba never really lived up to what we thought he could do, although he had some good games, but the trade worked out well in general. It's really a shame that Swift's arm hasn't held up, because he's a terrific pitcher when he's healthy."

In retrospect, Rosen understands the reaction. "The media following us doesn't see much of the other league, so there was no reason they would know much about Seattle pitchers." At the time, though, he reacted very uncharacteristically, defending the trade during a radio interview by criticizing Mitchell.

"I got hammered pretty good for that trade, and I reacted in a way I'm not proud

MATT WILLIAMS

Nobody spent more time on the San Francisco-Phoenix shuttle than Matt Williams, but not because his ability wasn't appreciated by Giants President Al Rosen.

"I always thought Matt would be a star from the first time I watched him play, in a college doubleheader," said Rosen. "That's when I decided he would be our No. 1 choice in the draft."

Even when Williams was struggling, and being shuttled back and forth, Rosen compared him to Mike Schmidt, a Hall of Famer and the man many baseball people think is the best third baseman of all time.

"I thought he had the same kind of power as Schmidt," said Rosen, "and that he would be a good RBI man, though probably not hit for a high average. I think time will prove him to be a better fielder than Schmidt, though Mike was a very good fielder. Matt has great hands. He did a fine job for us at shortstop in 1987 when Jose Uribe was hurt, though I always thought third base would be his best position.

"Early in his career, even though he'd shown he could play on the Major League level, we sent him down to Phoenix a couple of times because he just needed the minor league experience. He had a great deal of trouble with the curve ball, because he'd chase it out of the strike zone, and he just had to see more of that pitch to learn to hit it. He never complained about being bounced back and forth, though I'm sure he was smoldering underneath."

Smoldering is probably too strong a word. Matt is very competitive, but he understood what was happening.

"I don't know that I ever doubted my ability," he said. "When you look at my career, I hadn't played much more than 100 games in the minor leagues before I was in the big leagues. I just needed more experience, more at-bats.

"The one year I may have doubted myself was '89. Roger

(Craig) had given me the job at third base and I just couldn't hit, so I couldn't hold it. That was really disappointing, not just for me but because I hurt the team. I was getting up here in key situations and I wasn't doing the job."

The next year, Williams showed he belonged with a .277 average, 33 homers and 122 RBI. But he said, "It seemed every time I came up that year, there was a runner on second base for me to drive in, so my statistics should have been good."

That's a very typical comment from Matt, who is always embarrassed by praise. In 1994, before the strike ended the season at 112 games, he had hit 43 home runs, on a pace to hit 62 homers for a full season, one more than Roger Maris's record. But he wouldn't brag about that, either. "I wasn't hitting much over .260, so I'm not sure I was a better hitter that year," he said. "I was hitting the ball in the air more, which means more home runs but can also mean more fly ball outs. It seemed that year that, every time a pitcher made a mistake, laying the ball out over the plate, I jumped on it. It only takes 15-20 of those, where you hit it out instead of fouling off the pitch or hitting a line drive, to make a big difference in your home run total."

That kind of modesty endeared Williams to Giants fans, who saw him as a throwback to an earlier era when athletes were less flamboyant. Matt doesn't like to call attention to himself. When he hits a home run, instead of dropping his bat at the plate and watching it, he runs quickly around the bases, with his head down, because he doesn't want to embarrass the pitcher.

And, oh, yes, about that Mike Schmidt comparison: After the 1996 season, Matt had played in 1,120 games with 247 homers and 732 RBI. After the 1979 season, Schmidt had played in 1,114 games with 235 homers and 666 RBI. Al Rosen knew what he was talking about.

Don "Caveman" Robinson poses for a magazine cover shot.

Right hander Kelly Downs was acquired from the Philadelphia Phillies in 1984. Over a two-year stretch (1987-88), he won 25 games and posted six shutouts.

Gary Carter spent one season (1990) in a Giants uniform. The future Hall of Famer hit .254 in 92 games.

Bob Knepper returned for his second tour of duty with the Giants in 1990. He led the Giants with 16 wins and six shutouts in 1978.

DIRK SMITH, Director of Travel
DAVID LEWIS, Batboy (kneeling)
MARK LETENDRE, Head Trainer
BRIAN SAUNDERS, Batboy (kneeling)
DENNIS PARRY, Clubhouse Assistant
MIKE MULLANE, Bullpen Catcher

14 MIKE REMLINGER, Pitcher
7 KEVIN MITCHELL, Outfielder
35 STEVE DECKER, Catcher
31 DON ROBINSON, Pitcher
1 MARK LEONARD, Outfielder
12 DUSTY BAKER, Coach

40 BUDDY BLACK, Pitcher
29 MIKE LACOSS, Pitcher
60 MARTY DEMERRITT, Bullpen Assistant
19 DAVE RIGHETTI, Pitcher
21 TONY PEREZCHICA, Infielder
32 TREVOR WILSON, Pitcher

16 TERRY KENNEDY, Catcher
5 BOB LILLIS, Coach
37 KELLY DOWNS, Pitcher
34 NORM SHERRY, Coach
50 SCOTT GARRELTS, Pitcher
39 ROGER CRAIG, Manager

Roger Craig was the first manager to win two championships (1987 National League Western Division and 1989 National League) within four years of a 100-loss team.

Jeff Brantley became the Giants' stopper in 1990. His 19 saves ranked eighth in the league.

San Jose native Dave Righetti joined the Giants in 1991. He led the team with 24 saves.

"T.K." Terry Kennedy was with the Giants for three years (1989-91).

of," he said. "The next time I saw Kevin, I apologized for that. I shouldn't have reacted that way."

Rosen was right to make the trade, though. Swift as a starter and Jackson in the bullpen made it possible for the Giants to make a great run in 1993 while Mitchell failed to play as many as 100 games in the next three seasons and then went off to Japan.

A much bigger story surfaced during the 1992 season, making everybody forget about the Mitchell trade: Once again, it seemed the Giants were on their way out of San Francisco.

After 1989, there had been two more attempts to build a new park for the Giants, one in Santa Clara, the other in San Jose. The San Jose defeat, in June, 1992, was another shocker, because it came about, Corey Busch believed, for non-baseball reasons.

"We got caught up in the Ross Perot phenomenon," he said. "We had researched previous primary elections and were able to pinpoint the number of votes we needed to pass the initiative. We actually got about 300 more votes than we thought we need-

15 GREG LITTON, Infielder
42 BILL FAHEY, Coach
49 JEFF BRANTLEY, Pitcher
20 WENDELL KIM, Coach
8 KIRT MANWARING, Catcher
18 MIKE BENJAMIN, Infielder

9 MATT WILLIAMS, Infielder
46 JOSE SEGURA, Pitcher
17 KEVIN BASS, Outfielder
28 RICK PARKER, Outfielder
45 FRANCISCO OLIVERAS, Pitcher
22 WILL CLARK, Infielder

6 ROBBY THOMPSON, Infielder
10 DAVE ANDERSON, Infielder
25 MIKE FELDER, Outfielder
26 MIKE KINGERY, Outfielder
33 JOHN BURKETT, Pitcher

ROGER MACIAS, Batboy
51 WILLIE MCGEE, Outfielder
GREG LYNN, Assistant Trainer
MIKE MURPHY, Equipment Manager

STADIUMS

Corey Busch's first assignment when he came to work for the Giants, in April, 1979, was to find a way to get a new park. "Even in 1979, it was clear that this franchise couldn't succeed at Candlestick," he said. "Maybe in some cities you can succeed with a bad facility, but not in San Francisco."

Former Mayor George Christopher, who brought the Giants to San Francisco, proposed using a $55 million surplus in the city treasury to dome Candlestick, but the Giants weren't interested.

"A report we did showed that it didn't make economic sense," said Busch. "It wouldn't have been much cheaper than building a new park, and if you domed Candlestick, you'd still have a bad park."

Reluctantly, the Giants considered a domed stadium downtown. "We never really liked the idea of a dome," said Busch. "Baseball isn't meant to be played indoors. We thought we'd have to do it, but once we learned we could mitigate the wind for the fans comfort at China Basin, we abandoned the idea of a domed stadium."

Architects now try to diffuse the effect of the wind by putting up partial barriers, following nature's example in Golden Gate Park, where tree branches allow wind to come through while slowing it down. By contrast, at Candlestick, the wind hits the hill and builds up speed as it comes up and over, swooping down on the park and swirling around.

Before anything was put on the ballot, Lurie considered another idea: Sharing the Oakland Coliseum with the A's. It wouldn't have been a first in baseball history. The Giants and Yankees had both played in the Polo Grounds before Yankee Stadium had been built, and as recently as the 1960s, the Angels had shared Dodger Stadium while their park was being built in Anaheim. The A's didn't like the idea, though, and neither did the Coliseum Board, because it would have made it impossible to schedule the lucrative rock concerts during baseball season.

Still another idea was put forth in May, 1985, by real estate developer Peter Stocker, whose many projects included the Opera Plaza in San Francisco. Stocker planned to incorporate a hotel and retail operations in a park which would be built on Rincon Hill, with money which would be raised by selling permanent seat locations to fans. Stocker was ahead of his time. The ticket plan was a predecessor to the Charter Seat plan which would be used by the Giants for Pacific Bell Park, and his idea of incorporating a hotel and retail operations into the park was later used in Toronto, in a much more grandiose scheme, when Skydome was built. But Stocker's ingenuity wasn't enough. The operation lacked funding and collapsed in October of that year.

Ultimately, four ballot measures, two in San Francisco, were put forth by the Giants under Lurie and all failed. The first, Proposition W in 1987, was a bad idea. It lacked specifications, so nobody knew what it would cost to build a stadium, and it was resoundingly defeated.

The defeat of the 1989 plan was the most devastating. Learning from their earlier mistakes, the Giants and the city devised a specific plan. The city's participation, $30 million in loans, would be repaid by the club. Mayor Art Agnos campaigned tirelessly for the plan, the Giants were in the World Series just three weeks before the measure would go on the ballot and good fortune seemed to be smiling on them.

And then, the Loma Prieta earthquake hit. The ballpark campaign came to a halt, as Agnos headed up an emergency earthquake relief effort, joined by those who had been working for the ballpark.

"The day after the earthquake, we had campaign literature which was supposed to go to absentee voters," said Busch. "It didn't, so we lost our whole absentee voters campaign. We also lost three weeks of campaigning."

On election day, those going to the polls actually favored the ball park initiative, but the absentee vote was overwhelmingly negative, so the initiative was defeated by 1,800 votes.

Lefty Bryan Hickerson (1991-94) was used as a spot starter and middle inning reliever.

Utility man Greg Litton celebrates with Brett Butler after a victory in 1990.

Catcher Steve Decker (1990-92, 1996) is being interviewed on the Giants Radio Network after a victory at Candlestick Park.

Relief specialist Dan Quisenberry retired in late April 1990 after pitching five games.

Mike Remlinger made his Major League debut in 1991.

ed, but we got swamped because the turnout smashed all previous records. The extra people were the Perot people, who were sending a message by voting no on everything. Don't approve money for anything, including a new ballpark. It was over 45 minutes after the voting closed.

"That was a very sad moment because I knew it meant the end of my time in baseball, because I knew Bob would sell the club."

He was right. Frank Jordan, who had succeeded Agnos as mayor of San Francisco, came to Lurie and tried to persuade him to stay on as owner, but Lurie told him, "I'm 0-for-4 and I can't take Candlestick."

Lurie tried to find a local buyer, without success. Then, he got a call from a Florida group which wanted to buy the team and move it to St. Petersburg. They came to an agreement in August, with a sale price of $115 million, though Lurie cautioned the new buyers that if an ownership group surfaced in San Francisco, the league would make every effort to give them a chance to keep the team and, indeed, that he would prefer the team remain in San Francisco.

When the news broke, Lurie was pilloried in the newspapers and on the airwaves. One columnist, noting the city names, said Lurie should move to St. Petersburg in Russia and compared him to Stalin; the column was pulled by the newspaper's publisher before it could run.

"What happened after that was a nightmare," said Busch. "We knew there was no way anyone was going to come forward and offer to buy the team and keep it in San Francisco unless the team was going to leave, but from that point, Bob Lurie was a bad guy. No amount of explaining the situation would change that. Baseball fans buy tickets and souvenirs because it's an emotional thing, so you can't expect that they'll sit back and say, 'It's all right, we understand that the team is leaving.'

"In retrospect, the biggest mistake we made was in not saying to the Tampa guys

that, for a period of time, 30 days, 60 days, we will allow local buyers to come forward."

Forgotten, of course, was the fact that Lurie had saved the Giants from moving in 1976. The hero had turned into a villain, though with the passing of time, perhaps he can be given the credit he deserves.

Busch, his long-time friend as well as associate, talks of Lurie's passion for the game. "Bob Lurie was not just a wealthy businessman who looked at this as an investment. We lost sleep over these things, we sweated over them, we really cared. He loved the game, he loved the people, he loved the team. He got to live out a fantasy. He was fortunate enough to have the means to do that, but God bless him for being willing to spend his money to do it."

The Giants actually got off to a very good start before the bad news came in from San Jose, leading the National League West through May. The rest of the season, though, was a total downer. In June, the month the San Jose ballpark measure was defeated, the Giants plunged to 7-19, falling out of contention.

It was hard to fault the players. Day after day they had to face questions from writers, not about their performance but whether they thought the team would be moved. After Lurie reached his tentative agreement with the Tampa Bay investors in August, the questioning became more intense. Now it was, "What do you think of the move?" To play their best, players have to be focused on the game, but they were given little chance to do that.

The Giants finished a badly-beaten last at 72-90. On the last day of Candlestick, fans cheered them appreciatively, in recognition of what they had done in the past, if not that season. "That season was like a David Lynch movie," remembered Bob Brenly, then a coach. "We were saving balls that came out of the game, thinking these might be the last ones ever used at Candlestick. Usually, after the last game, there's a decompression period. Guys sit around their lockers, maybe have a beer or two, and talk about the season. This time, though, everybody was stampeding out of there in their cowboy boots. It was like everybody wanted to get out before the place burned down."

Meanwhile, though, another drama was playing out, as a serious attempt was being made to keep the team in San Francisco.

Giants fans in 1992 were worried that their team was going to leave San Francisco.

Clockwise from top left: Dusty Baker,
Peter Magowan, Barry Bonds, Shawn Estes,
Pacific Bell Park, Rod Beck and Willie Mays.

III

A DREAM BECOMES REALITY

• THE PETER MAGOWAN ERA •
1992-PRESENT

S an Francisco Mayor Frank Jordan had started to put together a local group which could keep the Giants at home immediately after the announcement of the tentative agreement Bob Lurie had reached with the Tampa Bay group. "Dan Geller (an investment banker) was actually the first to come forward," remembered Jordan. "He told me he'd contribute a million to get it started. Pretty soon we got commitments from Richard Goldman and Walter Shorenstein and Don Fisher."

Jordan would be ridiculed by the media in the weeks to come because most of the work he was doing was behind the scenes; publicly, little progress was being made. He had help from sports attorney Leigh Steinberg; with his national and Bay Area contacts, Steinberg could identify prospective partners for the San Francisco group. "Leigh was a real help," Jordan said, "because he was working behind the scenes with owners as well, and he could go on the talk shows and tell people that we were making progress, and that we could keep the team in San Francisco."

It was a difficult struggle, though. "Commissioner Fay Vincent came out here and we convinced him that we could raise the money to keep the team here," Jordan said. "But then, he was forced out, and we had to start all over again with (acting commissioner) Bud Selig. I remember thinking it was Murphy's Law: Anything that could go wrong did."

The Tampa Bay offer was for $115 million, but the San Francisco group was given the message that a San Francisco offer of $100 million would be enough to keep the team. "We had a helluva time getting up to $100 million," remembered Peter Magowan, who had been on the board of directors for 11 years and joined the investor group. "Given the makeup of the group, with guys like Charles Schwab and Walter Shorenstein, you would have thought it would be easy to get that money, but most of these guys were not really interested in baseball. They had a civic commitment to the city of San Francisco, but not really to baseball."

In the winter of 1992 new Giants ownership brought in a new manager: Dusty Baker.

For a time, it seemed that problem might be solved by George Shinn, the owner of the Charlotte Hornets, who wanted to invest $50 million and become the managing general partner of the new operation.

Shinn came out to San Francisco and paraded around the stadium, "St. George," said Magowan, sarcastically. "Shinn went all over the stadium, even to the left field bleachers, shaking hands," said Jordan. "He was being treated like the savior, and he was loving it." In his private box, Bob Lurie looked down at the scene with distaste, as did Al Rosen. Such public displays were not the style of either man, and they knew Shinn had not yet committed to anything.

He never did, though ultimately, it wasn't his decision. Other prospective owners realized that Shinn was not the answer, for a variety of reasons. One was personality.

When Shinn presented his ideas to the rest of the investors, they were horrified. He wanted to trade all the players with big contracts, including Will Clark and Robby Thompson, to get the payroll down. The other investors also began to hear from baseball people that an ownership group with Shinn at the top might not fly because they wanted to have local ownership. The local investors decided to drop Shinn.

The day after that decision, with newspaper headlines reading, "Giants Deal Collapses," Jordan was participating in the Columbus Day parade. Reporters asked him for comment, and Jordan said that the city still had a chance to keep the team.

"They treated me like an idiot," said Jordan, "but what they didn't know and I couldn't tell them was that I had a meeting the next day in New York with National League President Bill White. He told me that, if we came up with the money, the owners would vote to keep the team in San Francisco." It was more than sentiment for the owners. If the Giants moved to St. Petersburg, the other owners would get nothing, but if an expansion team were put there (as it would be later in the decade), owners would share in the expansion money.

With Shinn out, the local group needed more money, but as more investors came in and those who were already in boosted their financial commitment, the group was still $5 million short of its $100 million goal. Magowan and Baer went over to visit KTVU General Manager Kevin O'Brien. Baer reminded O'Brien that the station had telecast Giants games for more than 30 years. "We're on the five-yard line," he said. "We need to get into the end zone." O'Brien committed $5 million; the $100 million goal was reached.

Ironically, Lurie still had the biggest piece of the team, at $10 million. In his agreement with the Tampa Bay investors, it was stipulated that Lurie would have a $10 million share, and a fourth of that would be bought out in each of the next four years. The same provision was kept in the deal with San Francisco investors, so Lurie would retain a part of the Giants until just before the 1997 season.

With Shinn out, the question remained: Who would run the team?

Magowan was really the only candidate. He had the experience of being on the Giants board, and baseball had been a lifetime love; as a youngster in New York, he had seen the Giants play there before they moved to San Francisco.

"You have the experience of running a big company (Safeway) and a passion for baseball," Baer told Magowan. Baer knew about Magowan's passion from a personal standpoint. Larry had worked for the Giants in the early 1980s and then gone back to Harvard business school. "Peter used to send me these three-page, single-spaced letters before the start of the season with his evaluation of how the team would do," remembered Baer.

When the group presented their offer to the National League owners, it was tentatively approved, with a final decision to come in December. Confident of the final decision, Magowan started to make plans, and his first move was a bombshell.

"We didn't officially own the team yet, but we wanted to get Barry Bonds," remembered Magowan. Before any deal could be made, Lurie had to give his

Fans meet the newest member of the Giants prior to the 1993 season: Barry Bonds.

Much to the delight of Bay Area baseball fans, the Giants remained in San Francisco thanks to the efforts of Peter Magowan and some civic-minded San Francisco business people.

Barry Bonds earned his third NL MVP award in 1993. His 46 homers and 123 RBI led the league. His .336 average topped the Giants. And he won his fourth straight Gold Glove.

Giants President Peter Magowan addresses a crowd of more than 56,000 who came to the Giants' home opener in 1993—the first under the team's new management.

approval. Neither Magowan nor Baer contacted Lurie directly, though. Instead, Bob Quinn, who would be the general manager when the ownership change was made, talked to Al Rosen.

Quinn asked Rosen's opinions on the club's outfielders. Cory Snyder, Rosen thought, struck out too much and his best years were behind him. Mike Felder was a fourth or fifth outfielder, valuable in that role, but not as a starter. Chris James, too, was basically a reserve, not a starter, because he was a defensive liability. Rosen's opinions coincided with those of Quinn and Magowan.

"You've got to get a left fielder," said Rosen.

"What about Barry Bonds?" asked Quinn.

There was a long silence on the other end. Finally, Rosen said, "He's the best player in baseball. If you got him, that would transform the team."

Magowan thought that was tacit approval to make the deal, so he set up a meeting with Bonds' agent, Dennis Gilbert. It was one of the shortest negotiations in history. Magowan told Gilbert that Bonds was the best player and deserved to be paid the best. Ryne Sandberg was then the highest-paid player, at $7.1 million a year. Magowan proposed that the Giants would pay Bonds $7.2 million a year for five years, one year longer than Sandberg's contract. Gilbert said he wanted seven. Magowan then proposed six years, and the deal was made. "It probably took 45 seconds," said Magowan. "A $43 million deal!"

It was the second time the Giants had tried to get Bonds. When he graduated in 1982 from Serra High in San Mateo, only about 20 miles from Candlestick Park, the Giants had made him their No. 1 draft pick, but Bonds spurned them to go to Arizona State for the next three years. At the time, it was reported that the Giants' offer was about $5,000 short of what Bonds wanted, but he insisted in 1996 there was more to it than that.

"It was never about money." he said in an interview in Spring Training. "I didn't want to spend five years in the minors. I thought I could learn more going to a school with a good baseball program than I could in the minors."

He was probably right. He had three years at Arizona State, making the All-Pac

Big crowds like the 56,689 on Opening Day weren't uncommon in 1993—the year the Giants set a single-season attendance record with 2,606,354.

Bob Quinn replaced Al Rosen as Giants general manager in 1993. Quinn relinquished his duties after the 1996 season and now serves as vice president and senior advisor to baseball operations.

With 46 home runs in 1993, Barry Bonds became the first Giants player ever to hit 30 or more homers in his initial season with the team.

Peter Magowan and Dusty Baker share a laugh before a game.

10 team each year, and was named in 1996 to the All-Time College World Series team. He was drafted by Pittsburgh and played only 115 minor league games before being brought up to stay in 1986.

He never expected to play in a Giants uniform. When he became a free agent after the 1992 season, he and his agent were talking to other teams, primarily the Yankees. "We never thought about the Giants at all," he said. "When they approached us, I was totally in shock, but I was happy to sign with the Giants because it meant I would be coming home.

"I thought we would have a good team, too. When the Giants had Kevin Mitchell to go with Will Clark, they won the pennant. Now, they had Clark and Matt Williams. They just needed one other hitter to have a real good team again."

The reaction to the announcement that the Giants had signed Bonds was all that Magowan could have wished for; it was all over the talk shows and television, a front page story in the newspapers. A press conference was scheduled for the next day in Louisville.

When Magowan arrived in Louisville, he had an urgent message from Baer: "We've got a helluva problem. Baseball won't let us sign Barry Bonds."

Bonds was there with his father, Bobby, and his entourage, but everything was put on hold while Magowan and Baer met with interim baseball Commissioner Bud Selig, the two league presidents, Lurie, Rosen and a phalanx of lawyers in Selig's hotel suite. "There wasn't a smile in the room," remembered Magowan. Rosen poked a finger in Baer's chest. "You had no right to do this," he said. Lurie told the group, "I don't want to wind up still owning the club if this deal falls through and being on the hook for Bonds's contract."

Magowan was upset because other clubs were signing free agents; Atlanta had just signed Greg Maddux. "What are we supposed to do—just sit back and watch everybody else improving their clubs?" he demanded. But Lurie said he wouldn't permit the deal, and without his permission, the deal couldn't be made. The press conference was canceled, and Magowan went to Bonds to explain what had happened.

Will Clark ended his Giants career in 1993. He is among the San Francisco top-10 in eight offensive categories.

"I didn't sleep for the next two days and nights," said Magowan. "I tried to figure a way we could work this out."

Meanwhile, Bonds was in his hotel room. "They kept me there because they didn't want me talking to any reporters," he remembered. "So, I just watched TV for two days. I figured there was nothing I could do about it and they'd work something out."

Magowan did, with the approval of his partners and Gilbert. The ownership group agreed that, if their agreement with Lurie fell through, Bonds would be freed from his contract with the Giants and able to sign with any other club. If his new contract fell short of what he would have earned with the Giants, Magowan's group would pay the difference.

"It was the only way we could get him onto the team," said Magowan. Two days later, the press conference was finally held, as Bonds told everybody how happy he was to be with the San Francisco Giants. "Barry hit a home run in the first game and won the MVP, so we felt justified by what we had done," added Magowan.

Magowan's next move was hiring Dusty Baker as his manager. It was both a smart and popular move, because Dusty had been the batting coach for the Giants and had been seen as a logical successor to Roger Craig.

Dusty, whose best playing years had been with the Dodgers, nonetheless had

The Giants sent four players to the 1993 All-Star Game in Baltimore (left to right): Rod Beck, Robby Thompson, Barry Bonds and John Burkett.

(Left) Robby Thompson belted 19 homers in 1993—the most by a San Francisco second baseman until Jeff Kent's 29 in 1997.

(Top) Music legends The Grateful Dead and Tony Bennett provided the entertainment on Opening Day 1993.

Rod Beck's 48 saves in 1993 were five shy of the NL record (53) set the same year by Chicago's Randy Myers.

been a Giants fan in his youth, from the time when his close friend Bobby Bonds had signed with the Giants. That allegiance had been cemented when his family moved from Southern California to Sacramento.

His route to the Giants after his playing years was, he firmly believes, a matter of fate. The first step came in 1987 when Dodgers Vice President Al Campanis made his remarks on ABC-TV's *Nightline* show about blacks lacking the "necessities" to be managers. In the wake of that, Baker went to Dallas to meet with other former black players, including Curt Flood, Frank Robinson and Willie Stargell, to formulate a plan to get opportunities for blacks. "Some of it was just trying to get in the loop," said Dusty. "There were times when we'd hear about a job but it would be filled before anyone could call."

At the time, Baker wasn't even in baseball, having become a stockbroker after his playing days. At the conference, Al Rosen talked to him about joining the Giants organization, first mentioning the possibility of managing in the minor leagues. Dusty wasn't interested in that, but he was going through a lot of changes in his life, including a divorce and relocation from Los Angeles to Northern California.

"I went to Lake Arrowhead with my brother, who was getting divorced at the same time, with our daughters," he said. "When I'm having trouble, I either go to the mountains or the waters, to pray, kind of get guidance. So I'm standing in line and I hear, 'Hey Dusty,' and I turn around and it's Bob Lurie. It was his first time up, my first time up. You have to be blind not to see that this was a sign. So, that's when I made up my mind I'd try it for five years."

Not in the minors, though. Dusty came to the Giants as a first base coach the first year (1988), then a batting coach for four years.

After the 1992 season, Al Rosen called Baker and told him he wanted Dusty to manage in the fall league in Arizona. "I'd had another offer to manage in the Hawaiian League," said Baker, "so I was kind of lying low, wanting to do that. But there was a stock market scandal in Japan, which involved the guys who were putting together the Hawaiian League, so that league fell apart. So, I wound up managing in the fall league."

Rosen, of course, wanted Baker to have some managing experience, because he knew that Roger Craig would not return as Giants manager, whatever happened to

20-20: John Burkett's 22 wins led the National League in 1993, while Billy Swift contributed 21.

Born in San Mateo but raised in Washington state, Buddy Black was a member of the Giants' starting rotation from 1991-94.

Jeff Brantley was part of the Giants bullpen from 1988-93.

Mike Benjamin spent six years (1989-95) with the Giants and was the starting shortstop on Opening Day in 1991.

the club. Dusty was surprised, because Craig had another year on his contract. "I was in no hurry," he said. "I felt, what better guy to serve my apprenticeship under. I learned a lot from Roger, especially on how to handle pitchers."

When he was hired, though—on his sister's birthday, he remembers—he was ready. "I knew the personnel. I had coached most of the guys. They knew what made me happy, what made me angry." The managing experience in the fall league had helped, and Baker had also found his pitching coach, Dick Pole, who worked with him in that capacity in the fall and joined him with the Giants.

That was a magical year for the Giants. Not expected to do much, they led the league for most of the year, and, though they fell short by a game to the Atlanta Braves, they still won a San Francisco franchise-record 103 games in the regular season.

"I'm a baseball fan, first and foremost, and I would have paid to see that team play," said Bob Brenly, a Giants coach that year. "It's just such a shame that the team didn't get into the playoffs."

Off the field, the new management was also doing its best to make Candlestick more user-friendly, with better food and cleaner restrooms. Ticket prices in the upper deck sections were reduced, to make it easier for families to afford the games. Magowan read and answered letters from the fans, and Giants executives walked through the stadium wearing "We're Listening" badges, taking suggestions from fans.

Will Clark, Matt Williams and Barry Bonds provided much of the offensive punch for the Giants in 1993. The trio combined for 98 home runs and 306 RBI.

Former U.S. Olympian Billy Swift led the National League with a 2.08 ERA in 1992.

Mike Jackson was the Giants' middle-inning relief man from 1992-94.

PETER A. MAGOWAN

When he was a student at Stanford in the early 1960s, Peter Magowan wrote a letter to Chub Feeney, then general manager for the Giants, asking for a job in the Giants minor league system.

"I told him I had some ideas for improving attendance," remembered Magowan, now the managing general partner for the Giants.

Feeney wrote back and told him there were no jobs available, that there were few jobs in the organization and there was almost no turnover in those jobs. His advice to Magowan was to forget about a future in baseball.

But, he added if Magowan wanted to talk to him about that, to give him a call, which Magowan did. "We had a nice talk, and was the start of a relationship that lasted 30 years," he said.

It took more than a letter to discourage Magowan, whose love of baseball stems from a childhood passion. He grew up in New York rooting for the Giants, and that rooting interest continued even when the team moved to San Francisco. "I was going to Groton Academy and listening to the re-creation of the Giants games on the radio at night," he said. "The games didn't start until 11 p.m. East Coast time and we had to be up at 6:45 a.m., so I had some short nights."

He remembers his grammar school teacher allowing her students to listen to the dramatic final game of the 1951 playoff between the Giants and Dodgers, won on Bobby Thomson's home run in the bottom of the ninth. "That was the most exciting day of my life," he said. "My father went to that game with three business colleagues, and all three left before the start of the ninth inning. He told me there was a lesson in that: Never give up. I thought of that many times when it seemed our bid to keep the Giants in San Francisco would fail."

Magowan, who moved to San Francisco in 1978 to become CEO for Safeway, had been on the Giants board of directors for 11 years when Bob Lurie made a tentative agreement to sell the club to a Tampa Bay group. Magowan quickly pledged his money and support to a new ownership group which was eventually successful in buying the club and keeping it in San Francisco.

Because of his experience and his love of the Giants, Magowan was a natural for the managing general partner position, and he resigned as Safeway CEO to devote full time to the Giants job. "I knew I couldn't do both because I get involved in everything," he said. "I was 50 at the time and thought it was the right time for me to make this change."

Giants fans can be grateful he didn't take Chub Feeney's advice.

Four Giants—the most ever in a single-season—won Gold Gloves in 1993. From left to right: Barry Bonds, Matt Williams, Robby Thompson and Kirt Manwaring.

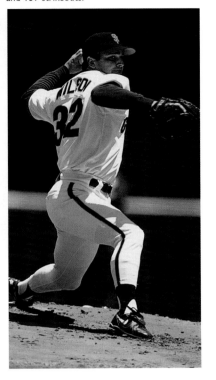

Trevor Wilson led the Giants in 1991 with 13 wins, a 3.56 ERA and 139 strikeouts.

"Some of the changes we made were suggestions from fans," said Baer. "The green left field fence was the idea of 16-year-old in the East Bay. The bleachers were the idea of a woman in Millbrae."

All those changes were helpful and even exciting—the left-field bleachers became the place to be in the early weeks—but they weren't as important as what was happening on the field. With Bonds off to the best start of his career, hitting over .400 for the first seven weeks of the season, the Giants surged into first place.

"I had to do well," laughed Bonds, "because I was playing before people who had seen me grow up. There was a lot of pressure on me, because you know what they would have said if I hadn't done well. But it wasn't just me. Everybody was playing well that year."

When Baker thinks of that year now, the signing of Bonds is the first big memory, but there are others as well.

"I have a picture on my wall of our defense. We had Gold Glovers at third, at second, in left and catcher. We had former Gold Glovers with Will Clark and Willie McGee, and we had D-Lew (Darren Lewis) in center, who should have been a Gold Glover. (Lewis, in fact, broke a Major League record that year with 267 consecutive errorless games.) Royce Clayton was a future Gold Glover. Defense is so important. Unless you have a strikeout pitching staff, guys who can get out of trouble with strikeouts, you've got to be able to catch the ball, so the other team doesn't get extra opportunities. That was especially important for us that year, with guys like Swiftie (Bill Swift) who got hitters to hit the ball on the ground."

Swift was an interesting case. He had undeniable ability, but he had arm problems virtually every year he pitched, including his first year with the Giants, when he broke down late in the season, after putting together a 10-4 record. Baker, with Pole's help, carefully monitored Swift's pitches and appearances, and Swift had by far his best year, winning 21 games.

The bullpen was another strong factor, not just closer Rod Beck with his 48 saves but setup men Kevin Rogers and Mike Jackson. When a Giants starter got through seven innings with a lead, he knew the bullpen would take it the rest of the way.

"We had great leadership, too," said Dusty. "Guys like Willie McGee and Robby Thompson. Dave Righetti and Buddy Black played a big role with the pitchers. Blackie (Bud Black) was good with the young guys, Trevor Wilson and Bryan Hickerson, and Rags (Dave Righetti) with the guys in the bullpen."

Dave Burba spent four years (1992-95) in a Giants uniform.

Richmond native Willie McGee joined the Giants in 1991 and led the team with a .312 batting average.

Will Clark addresses the Giants of the future during a 1993 "Little League Day."

Royce Clayton was the Giants' first selection in the June 1988 draft.

San Jose native Dave "Rags" Righetti led the Giants with 24 saves in 1991, the most by a San Francisco left hander.

Though they'd been down-rated before the season started because of their poor season in 1992, the Giants were actually a very solid team that year, with few weaknesses. Even the bench was strong, with Mark Carreon and Dave Martinez available for pinch hitting and spot starting.

Atlanta was the overwhelming favorite to repeat as National League champion, but the Giants' fast start swept them into a 10-game lead by the end of July. Probably the most telling indication of how well the Giants were playing was a wild game in April against Atlanta when they battled back from a five-run deficit twice to beat the Braves, 13-12. Matt Williams hit two homers, including the game-winner.

In early July, Williams went on the disabled list with a pulled stomach muscle, at a time when he was having his best season, hitting .295 with 21 homers and 65 RBI. In retrospect, Baker thinks that was the point when he knew what kind of season the club was going to have, because the Giants got some very unexpected help.

"We were going east without Matty, to Montreal, New York and Philly. That's a trip that has ruined a lot of West Coast teams, and we were going on it without a guy who had been doing almost as much damage as Barry."

Dusty turned to Steve Scarsone and Mike Benjamin, alternating them depending on the pitching; Scarsone had trouble with a high fastball pitcher but Benjamin had his best success against that kind of pitcher. "Scars got hot in Philly. He cooled off, but then Benjy got hot, but then he got hurt. We called up Eric Johnson and Paul Faries and they came in and did a great job. When you lose one of your stars and can hold your ground, you're really in great shape."

Even as he managed the division leader, though, Baker could see trouble ahead, when the Braves picked up first baseman Fred McGriff from the San Diego Padres in mid-season, plugging the one hole in their starting lineup.

In the aftermath of that deal, Dusty had one of his few run-ins with the media.

Giants President Peter Magowan's first move was signing former Serra High School star Barry Bonds before the 1993 season.

This writer was present when he said, "I hope the Braves got him a week too late." When it was reported, some writers and broadcasters left out the "I hope" part. "When I heard that, I said, 'Hey, wait a minute, I'm not going to say that,'" remembered Dusty. "The last thing I wanted to do was make the Braves mad. I was always worried about them, because I knew they were the kind of team that could win four or five years in a row."

The Braves started making their move—they would win 39 of their last 50 games—and the Giants got hit by serious injuries to the starting rotation, losing left-handers Wilson and Bud Black. By season's end, they had only two reliable starters, Swift and John Burkett, who had a career year with 22 wins.

In late August, the Braves came to Candlestick and swept a three-game series. In mid-September, the Giants lost eight in a row to slip out of first place for the first time.

To make it worse, as the Giants started to snap out of their malaise, they lost the man who best symbolized the heart of the team, Robby Thompson, who was hit in the face by a pitch in a Sept. 24 game against San Diego by the Padres Trevor Hoffman, suffering a fractured cheekbone.

Thompson would finish with one of the best seasons by a Giants second baseman in San Francisco history, with a .312 batting average, 19 home runs and 65 RBI. He had a 21-game hitting streak, longest of the season in the National League and the longest in Giants history since Jack Clark had set the San Francisco record with 26 in 1978. He homered in five straight games, August 20-24, one short of the club record set by Willie Mays in 1955, when the Giants were still in New York.

The gutty Thompson would come back after only eight games to play in the final game of the season, which was typical of him. Throughout his Giants career, he had played despite a chronic back ailment and other injuries too numerous to men-

Todd Benzinger (1993-95) gave the Giants a solid performer at first base and the outfield.

"Flea." Bob Lillis proved to be a valuable bench coach for Roger Craig and Dusty Baker.

tion. Sadly, though, this injury marked the end of Thompson as a front-line player. He signed another contract after the season and played three more years, but he was never the same player again. That injury, coupled with others that hit in the next three seasons, so limited him that he played fewer than half the Giants games over that period. The Giants bought out the last year of his contract after the 1996 season.

Meanwhile, the Giants shook off Thompson's injury and their earlier problems to win 10 of their last 11 games and 16 of 18. "You knew a down time would come," said Baker, "but what I was most proud of that year was the way we came back." With four games left, the Giants were tied with the Braves, but they had a four-game series left in Los Angeles against the Dodgers, while the Braves were hosting the expansion Colorado Rockies, who could not win a game from Atlanta all season.

It was obvious the Giants had to sweep the Dodgers, and they came close, winning the first three games of the series. One more win and they could force a playoff; they had already won a coin flip, so the game would be at Candlestick Park.

For the last game, Baker faced a very tough pitching choice: With neither Swift nor Burkett available, he had mediocre veterans Scott Sanderson and Jim Deshaies or rookie Salomon Torres. He remembered a similar situation from his playing days in Los Angeles.

"In 1980, we were down three games with three games to go and swept Houston. We had a one-game playoff. The safe thing would have been to start the veteran, Dave Goltz. We (players) begged Tommy to start Fernando Valenzuela. Tommy chose to go with Goltz, and we got beat.

"That was in my mind. I went with the talent."

It probably didn't matter. Torres got rocked by the Dodgers, but the Giants couldn't muster any offense, either. They lost, 12-1, and the Braves won the pennant. Only twice in National League history had a team won more games and finished second, the 1909 Chicago Cubs and 1942 Brooklyn Dodgers, both of whom won 104 games. For Baker, it was a bad case of deja vu. In 1982, when he was with the Dodgers, they had won a coin flip and would have faced the Braves in a playoff at Dodger Stadium, but Joe Morgan's home run at Candlestick had beaten the Dodgers and knocked them out of the playoff.

Robby Thompson hit safely in a National League-best 21 straight games in 1993.

Dave Martinez filled a utility role during his two seasons with the Giants (1993-94).

In 1993, John Burkett became the first member of the Giants to lead the National League in wins (22) since 1973.

Darren Lewis (above and right) won a Gold Glove in and led club in steals in 1994.

Matt Williams led the National League with 43 homers in 1994.

Mark Carreon rotated between first base and the outfield during his time (1993-96) with the Giants.

For everybody in the Giants organization, it was a bitter case of what might have been. "I was having dinner downtown the next night," remembered Giants Executive Vice President Larry Baer. "It was a beautiful night, but all I could think of was we could have been playing the Braves at Candlestick with Swift pitching. I liked our chances with that matchup."

Meanwhile, Baker had been out at Candlestick. "I went out every day for a week," he said. "How do you just turn it off?"

That loss, in retrospect, was almost an omen for the Giants, because in the next three seasons, almost everything that could go wrong did.

The problems started in the off-season, when Will Clark left as a free agent to sign with the Texas Rangers. Clark had suffered with nagging injuries the previous two seasons and had his worst year since his rookie season in 1986, finishing with a .283 average with just 14 home runs and 73 RBI. Down the stretch, though, Clark had some key hits, and he was always a club leader. He wasn't popular with his teammates because he would get on players he thought weren't giving their best, but he was a tremendous competitor, and that attitude had much to do with the Giants' success while he was with the team.

Because of Clark's physical problems, the Giants didn't negotiate an extension of his contract during the season, preferring to wait until after the season when it would be easier to evaluate his future. By then, though, both the Rangers and the Baltimore Orioles got in the bidding for Clark, and the Rangers' offer of five years at $30 million was far better than the Giants' best offer of three years for $15 million.

The judgement by the Giants management proved right: Clark was continually on the disabled list in Texas, never matching his superstar statistics of previous years.

Giants fans took a liking right away to new Manager Dusty Baker in 1993. Winning 103 games didn't hurt, either.

Mark Portugal was a member of the starting rotation from 1994-95.

Many Giants fans will agree that announcer Hank Greenwald was born with a bat in his hand. He entertained fans with his wit and baseball knowledge from 1979-86 and 1989-96.

In an attempt to bolster their pitching, the Giants signed Mark Portugal as a free agent for $4 million a year. Portugal was a noted Giant-killer, having gone 11-2 against them while with Houston. He had been exactly a .500 pitcher, 45-45 in the Majors, until going 18-4 in 1993. The Giants hoped that had been a breakthrough year for Portugal and he would have more seasons like that, but in 1994, he reverted to his previous form with a 10-8 season.

Even though Clark was not the hitter in 1993 that he had been earlier in his career, he still had been a factor because pitchers worried about him and worked hard to get him out. Clark's replacement, Todd Benzinger, did not worry pitchers, and the Giants run production fell off.

The pitching also declined. Bill Swift, who had been possibly the league's best pitcher the year before, had more arm problems and fell from 21-8 to 8-7. John Burkett had an even steeper decline, from 22-7 to 6-8, though Burkett's decline was more a result of a much less potent attack behind him; his ERA was actually slightly better than the season before, 3.82, compared to 3.85. Mike Jackson, who had made 81 appearances the season before as an invaluable setup man for stopper Rod Beck, made only 36 appearances in what would be a much-shortened season.

Outfielder Barry Bonds, the new ownership group's first major signing, developed a following during his MVP season of 1993. He donated 50 tickets to special families that comprised "The Bonds Squad."

Mayor Frank Jordan (left) presents a proclamation to Giants President Peter Magowan recognizing the initial "Until There's a Cure Day."

Pitcher Rod Beck and his wife, Stacey, are very active in "Until There's A Cure Day" events.

In 1994, the Giants became the first professional sports team to host a benefit game to help in the fight against AIDS. "Until There's A Cure Day" has been an annual event ever since.

Giants Manager Dusty Baker poses with the special AIDS ribbon Giants players and coaches wore on their uniforms for "Until There's A Cure Day."

Giants and Colorado Rockies players and participants form the Human AIDS ribbon at the close of the first "Until There's A Cure Day."

With all these problems, the Giants sank into a deep hole in the first half of the season, as much as 15 games below .500, at 35-50.

And then, they signed Darryl Strawberry, the very talented but very troubled player who had worn out his welcome with the New York Mets and Los Angeles Dodgers. Even though they still had to pay his multi-million dollar salary, the Dodgers had cut him earlier in the season after just 32 games.

Strawberry's signing was very controversial. There were many skeptics when he said he was off drugs, though his older brother, a police officer, would travel with the team to help him stay on his program. There was a question about how much Strawberry had left physically.

But, there was no question of the impact he had on the Giants. In truth, he didn't do very much offensively, hitting only .239 in his 29 games in a Giants uniform, but he galvanized the team. He looked awesome in a uniform whose shirt sleeves were cut high to emphasize his huge arm muscles. With his long, looping swing, reminiscent of Willie McCovey, he seemed capable of hitting the ball out at any time. Pitchers approached him warily. Like Clark the year before, he was a psychological factor even when he wasn't a physical one.

With Strawberry in the lineup, the Giants drew three straight crowds of more than 50,000 in a series against the Dodgers, had another 50,000-plus crowd against Colorado, and a crowd just 373 under that magic figure in the next series.

Suddenly the season was turning around. The Giants shaved nine games off the Dodgers' lead in only three weeks in July. They were only three games back of the division-leading Dodgers on Aug. 11, and Dusty Baker was looking forward to the rest of the season. "All we had to do was gain one game a week and we'd be tied going into September," he said. "I liked our chances in that situation."

Individually, too, one player was red-hot: In a season when many hitters were setting home run records, Matt Williams was the hottest with a Major League-leading 43 home runs, a pace which would have produced 62, one more than Roger Maris' record. In typical self-effacing fashion, Matt downplayed that.

"I don't think I was hitting any better than in other years," he said. "My average was in the .260s (.267). I was hitting the ball in the air more, which meant more home runs but maybe more fly outs, too, and I was hopping on mistakes. It seemed that year, every time a pitcher hung a pitch out over the plate, I jumped on it and hit it out. In the course of a season, it only takes about 15-20 times like that when you hit the ball in the air instead of maybe fouling off the pitch or hitting a line drive to make a tremendous difference in your home run total."

Darryl Strawberry spent part of the 1994 season with the Giants.

Skipper Dusty Baker fills out the lineup card.

Trevor Wilson was part of the starting rotation in 1993, winning seven games.

The brothers Leiter: right hander Mark (left) and lefty Al. Mark Leiter pitched two years for the Giants (1995-96).

Kirt Manwaring (1987-96) is the only catcher in San Francisco Giants history to have led the team in triples (five in 1992).

Ted Robinson joined the Giants announcing team in 1993.

We'll never know, though, if Matt would have hit 62 home runs or if the Giants would have caught the Dodgers, because on August 12, 1994, Major League Baseball went on strike. There would be no more baseball until the next April. No World Series, not even a Spring Training with regular players.

The strike was a blow to the whole game, and no team suffered more—and more unfairly—than the Giants. "We were making our move and we were on a pace to have the second best attendance year in our history, second only to the 2.6 million the year before," said Larry Baer. "All the time in the baseball owners' meetings, Peter (Magowan) was saying, 'We've got to keep playing. No matter how long it takes to settle this, we've got to keep playing.' But not enough people were listening."

Normally, the World Series creates an excitement for baseball that lasts through a winter of stories about trades, free agent signings and rookie "phenoms." Spring Training becomes another source of excitement, a symbolic fresh start, leading up to Opening Day.

The strike killed all of that. Instead of stories about players, fans were seeing stories and pictures featuring interim Commissioner Bud Selig and Players Association chief Donald Fehr. Instead of reading about exciting new players, they were hearing about players who would not even have been on the 40-man rosters. Baseball was planning a season with "replacement" teams, consisting primarily of rookies from the minor leagues or veterans long past their prime looking for one last shot.

Those teams played only in Spring Training because a court-enforced settlement ended the strike in early April. Teams held another short Spring Training with their regular teams, and the Giants began what would be just a 144-game schedule on April 22 in Atlanta, facing Greg Maddux and, predictably, losing.

The ace starting pitchers from the 1993 team were both gone: Bill Swift as a free agent to Colorado and John Burkett in a trade with the Texas Rangers.

The Giants, though, got off to a reasonably good start; when they beat Colorado, 3-1, on June 6, they were 20-16 and one game ahead in the NL West. It was a very costly win, though, because they lost Matt Williams, who was having a spectacular year, leading the league in batting average (.381), home runs (13), RBI (35) and slugging percentage (.754). Williams fouled off a pitch and broke a bone in his right foot. Not knowing the extent of his injury, Williams stayed in the game and singled in that at-bat, but he came out for a pinch-runner after reaching first.

"That was my most frustrating season," Williams said, "because I felt I had finally put it all together, hitting for average and power, and then I foul a pitch off my back foot, which nobody ever does."

Williams missed 68 games before returning in mid-August. He still finished at .336, his best average with the Giants, and led the club with that and his .647 slugging percentage, also hitting 23 homers and driving in 65 runs. The Giants had a terrific one-two punch with Williams and Barry Bonds, who finished at .294 with 33 home runs and 104 RBI, but Bonds couldn't carry the team by himself. Without Matt, the Giants went 28-40 and fell to last place, seven-and-a-half games out. His return couldn't bring them out of their slump, and they finished at 67-77.

(Top) Mark Dewey had two stints with the Giants (1990, 1995-96).

(Left) Manager Dusty Baker achieved this plateau on Aug. 6, 1995 vs. the Dodgers.

William VanLandingham, owner of the longest name in Major League Baseball history, won eight of his first 14 starts during 1994, his rookie season.

The 1993 Giants look like they're dressed for "Casual Friday" at the office.

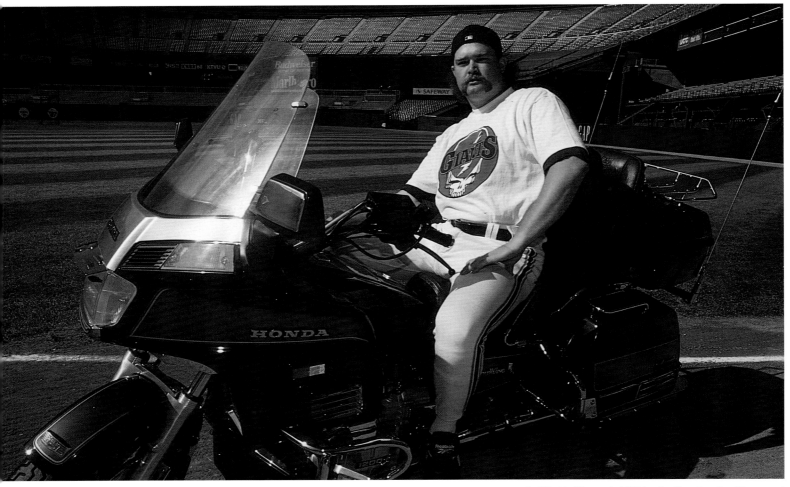

Rod Beck's 48 saves in 1993 is a San Francisco franchise record.

Jeff Reed proved to be a valuable backup to Kirt Manwaring from 1993-95.

Attendance also dropped to an average of 17,243 a game, slightly more than half the 1993 average and the lowest since the 1985 Giants, the team that lost 100 games. Attendance was off throughout baseball that year, of course, but the Giants' dropoff was the biggest percentage decline in the National League.

Fans were taking out their resentment because the game had been taken away from them. It may have been unfair to the Giants, because Magowan had not wanted the strike and the club management had worked hard from the start to please the fans, but the fans were in no mood to worry about that. They didn't care who was at fault. They were showing their anger in the only way open to them.

Meanwhile, the Giants were caught in an awkward transitional period. Under the direction of Brian Sabean, they had been revamping their minor league system, but the best prospects were still at least a year away from the Major Leagues. They tried to fill in for the 1996 season with veterans, but injuries sidelined free agent acquisitions Shawon Dunston (shortstop) and Stan Javier (center field). In right field, Glenallen Hill broke his wrist diving for a ball.

Most damaging of all, Williams again had his season shortened by injury, this time a shoulder operation. The injury the year before had been a fluke, but this was more serious because it was damage done over a period of time. He again hit over .300, at .302, but played in only 102 games, hitting 22 homers and knocking in 85 runs.

The only bright spot in the year was Barry Bonds, who had another year which would have merited Most Valuable Player consideration if the Giants had been contenders, finishing at .308 with 42 home runs, 122 runs scored and 129 RBI, despite being walked a National League record 151 times.

Bonds also reached two important milestones, one career, one season. On April 27, when he hit homers 300 and 301 off former Giants pitcher John Burkett, then with the Florida Marlins, he became one of only four players in Major League history to hit more than 300 home runs and steal more than 300 bases. The previous three were Willie Mays, Andre Dawson and Barry's father, Bobby.

Bonds also became the second player (Jose Canseco was the first) to steal 40 bases while hitting 40 home runs in a season. Bobby Bonds, who had a Major League record five seasons with at least 30 homers and 30 stolen bases, had just missed 40-40 when he slugged 39 homers while stealing 43 bases in 1973.

Barry entered September with just 25 stolen bases, so he had little thought of reaching 40. "My teammates told me to go for it," he said. "I hadn't even been thinking about that. I figured that, as long as it didn't hurt the team, I'd give it a try."

Bonds wound up with 15 stolen bases in September, just reaching the magic 40 mark. For the season, he was caught stealing only seven times, so he had an outstanding success rate of more than 85 percent.

The next spring, though, he said that would probably be the only time he'd ever steal that many bases again. (With Pittsburgh, he had stolen as many as 52 in a season.) "Maybe if I got close again, I'd go for it," he said, "but I don't think so. It's too hard on my body. I'm getting at a stage of my career where I have to think about conserving my energy. Dusty reminds me all the time that as I get older, I

BARRY BONDS

Willie Mays is the best player ever to wear the San Francisco Giants uniform, but Barry Bonds (upper right) isn't far behind. Like Mays, Bonds can win games with his bat, his glove or his feet. The two are close personally as well. Mays and Barry's father, Bobby, were close friends, and Mays is Barry's godfather.

"People have always expected more of me than they have of other players," said Barry. "I wasn't ever just another player. I was Bobby Bonds' son, Willie Mays' godson."

He hasn't disappointed. By the time the Giants opened their 40th season, Barry Bonds seemed well on his way to the Baseball Hall of Fame.

Bonds makes it look easy, but in fact, his success is due at least as much to his dedication and hardwork as to his natural ability.

In the off-season, Bonds pursues a rigorous training regimen with personal trainer Ray Farris, who also works with San Francisco 49ers star receiver Jerry Rice. He often exceeds even the demands put on him by Farris.

"He keeps telling me I should take a day off and let my body recuperate," said Bonds in the spring of 1997, "but then he says, 'But, I'm not going to tell you not to go to the track because you know if I do, you'll just go without me.'

"I feel like I'm a finely-tuned machine. I'm going to keep challenging myself to do even more. Maybe I'll break down some day, but I'm going to keep going as long as I can."

Bonds is into the game mentally, too. Before a game, for instance, he'll sit in as pitchers go over the opponents' lineup with Pitching Coach Dick Pole because he wants to know how they'll pitch each batter, which gives him an edge in positioning himself in the field.

In the half hour before the game, he sits in front of his locker and visualizes how the game will go. "It's something I learned from Mike Schmidt, when he was with the Phillies and I was with the Pirates starting out," said Bonds. "Sometimes, too, I'll take myself completely away from the game, thinking of something that has nothing to do with the game, just to relieve the pressure a bit, but I always come back to the game, trying to prepare for everything that might happen."

Bonds has been a controversial figure with the Giants, primarily because of his problems with the media. He marches to his own drummer. Sometimes, he'll refuse to talk to reporters; other times, when the mood strikes, he'll talk for 45 minutes on a wide-ranging set of topics. He can go 0-4 and talk, or he can go 4-for-5 and not talk. "I didn't win this game by myself," he'll tell reporters. "Go talk to some of the other guys who contributed."

The one constant about Bonds is his commitment to children. "He's never refused to do anything we ask him to do with kids," said club Executive Vice President Larry Baer.

The Giants ask each of their players to commit to a charity. When Bonds came to the club, he chose the Adopt a Special Kid charity, to which he's contributed both his time and money, more than $100,000. He was honored by the charity at a dinner in the fall of 1996 because of his help.

When a child with leukemia needed blood donations in the winter of 1997, Bonds agreed to visit the child in the hospital and help get the word out, but he insisted that only one reporter be allowed at the hospital. He donated blood himself after his visit.

That's typical of Bonds, who has never sought public attention for his charity work, which also includes being a board member for United Way and fund-raising appearances for Easter Seals. "He's not doing it to enhance his image," said Baer. "He's always said that he wants to do things where he can make an impact."

On the field, he's always made an impact, and that impact has been almost daily. In his first four seasons with the Giants, he missed only six games, and he set a franchise record with 357 consecutive games, his streak finally ending in the 1996 season.

The contract extension Bonds signed in the winter of 1997 guaranteed that he'd be in a Giants uniform when they open Pacific Bell Park in the year 2000, so as fans see the statue of Willie Mays in front of the stadium and remember his great feats they can marvel at the ones Barry Bonds is still performing on the field.

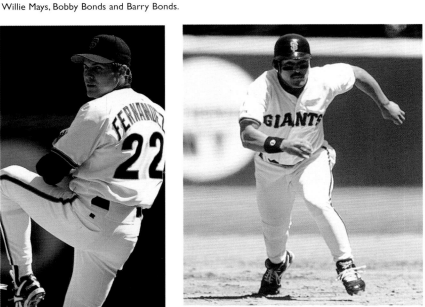

Members of the exclusive 300 home run/300 stolen base club pose in 1996 (left to right): Andre Dawson, Willie Mays, Bobby Bonds and Barry Bonds.

The Giants paid tribute to a remarkable feat by Barry Bonds in 1996—42 homers/40 stolen bases—on Opening Day 1997.

Osvaldo Fernandez defected from Cuba in 1995 and signed with the Giants before the 1996 season.

Outfielder Marvin Benard hit .248 in 135 games in 1996.

Veteran Mark Gardner won 12 games in 1996.

bruise more easily and it takes longer for me to recover. I think I can help the team more with my slugging than by stealing bases."

Because of that, Bonds's chief career goal had become 500 home runs, a figure which is a sure guarantee of election to the Baseball Hall of Fame. Since he seemed certain to get more than 400 stolen bases—he had 380 going into the 1997 season—even 400 home runs would put him in an exclusive category, because nobody had ever combined 400 home runs and 400 stolen bases.

Bonds also had one more goal: to win the Most Valuable Player award at least one more time. With two MVP awards with Pittsburgh and one with the Giants, Bonds was tied with seven others in Major League history who had won three. Nobody had won four.

His chance to do that was linked to an improvement of the team, because historically, the award goes to a player on a contending team. In 1996, numerous injuries had forced the Giants to fill in with minor leaguers, most of whom were not ready for the Majors yet, and they finished last in their division again, losing 94 games.

As early as July, this writer sat with Sabean, who would be promoted to general manager at the end of the season, and heard Sabean say, "We've only got four legitimate Major Leaguers out there."

Sabean was determined to re-shape the Giants, to make them both younger and better. "It can't be done overnight," he said. "We've finished in last place the last two years, and you can't just wave a magic wand and make this a first place team."

His moves had actually started midway through the 1996 season because he was the one who suggested a series of trades: Mark Carreon for left-handed relief pitcher Jim Poole, who strengthened the Giants' weak bullpen; veteran starter Mark Leiter for young lefthander Kirk Rueter and Kirt Manwaring for Rick Wilkins. At the time, the last trade seemed merely an exchange of catchers past their prime, but Wilkins, finally recovered from neck problems, regained his hitting stroke with the Giants and played well defensively.

One thing that bothered Sabean about the makeup of the Giants was the fact that

Fremont's Shawon Dunston left the "Friendly Confines" of Wrigley Field and the Cubs for a season with the Giants in 1996.

The Giants proudly boast one of the Bay Area's premier community outreach programs. Part of their program includes renovation of neighborhood baseball fields. Giants pitcher William VanLandingham, former Giants infielder Steve Scarscone, Giants Community Representative Orlando Cepeda, ex-Giants pitcher Mike Krukow and Community Representative Vida Blue break ground at San Francisco's St. Mary's Playground.

The San Francisco Giants were the first Major League Baseball team to have every player, coach and uniformed staff member actively involved with at least one local non-profit organization. Former Giants pitcher Mike Krukow (left) and ex-Giants infielder Steve Scarscone are serving meals at San Francisco's St. Anthony's Dining Room during the 1995 holiday season.

Matt Williams ended his Giants career with 247 homers—third on the all-time San Francisco list.

The Giants' efforts in the 1996 "Yes on Proposition B" ballot initiative, along with the support of San Francisco voters, paved the way for the new Pacific Bell Park in China Basin, which is scheduled to open by Opening Day 2000.

Giants Executive Vice President Larry Baer, Pacific Bell President of Consumer Communications Services John Polumbo, and Giants President Peter Magowan announce the partnership of Pacific Bell and the Giants.

The efforts of San Francisco Mayor Willie Brown were instrumental in paving the way for the Giants' new home in China Basin.

Giants President Peter Magowan and his wife, Debby, celebrate after the Proposition B victory.

Willie Mays gave his support towards the Giants new stadium.

San Francisco Giants Vice President and General Counsel Jack Bair with one of the star volunteers from the "Yes on B" campaign, Mike Crockett.

so much of the payroll was concentrated on three players—Bonds, Williams and Thompson—in 1996, making it difficult to get quality players at other positions, even though the Giants' $34 million payroll was in baseball's top-10.

Bonds was arguably still the best player in baseball, so he had to be kept. There were rumors the Giants were trying to trade him, but there was never any substance to that. The Giants, in fact, had made a Bonds home run into the bay the concluding scene of their video advertising the park to be built in China Basin.

Thompson was through as a front-line player, and the Giants exercised an option to buy out his contract.

Williams was a tough call. Matt was a very popular player because he was such a nice person as well as a great player, but injuries had reduced his playing time sharply the past two seasons, and there was some question whether his shoulder would permit him to play third base. His back-loaded contract would go up to $6.75 million in 1997.

Sabean decided, with Magowan's backing, it would make more sense to trade Williams for players who could strengthen several positions. So he traded Matt to Cleveland for shortstop Jose Vizcaino, second baseman Jeff Kent, pitchers Julian Tavarez and Joe Roa and $1 million. Vizcaino and Kent significantly improved the Giants at two positions, but Sabean was most pleased with the acquisition of Tavarez. Despite a sub-par 1996 season, Tavarez's potential was so high Atlanta had offered to trade first baseman Fred McGriff to Cleveland for him. He was projected as a setup man for closer Rod Beck for the 1997 season, but he was also seen as a possible closer or a starter in the future.

The trade was criticized sharply in newspapers and over the air, but it was the

State Senator Quentin Kopp and KNBR Radio's Ralph Barbieri, at the introduction of the new Pacific Bell Park.

Former San Francisco Supervisor Roberta Achtenberg (left), California State Senator Quentin Kopp, Giants President Peter Magowan and Giants Executive Vice President Larry Baer gaze at a model of the new Pacific Bell Park.

Giants Executive Vice President Larry Baer, a native San Franciscan, was a major force in the 1996 ballpark campaign.

only way Sabean could improve the team at several positions. Though largely overlooked at the time, the $1 million Cleveland threw in later enabled Sabean to sign free agent Darryl Hamilton, another significant upgrade, to play center field.

In between those moves, Sabean re-signed Wilkins and Hill, who could have been free agents. He also traded pitcher Allen Watson for first baseman J.T. Snow, plugging what the Giants GM had called "our black hole," and minor leaguer Jesus Ibarra, a strong hitter who was a very weak defensive player, for third baseman Mark Lewis, while signing reliever Doug Henry as a free agent.

The 1997 Giants would indeed be the New Giants.

Prognosticators thought no more of the new Giants than the old ones; the team was picked to finish last in the National League West. In the clubhouse, though, there was a quiet confidence.

"I looked around the clubhouse in Spring Training and saw guys I knew could play," Jeff Kent would remember later. "I knew I could play. I had played with Jose Vizcaino in New York, and I knew he could play. I knew J.T. Snow and Darryl Hamilton could play. We had a lot of guys who had proven themselves, but nobody gave us much credit for that."

Kent spoke from personal experience because he had come with a reputation of being an underachiever and a negative in the clubhouse; with the Giants, he would be just the opposite.

The underachieving reputation probably stemmed from his first year in New York when he had started off very strong, hitting .375, with eight homers and 26 RBI in April, but ended the season with just 14 home runs.

Ex-pitcher Mike Krukow has been one of the Giants' television and radio voices since 1993.

General Manager Brian Sabean worked his trading magic to make the Giants winners in 1997.

Bay Area native Jon Miller replaced the retired Hank Greenwald as the "Voice of the Giants" in 1997.

J.T. Snow was a two-time Gold Glove winner at first base for the Anaheim Angels. Snow, the son of ex-Los Angeles Rams wide receiver Jack Snow, was traded before 1997 from Anaheim for pitcher Allen Watson and a minor leaguer.

"It's tough in New York," he said. "When you're down, not many people will back you up. When you're on top, they call you Superman or hero. In New York, there's no in-between."

Kent is intense, very demanding of himself, a trait he acquired in childhood as the first-born son of a policeman father who was never satisfied with his son's performance. "If I pitched a one-hitter in Little League, he'd say, 'I think you could have gotten that guy out with a curve ball.'"

The Giants' chances looked worse when Shawn Estes was sidelined in the spring with tightness in his left bicep. An even more serious blow came when a Randy Johnson fastball hit the wrist of J.T. Snow and bounced off to hit just below Snow's left eye. J.T. fell to the ground, legs kicking in agony, and the same thought went through everybody's mind: Is his career over?

"All I could think of was Dickie Thon or Tony Conigliaro, whose careers were ruined when they got beaned," said Manager Dusty Baker.

"I was lucky that I was able to get my wrist up so it didn't hit me directly in the face," Snow would say later. "If it had hit me directly, I don't think I'd be standing here today. After that, it was just a matter of getting well. You can't go up there with fear or you'll never get a hit."

Because of that injury, Snow had almost no Spring Training, and the combination of a lack of work and having to learn pitchers in a new league caused him to have a slow start at the plate, hitting under .200 for the first month and not hitting a home run in his first 50 games, but even when he wasn't hitting, Snow saved wins for the Giants with his incredible fielding, often going into the hole between first and second to cut off what seemed to be base hits and digging errant throws from infielders out of the dirt for outs.

Amazingly, J.T. was in the starting lineup for the first game, which was virtually the only good news for the Giants, who lost the season opener to the Pittsburgh Pirates, 5-2.

Former University of California star Jeff Kent came from Cleveland in the Matt Williams trade. Kent set San Francisco team records for offensive output by a second baseman with 29 homers and 121 RBI.

Julian Tavarez appeared in 89 games during 1997—a San Francisco record.

LARRY BAER

Larry Baer was the first to get the ball rolling on keeping the Giants in San Francisco in 1992, even though he was working in New York.

Baer had been the marketing director for the Giants, 1980-83, before going to Harvard Business School and then to CBS. By 1992, he was special assistant to CBS Chairman Laurence Tisch, but he was keeping an eye on his old team from 3,000 miles away.

"I had a friend at San Francisco City Hall, Ron Blatman, and when the Giants lost the San Jose election in June of 1992 to build a new ball park, he told me they were really worried in City Hall because the feeling was Bob Lurie might sell the team and move the Giants out of town," remembered Baer.

"So, I called Donald Fisher, who called Charles Schwab, and then we talked to Richard Goldman, who was chief of protocol at City Hall, and they all said they'd try to do whatever was necessary to keep the team in San Francisco."

When Lurie did make his tentative deal with a Tampa Bay group, Mayor Frank Jordan brought in Walter Shorenstein and sports attorney Leigh Steinberg, both of whom made several contacts to bring a group together.

Meanwhile, Baer was making his own calls and holding many cross-country conversations with Peter Magowan, who had been on the Giants board of directors for 11 years.

"Peter and I had become friends when I was working for the Giants," said Baer. "We used to play tennis. We kept in touch when I went back to New York. When we were putting the group together, he'd call me from San Francisco before he went to bed at 11 o'clock. Of course, that was 2 a.m. in New York, but he'd tell me, 'We've got to do more. We've got to get this done.'"

Baer eventually convinced Magowan he should be the managing general partner, but Magown agreed only if Baer would become the the team's executive vice president.

The two have made a great combination. Baer worked extensively on the ball park campaign, talking to civic groups every day. Since the measure passed by nearly a two-thirds margin, he has worked on financing for the park, starting with the big package from Pacific Bell, whose name will be on the park.

"It's been a roller coaster ride," said Baer, "from '93 when everything went right to the strike year and the last place finishes in '95 and '96. During the strike, Peter would kid me, saying, 'Look what you got me into.' But during the '97 season, he told me he was glad I'd kept after him to take over."

Utility infielder Bill Mueller hit .292 in 128 games during 1997—his first full season in the Majors.

For 20 years (1958-78), Giants fans were entertained and informed by the wit and charm of Lon Simmons. After being away from the team's airwaves for nearly two decades, Simmons returned on a part-time basis in 1996.

From 1993-96, no one in Major League Baseball had more saves (144) than the "Shooter," Rod Beck.

Very quickly, though, the Giants turned it around, winning four of their next six and then ripping off a nine-game winning streak to put them at 13-3, best in baseball at that point. In game 11, the fourth of their winning streak, the Giants moved into a tie for first with the Dodgers and Rockies.

There were heroes throughout the clubhouse the first month. Estes won his first four decisions, the fourth being a four-hit shutout over the Houston Astros that was not only his first Major League shutout but the first complete game of his professional career. Rod Beck had 11 saves in his first 11 appearances.

Barry Bonds hit a game-winning triple in game three against the Mets, a first-inning homer in a 3-0 win over the Phillies in game eight and a three-run inside-the-park home run in the first inning of a 4-3 win over the Braves in game 18. Glenallen Hill hit two two-run homers to beat the Phillies in game 13. Mark Lewis, playing his first game after coming back from elbow surgery, hit two home runs in a 7-6 win over the Mets in game 10. Rick Wilkins hit a two-run pinch-hit double to beat the Mets in game four.

Nobody was more important in that early going, though, than Kent. Because pitchers were so concerned about Bonds, they often pitched around him. Kent, hitting behind Bonds, made them pay. He knocked in five runs in the Giants second game, went 2-for-3 in the third game and knocked in two more runs in game six, all Giants victories. He had home runs in three straight games on the first Eastern road trip, as the Giants beat the Mets in the first two games and the Phillies in the third. He closed out the month with a grand slam that helped beat the Phillies, 6-1. He would finish the season with three grand slams, all of them coming after intentional walks to Bonds.

The Giants rode that momentum to a six-game lead at the All-Star break over the Dodgers. Two patterns had emerged in the Giants play. They had shown an ability to come from behind; eventually, 47 of their victories, more than half, would come that way. Possibly even more important was their ability to come back after lopsided losses. They would eventually have an incredible 17 games in which they gave up 10 or more runs, but they usually came back to win the next day.

"We don't beat up on ourselves when we lose one of those games," said Kent, "and we don't try to go out there for revenge. Getting angry is usually counter-productive in baseball. You have to just stay focused and play your game, and that's what we do."

Though happy with the team's performance, Giants General Manager Brian Sabean

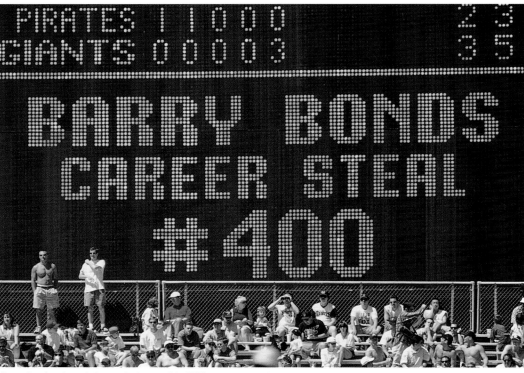
Barry Bonds achieved this mark during a July 1997 series against the Pirates in San Francisco.

Before the 1997 season, Giants fans needed a scorecard to identify their infield. By season's end, everyone knew (left to right) Bill Mueller, Mark Lewis, Jeff Kent, Jose Vizcaino and J.T. Snow.

BRIAN SABEAN

After Brian Sabean made his first big trade for the Giants, sending Matt Williams to Cleveland for Jeff Kent, Jose Vizcaino, Julian Tavarez, Joe Roa and $1 million, he had a meeting with writers to explain the trade. Taking his cue from a letter to the editor which had called him an idiot, Sabean told the writers, "I am not an idiot."

"I meant it to be humorous," said Sabean, "but nobody took it that way. That became the headline on stories the next day.

"I can't say I was surprised by the reaction to Matt's trade. He was very popular with the fans, and people think when you trade a player like that, you should get a Rotisserie player in return. But that's not the way it works in baseball today. Look at what the A's got for Mark McGwire. We got proven players in the trade, and we got money we could use to do other things (specifically, to sign Darryl Hamilton as a free agent).

"But it was a month before we made our next trade, to get J.T. Snow, and that was a long, long month."

Though only 40 when he was named general manager on Sept. 30, 1996, Sabean had impressive credentials for the job. Before joining the Giants, he had spent eight years in the New York Yankees organization, ending with three years as vice president of development/scouting, as he played a significant role in strengthening the Yankees farm system. He had spent four years as assistant to

Giants General Manager Bob Quinn, obviously being groomed for the general manager job he assumed after the 1996 season.

Though he is known as an astute evaluator of playing talent, Sabean insists he's just part of a team.

"It's not like I'm just sitting here and making decisions," he said. "We have scouts out there sending in information we can use, not just statistics. Bob Quinn still has an office next to mine, and I listen to him. Ned Colletti and Dick Tidrow are experienced, competent baseball people, and I can depend on their advice.

"When it comes to making a trade, we split up the phone calls, because it would drive you crazy to have to be on the phone all the time. When we find out who's available and who we'd have to give up, we get together and share our information. Usually, we can come up with a consensus."

After the 1997 All-Star Game, Sabean went to the Giants ownership group and asked for more money to make trades to improve the team. "They got pretty excited when I gave them names of some of the players I thought we could get," said Sabean. "They told me to go ahead and we bumped up the budget about $2.5 million."

Just before the trading deadline at the end of the month, Sabean pulled off a deal which astounded the baseball world, acquiring veteran pitchers Wilson Alvarez, Roberto Hernandez and Danny Darwin from the Chicago White Sox, shoring up a pitching staff which had been staggering.

Shorstop Jose Vizcaino, along with Julian Tavarez, Jeff Kent and pitcher Joe Roa, were acquired from Cleveland for Matt Williams and Trenidad Hubbard.

Every winter, Giants players and staff travel throughout Northern California as part of the "Giants Caravan." School visits are a major part of the week-long caravan. Here, pitcher Shawn Estes makes a new friend.

Former infielder Duane Kuiper became one of the Giants radio and television announcers in 1987.

feared the team would not be good enough to win without some improvement, and he engineered a series of trades in July which would give the Giants enough to prevail down the stretch.

The first trade, on July 16, was hardly noticed, as he sent young catcher Marcus Jensen to Detroit for catcher and former Stanford University quarterback Brian Johnson, but it would later pay huge dividends. Baker had always liked Johnson for his intelligence and character as well as his ability, so he was a good fit.

The next trade sent minor leaguers Brandon Leese and Bobby Rector to Florida for righthander Pat Rapp. Sabean hoped Rapp could fill a spot in a rotation weakened by the loss of Osvaldo Fernandez through elbow surgery.

Then came the blockbuster trade, as the Giants acquired pitchers Wilson Alvarez, Danny Darwin and Roberto Hernandez from the Chicago White Sox for minor league pitchers Keith Foulke, Lorenzo Barcelo, Bobby Howry and Ken Vining, shortstop Michael Caruso and outfielder Brian Manning.

Alvarez was an All-Star starter, Hernandez led the American League in saves in 1996 and Darwin was a spot starter and provided bullpen help.

The trade also created a potential problem with two All-Star closers, Beck and Hernandez, on the team. Hernandez told Baker immediately, "I'll do whatever you want. I know Beck is your closer, so if you want me to be the setup man, that's what I'll do."

There would still be some anxious moments because Hernandez, with a fastball that occasionally reached 100 mph on the radar gun postings, quickly became a fan favorite. But Dusty defused possible explosions, as he did all season.

The players deserved credit for what they were doing, but Baker's deft managerial touch also had much to do with the Giants' success. First, he brought together a group of strangers in Spring Training and molded them into a team. Then, he made a series of changes throughout the season, while managing to keep almost everybody happy.

He had started the season thinking Wilkins would be his starting catcher and an important power hitter, but Wilkins fell into a slump at the start of the season and could not get out of it. Dusty went first to Damon Berryhill and then to Johnson when he arrived in July.

These late-season acquisitions plugged major holes in the Giants pitching staff.
Left to right: Danny Darwin, Wilson Alvarez, Roberto Hernandez and Pat Rapp.

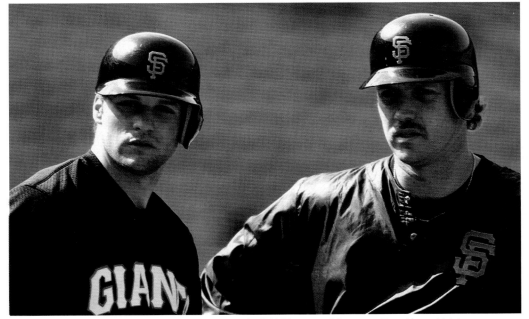

Glenallen Hill set a career-high with 24 homers during his first season (1995) with the Giants.

Shawn Estes (left) won 19 games in the Giants' "worst to first" 1997 season, while veteran Doug Henry (right) was invaluable in middle-inning relief.

Stan Javier, son of former St. Louis Cardinals infielder Julian Javier, signed with the Giants in 1996 after two seasons in Oakland.

Glenallen Hill opened the season in right field, but Stan Javier played so well when he was in the lineup that he eventually became the starter. Hill erupted, but Baker called him into the office for a talk. "We're cool," said Dusty. "I told him he'll have plenty of chances to play."

Jim Poole started the season as the main left-handed reliever, but when he didn't do the job, Dusty gave it to Rick Rodriguez. Doug Henry had a great first half, but when he faltered, Julian Tavarez got more chances, eventually leading the league in appearances.

There were also the Baker hunches, usually based on solid information. He started Rich Aurilia at shortstop in a June 14 game in Anaheim, for instance, because Aurilia had played against Angels starter Allen Watson in high school and hit well against him. Aurilia hit a grand slam homer in a 10-3 Giants win.

The Giants needed all of Dusty's magic because their lead kept shrinking after the All-Star break and eventually disappeared. When they lost to Pittsburgh in game 130, they fell into second place behind the Dodgers.

From that point, it was a dogfight. The Giants climbed back into a tie for the lead on Sept. 11 and took a game lead the next day, but then fell back. When the Dodgers came into 3Com Park on Sept. 17 for a two-game series, they led the Giants by two games with just 11 to go.

Nobody who was there—and there were crowds of more than 50,000 for both games—will ever forget those two games, memorable in different ways but as exciting as baseball games can ever be.

MASCOT

As part of the celebration of the 40th season, the Giants introduced their first legitimate mascot, a seal.

In 1984, the Giants had poked fun at the proliferation of baseball mascots with The Crazy Crab, but this time, they were serious.

"It's for the kids," said club Senior Vice President Pat Gallagher. "We talked to a lot of people about it in the off-season and got an overwhelmingly positive reaction."

Why a seal? "Part of it was the seal has a baseball background," said Gallagher, "because the San Francisco minor league team was the Seals. A seal is non-threatening, so we knew he wouldn't scare the kids. And, since we'll be moving into a park in China Basin, where there are a lot of seals, it just seemed the natural thing to do."

Bonds, who had been criticized for not hitting in the clutch in the two weeks before, hit a towering blast into the second deck in right field in the first inning, providing the only two runs the Giants needed in the first game. Kirk Rueter pitched seven strong innings, giving up just one run and four hits, and Hernandez came on to pitch two scoreless innings to save the win.

One game back.

It was the second game, though, that was really one for the ages. It seemed the Giants might put it away early as Snow hit a solo homer and Bonds hit a three-run blast, putting the Giants up 5-1. But the Dodgers came back to tie with two-run rallies in the sixth and seventh, the last two runs coming on a single by Mike Piazza.

In the top of the 10th, with Beck in the game, Piazza seemed fooled on a split-fingered fast ball on the outside of the plate, reaching out but getting just enough on it to dump a ball into right field for a single. Eric Karros and Raul Mondesi followed with singles. The slow Piazza held at third on Mondesi's hit, but the Dodgers had the bases loaded with nobody out.

It had been a rough stretch for Beck, who had come in with a 4-1 lead in the ninth against the Braves in Atlanta on Sept. 15 and given up three singles and a home run to Fred McGriff which gave the Braves a 5-4 win.

Beck was both the Giants' career leader in saves and the National League leader in that department for the season, but that was overshadowed by his recent troubles. When Baker walked to the mound, many in the crowd hoped he'd go to Rodriguez, warming up in the bullpen. The thought never crossed Dusty's mind. He just told Beck he could do the job and to "dig deep."

Beck got a big out by striking out Todd Zeile. Veteran Eddie Murray, who had just been picked up by the Dodgers, came up as a pinch hitter. Murray was a notorious first-pitch fast ball hitter, so Beck threw him a split-fingered fast ball, breaking down, and Murray hit it to Kent, playing on the infield grass. Kent threw home for

Barry Bonds gives blood at the Oakland Blood Bank.

Kirk Rueter came in a mid-season trade with Montreal in 1996.

Utility infielder Rich Aurilia has been a valuable reserve.

The Giants congratulate Barry Bonds after a home run in a critical game against the Dodgers on Sept. 18, 1997.

Brian Johnson's solo homer in the 12th won a crucial game against the Dodgers on Sept. 18, 1997.

The aces of the 1997 Giants pitching staff: lefties Shawn Estes (left) and Kirk Rueter.

Free agent Darryl Hamilton brought stability to center field in 1997.

Versatile infielder Mark Lewis came to the Giants before the 1997 season. He platooned with Bill Mueller at third base and also was a backup second baseman.

one out and then Johnson rifled the ball to Snow at first base to conclude an unusual double play. The Giants were out of the inning.

Two innings later, they won the game. Leading off in the 12th, Johnson hit a first-pitch fast ball from Dodger reliever Mark Guthrie into the left field bleachers. The Giants burst out of the dugout to greet Johnson as the Dodgers seethed in frustration, aware that momentum had swung.

The Giants went on to win three-of-four from San Diego—with Bonds delivering an unusual pep talk before the first game—while the Dodgers were losing three in a row at home to the Rockies. In Denver, the Giants split with the Rockies, with Johnson again the hero with a ninth-inning home run that was the winning run, and they came home with a two-game lead to face the Padres again in the season-ending three-game series. Anticipating the championship to come, players were calling it "Dustiny."

In the dressing room before the Friday night game, the players talked of the way the team had come together, on-and-off the field. "This is even better than the '93 team," said Beck. "With that team, it wasn't exactly 25 cabs for 25 guys but it might be 15. With this team, it's more like one bus for everybody."

"The one worry I had in Spring Training was whether we'd have chemistry, with

Roberto Hernandez won five and saved four after being acquired from the White Sox.

Brian Johnson contributed 11 home runs and 27 RBI after joining the Giants from Detroit.

so many changes," said Kent, "but everybody came together very quickly. I think it's because everybody has respect for everybody else. On some teams, there are little things that get on people's nerves, like, one player won't like what another one is playing on the radio. We don't have any of that."

One win by the Giants and a win by the Rockies over the Dodgers in Colorado would clinch, but Baker wasn't counting on that. "I know the Dodgers are going to win tonight," he said before the Friday night games.

Dusty was right, but that only delayed the inevitable. The Giants swamped the Padres on Friday night, 17-4, as Shawn Estes shook off his shoulder problems and pitched three-hit ball for seven innings, and then clinched with a 6-1 win on Saturday. Bonds hit his 40th homer, which put him over the 100 RBI mark. For the first time in 50 years, the Giants had three hitters with more than 100 RBI—Kent (121), Snow (104) and Bonds (101).

Fittingly, two of the pitchers the Giants obtained in mid-season were critical in the clincher, as Alvarez pitched two-hit ball for the first seven innings and Hernandez came on in the eighth, giving up a run but sending the Giants into the ninth with a 6-1 lead.

Then, Baker again showed how much he cares for his players. Before the game, he told Beck, "If there's any chance to do it, I'll have you out there at the end." Hernandez could certainly have finished the game, but Dusty kept his promise to Beck and sent him to the mound in the ninth. "Nobody deserved to close this game out more than Rod Beck for what he's done for this city and this organization," said Baker after the game.

Beck didn't disappoint, putting the Padres down 1-2-3. The sellout crowd was on its feet for the final batter, exploding in noise as Beck struck him out. Beck threw his arms in the air in celebration, and Baker thrust his right arm into the sky. Players in the dugout and pitchers in the bullpen raced onto the field to join their teammates. In left field, Barry Bonds knelt briefly in a private prayer and then raced towards the infield, where the Giants were all hugging one another.

When players headed to the clubhouse, Bonds jumped on top of the dugout and did high fives with fans and then hugged them, before he too jumped down and headed to the clubhouse where champagne was being sprayed on everybody, including team President Peter Magowan, General Manager Brian Sabean and Executive Vice President Larry Baer. It was a scene of extreme exuberance rarely seen in Bay Area sports history.

Bonds poured champagne down Beck's throat. "You started it and you ended it," he said.

The magic died, though, in Miami, where the Giants and Marlins started the first

SHAWN ESTES

By learning to control his temper, Shawn Estes became a big winner for the Giants in 1997.

Through his high school career and in the minor leagues, Estes always had the potential to be a star, but his temperament always defeated him. Even in Little League, he would pitch a fit if everything didn't go right, and that pattern continued into his professional career.

"I wouldn't have wanted to be on a team with me," Estes admitted during the 1997 season. "I was never on a winning team where I was the guy. You could say I choked.

"I always had to have it right now. Every game had to be a no-hit shutout. There were so many high demands that I didn't allow myself to take baby steps. Everything was a sprint to me. I never took a deep breath."

The Giants had traded for Estes and shortstop Wilson Delgado in May of 1995, giving up Salomon Torres, who had not been the same since he had lost the last game of the 1993 season.

Estes seemed just another erratic lefthander, just 9-20

in four-and-a-half seasons in the Seattle system. But once the Giants got him, he blossomed quickly. In 1996, he was 9-3 at Phoenix in half a season, and when he was brought up in July, he was in the big leagues to stay.

The Giants tried not to put too much pressure on Estes at the start of the season, especially after he spent the first 10 days of the season on the disabled list because of tightness in his bicep tendon. But he quickly became the Giants ace, going 12-2 before the All-Star break.

At times he still struggled with his control; in the next-to-last weekend of the season, he threw 11 straight balls to lead off a game against San Diego.

But that kind of a game was a rarity for Estes, who baffled hitters with a combination of a 92 mph fastball and a sharp breaking curve that came in at nearly the same speed. He ended the season with 19 wins, more than any Giants lefthander since Ron Bryant won 24 in 1973. At 24, he seemed a poster boy for the Giants as they looked forward to a bright future in Pacific Bell Park.

Scenes from a celebration: The Giants rejoice after clinching the 1997 National League Western Division pennant.

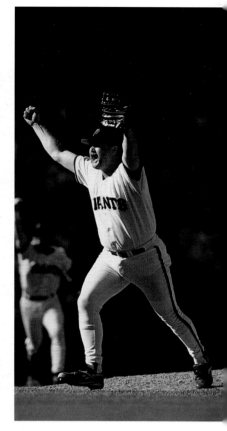

Barry Bonds stands on top of the Giants Dugout and shares in the celebration after the Giants clinched the 1997 National League Western Division Pennant.

Ready to lead the Giants into the Millennium: Peter Magowan and Brian Sabean.

round of playoffs. Perhaps the year-long struggle and the tension of the final two weeks had taken too much out of the Giants. Perhaps the store-bought Marlins were just a little better; Florida Owner Wayne Huizenga had bought up free agents like so many toys in the offseason and had put together a very good team. For three straight games, the Giants had chances to win, but couldn't come up with the hit or pitch they needed.

The first game was a classic pitchers' duel between Rueter and Marlins' ace Kevin Brown, scoreless for the first six innings. The Giants broke through in the top of the seventh with a home run by Mueller, and Bonds followed with a double that hit the top of the left field wall.

But the Giants couldn't get Bonds in, and in the bottom of the inning, Charles Johnson tied the score with a home run. In the ninth, with Julian Tavarez pitching, Jeff Conine singled and Tavarez hit Johnson, who was trying to bunt. Baker brought in Hernandez, but Craig Counsell bunted the runners up and pinch hitter Jim Eisenreich was walked to load the bases. Devon White bounced a ball to Kent, with the infield drawn in, the same kind of play on which the Giants had gotten out of in the 10th inning of the second win over the Dodgers. But the grounder wasn't hit as sharply this time and White is a much faster runner than Eddie Murray. The Giants got one out at the plate but couldn't turn the double play, and the next batter, Edgar Renteria, hit a ball through the right side to score the winning run.

The second game was a totally different game, but with the same result. Neither starting pitcher—Estes for the Giants, Al Leiter for the Marlins—was effective, and both were knocked out early. Brian Johnson homered for the Giants in the second inning, but Bobby Bonilla and Gary Sheffield both homered for the Marlins, who took a 6-4 lead into the seventh.

The Giants weren't conceding. In the seventh, Vizcaino and Bonds hit back-to-back doubles to close the gap to one run. In the ninth, with Hamilton and Javier

on base with one out, Bonds hit a ground ball to shortstop. Second baseman Craig Counsell, with Javier bearing down on him, threw wildly to first and Hamilton scored to tie the game.

But in the bottom of the inning, with Hernandez pitching, Sheffield singled and stole second and Bonilla walked. Moises Alou followed with a single to center Dante Powell, playing because Hamilton had injured his leg scoring the tying run, threw a bullet to the plate and Brian Johnson was confident he'd be able to tag out Sheffield. But the throw hit the pitching rubber and bounced high into the air, coming down only after Sheffield had crossed the plate. That seemed a symbol for what was happening to the Giants: the breaks just weren't going their way.

The Giants' hopes were dim when they returned to 3Com Park but the fans weren't deterred. The crowd of 57,188 was the largest at the park since Opening Day in 1994, when the Giants drew 58,077.

It was another frustrating game for the Giants. Kent, who had been playing with a wrist so badly injured that he required cortisone shots to keep playing, hit a solo homer in the fourth to give the Giants a 1-0 lead. With Alvarez, known as a big game pitcher, throwing goose eggs through five innings, the Giants had hopes.

But in the sixth, after getting the first two outs, Alvarez weakened and gave up singles to Alou and Jeff Conine and then walked Charles Johnson. The next batter, Devon White, had struggled at bat during the season, hitting only .245, and in the playoffs had gone hitless in the first two games. All that was forgotten, though, when he hit an Alvarez fastball deep into the left field seats for a grand slam, giving the Marlins a 4-1 lead.

The Giants had one last shot in the bottom of the inning. Mueller led off with a single and was running on a 3-2 pitch to Bonds. But Bonds was frozen by a pitch by Alex Fernandez that started inside and broke across the plate. He took strike three and Charles Johnson fired a strike to get Mueller at second base for a

The Giants line up prior to Game Three of the 1997 National League Division Series.

2000

double play.

"That was devastating, to see Barry go down like that," said Baker later. "Any betting man would have bet he'd put the ball in play."

Kent followed with his second solo homer, but the Giants never got closer. The Marlins added a couple of runs in the seventh off Hernandez, and the final score was 6-2.

It had been a bad series for Hernandez, but he appreciated just being there. "It was fun, a second chance for me and a lot of guys this season," he said. "But the ride ended too quick. Much too quick."

Baker walked through the clubhouse, shaking hands and saying goodbye to his players. Finally, he had talked to everybody. "It just doesn't seem like the season is over," he said.

But, it was.

Yet a promising new era of San Francisco Giants baseball had begun, headed by one of the best GM-Manager tandems in the Major Leagues. There was a new winning spirit which boded well as the Giants entered the final two years of transition into the new ballpark at China Basin.

SF

Index

Peterson, Charles "Cap" 64, **65-66**

Pierce, Billy 14, 16, 18, 41, **41**, 42, **42**, 48, 51, 65

Pole, Dick 173, 175, 187

Polumbo, John 190

Pompez, Alex 26, **27**

Portugal, Mark 180, **180**, 181

Posedel, Bill 12, 32

Poulson, Norris 21

Powell, Dante 202

Pregenzer, John **54**

Price, Joe **142**, 143

Quinn, Bob 166-167, 195

Quisenberry, Dan **160**

Rabb, Johnny **106**

Rader, Dave **91**, **105**

Rajsich, Gary 124

Rapp, Pat 196, **196**

Rector, Bobby 196

Reed, Jeff 186

Remlinger, Mike 156, **160**

Renteria, Edgar 202

Reuschel, Rick 140, **140**, 142, 144, 150

Reynolds, Harold 134

Richardson, Bobby 46, 52-53

Richardson, H.B. "Spec" 90, **90**, 91, 92, 94, **95**, 100, 104

Righetti, Dave **158**, 174, **176**

Rigney, Bill 4, 12, **12**, 13, 22, **22**, 23, **24-25**, 26, 28, **29**, 30-33, **33**, 34-35, **35**, 57, 62-64, 67, 75, 88, 90, **90**

Riles, Ernest **145**

Roa, Joe 190, 195, **196**

Robertson, Bob 73

Robinson, Craig **92**, **94**

Robinson, Don 138, 144, **154**, **156**

Robinson, Frank 4, 63, 64, **86**, 98, 101, **101**, 104, **104**, 106, 108, **108**, 109, **109**, 110, 112, **116**, 118, **118**, 119-121, 125, 171

Robinson, Jackie 26, 57

Robinson, Ted **184**

Rodgers, Andre 30, 32, 34, 36

Rodriguez, Rick 197-198

Rogers, Kevin 174

Roseboro, John 60-61, **61**

Rosen, Al 4, 90, 92, 124, 126, 128, **128**, 130, 132, 134, 137, 138, 140, **141**, 142-144, 145, 148, 156, 158, 164, 166-167, 169-171

Rueter, Kirk 188, **198-199**, 202

Ryan, Rosy 34, 81

Sabean, Brian 186, 188-190, **192**, 194-196, 200, **202**

Sadecki, Ray 64, **64**, 65

Sadek, Mike **88**, **98**

Sanford, Jack 16, 28, 34, 36, **37**, 38-39, 42, 46-47, **47**, 50, 52-53, 80

Sasser, Mackey 138

Sauer, Hank 4, **12**, **74**, **81**

Scarsone, Steve 176

Schmidt, Bob 27, **36**

Schmidt, Mike 118, 156, 186

Schwab, Charles 163, 193

Schwarz, Jack 4, **12**, 21, 26-27

Selig, Bud 162, 168-169, 184

Shaw, Bob 59

Sheehan, Tom "Clancy" 32, 35, **35**, 38, 63-64, 74-75, 78, 81

Sherry, Norm **147**

Shinn, George 164

Simmons, Lon 4, 14, **14**, 16, 19, 28, 32, 34-35, 38-39, 41, 57, 61, 75, 80-81, 84, **194**

Smith, Reggie 107, 110, **110**, 112, **112**, 114, 118

Snider, Duke 16, **62**, 63

Snow, J.T. 191-192, **192**, **195**, 198-200

Snyder, Cory 167

Sorrell, Billy **64**

Spahn, Warren **31**, 58, **62**, 80

Speier, Chris 4, 10, 11, 64, 68, **68**, **69**, 70, 78, 83

Starrette , Herm **116**

Steinberg, Leigh 4, 162-163, 192

Stennett, Rennie **106**

Stevens, Bob **29**

Stone, Steve **91**

Stoneham, Horace 12, 20-22, **22**, **24**, 30, 32, 34-36, 38, 54, 57, **58**, 63, 65-66, 71, 74-75, 78-84

Strain, Joe **106**

Strawberry, Darryl 182-183, **183**

Sularz, Guy "G-Man" **99**

Summers, Champ **107**

Swift, Billy 10, 156, 158, **172**, 174, **174**, 175-176, 178, 180-181, 184

Tavarez, Julian 190, **193**, 195, **196**, 202

Thomas, Derrel 94, 98, **98**

Thomas, Valmy 28, **26**

Thomasson, Gary **83**, 94

Thompson, Robby **129**, 133, **133**, 134, **134**, **136**, 150, **152**, 164, **170**, 174, **174**, 176-178, **178**, 190

Thon, Dickie 192

Trevino, Alex 130

Trillo, Manny 118, **125**

VanLandingham, William **184**, **189**

VanOrnum, John **116**

Vincent, Fay **153**, 154, **154**, 163

Virgil, Ozzie 78

Vizcaino, Jose 190, 191, 194, **195-196**, 202

Wagner, Leon 26-28, **28**, 58

Walter, Bucky **31**

Washburn, Ray 65

Watson, Allen 190, **192**, 196

Westrum, Wes 12-13, **71**, 81

White, Bill 28-29, 164

Whitfield, Terry 95, **96**, **106**

Whitson, Ed 92

Wilkins, Rick 189, 191, 194, 196

Williams, Bernie 70, **93**

Williams, Charlie 78, **79**, **82**

Williams, Matt 4, 10, 150, **150**, **154**, 155-156, **156**, 168, **173**, **175**, 176, **180**, 182, 184, 186, **189**, 190,

192, **196**

Williams, Mitch 150

Williams, Stan 16, 18

Wilson, Lionel **154**

Wilson, Trevor 175, **175**, 176, **183**

Wirth, Alan 94

Wohlford, Jim **120**

Worthington, Al **29**

Youngblood, Joel **117**

Zanni, Don 40

Zimmer, Don **140**

PHOTOGRAPHY CREDITS

Associated Press 54, 55 (TL)

Orlando Cepeda 27 (B), 52, 53

Dick Dobbins 26, 31 (TR), 32, 33 (T), 37 (T), 39, 44 (B), 48 (B), 55 (TR, BL), 62 (BR), 66 (B), 69 (T), 85, 86 (TL, BL), 156

Jon Francis 119

Garibaldi Studios 155 (R), 157 (TL), 158 (B), 159

Stephen Green 150 (A), 151

Bodie Hyman 122-123

Fred Kaplan 34, 35 (M), 60 (B), 62 (T), 67 (B), 70 (A), 74 (T), 83 (TL, TM), 91 (M)

Tony Khing 21 (T)

Nick Lammers/Alameda Newspaper Group 198 (T)

Brad Mangin 174 (L), 179 (TR)

National Baseball Library 49, 50, 51 (T), 62 (BL)

Russ Reed, 79 (BL), 90 (M)

San Francisco Chronicle 25 (B)

San Francisco Examiner xi, 202 (T)

San Francisco Giants Archives ii, v (B), vi-vii, ix, 12 (TL, BL), 14, 15, 18, 19, 22, 23 (A), 24 (A), 25 (T), 28 (A), 29 (A), 30 (A), 31 (TL, B), 33 (BL, BR), 35 (T, BL, BR), 36, 37 (BL, BR), 38 (A), 41 (A), 42 (A), 43 (B), 44 (TL, TR, M), 45, 46 (B), 47, 48 (T,M), 51 (B), 55 (BR), 57 (M,B), 58, 59 (A), 60 (T), 61 (A), 63, 64 (T,B), 66 (T), 67 (TR), 68 (A), 71 (TL, TR, BL, BR), 72 (A), 73 (TL, TR, M), 74 (BL, BR), 78 (A), 79 (BR), 81 (TR), 83 (M), 86 (M, BR), 89 (A), 92 (TL), 93 (TR, B), 94 (BL), 134, 139, 161 (B), 162 (BR), 167 (T), 170, 171 (TR), 175 (L) 176-177 (A), 178 (L), 181 (TR), 185 (BR), 194 (M), 197 (B)

SF Giants/Dennis Desprois x, 43 (T), 79 (T), 46 (T), 69 (M), 71 (M), 79 (T), 81 (M), 82 (A), 83 (BR), 84 (TR, B), 86 (TR, ML, MR, BM), 88, 90 (T,B), 91 (L, T), 92 (TR, B), 93 (L, M), 94 (T, ML, MR, BR), 95-101 (A), 104-118 (A), 120-121 (A), 124-133 (A), 135-138 (A), 140-144 (A), 145 (L, TR, MR), 146 (TL, TR, M), 147 (TL, TR, M, BL), 148 (A), 149 (B), 152 (A), 153 (TL, TR, B), 154 (A)

SF Giants/Andy Kuno vi (I), vii (I), 191 (TR), 192 (ML), 201 (M, BR)

SF Giants/Melissa Mikulecky 182 (BR), 190 (TL, TR, MR, B), 191 (TL, BL), 195, 196 (M)

SF Giants/Martha Jane Stanton 145 (B), 146 (B), 147 (BR), 149 (T), 155 (T, B), 157 (TR, BL, BR), 158 (ML, M, MR), 160 (A), 161 (T), 162 (all but BR), 164, 165, 166 (T, BR), 167 (B), 168, 169 (A), 171 (TL, B), 172 (A), 173, 174 (R), 175 (TR, B), 179 (TL, BL, BR), 180 (A), 181 (TL, M, B), 182 (TL, TR, BL), 183 (A), 184 (A), 185 (T, M, BL), 186-189 (A), 190 (ML), 191 (BR), 192 (TL, TR, B), 193 (A), 194 (T, BL, BR), 196 (T, BL, BR), 197 (TL, TR, M), 198 (M, BL, BR), 199 (A), 200 (A), 201 (L, TR), 202 (B), 203, 204

San Francisco Public Library 25 (TR)

UPI 17, 20, 57 (T)

Ray Ward Front cover, 76-77, 102-103,

Woodford Publishing, Inc. 12 (all but TL and BL), 27 (T), 56, 65, 67 (L), 73 (B)

Michael Zagaris 64 (M), 81 (TL, B), 83 (BL), 84 (TL), 91 (B), 153 (M), 166 (BL)

Many thanks to Dick Dobbins for most of the memorabilia pictured in this book.
A= all, I= inset T=top, L= left, R= right, M= middle